Ireland's Huguenots
and their Refuge,
1662–1745
An Unlikely Haven

To my beloved wife
Mary Claire

Ireland's Huguenots and their Refuge, 1662–1745

An Unlikely Haven

RAYMOND HYLTON

sussex

ACADEMIC
PRESS
Brighton • Chicago • Toronto

2 4 6 8 10 9 7 5 3

First published in hardcover 2005, and in paperback 2013, in Great Britain by
SUSSEX ACADEMIC PRESS
PO Box 139
Eastbourne BN24 9BP

Distributed in North America by
SUSSEX ACADEMIC PRESS
Independent Publishers Group
814 N Franklin St, Chicago, IL 60610, USA

British Library Cataloguing in Publication Data
A CIP catalogue record for this book is available from the British Library.

Library of Congress Cataloging-in-Publication Data
Hylton, Raymond.
Ireland's Huguenots and their refuge : an unlikely haven / Raymond
    Hylton.
p. cm.
Includes bibliographical references and index.
ISBN 978-1-902210-78-0 (hbk. alk. paper)
ISBN 978-1-902210-79-7 (pbk. alk. paper)
    1. Huguenots—Ireland—History. 2. Ireland—Church history.
    I. Title.
BX9458.I7H95 2005
284′.5′09415—dc22
                                                                    2004026126

Typeset and designed by G&G Editorial, Brighton.
Printed and bound by CPI Group (UK) Ltd, Croydon, CR0 4YY
This book is printed on acid-free paper.

◈ CONTENTS ◈

◈ ILLUSTRATIONS ◈

Illustrations are located on pages 60–3, 98–101 and 150–3.

Huguenot Nightmare (1), St. Bartholomew's Day in Paris: The royally-sanctioned slaughter of some 10,000 Huguenot men, women & children on 24 August 1572 ran deep into the ancestral memory of Huguenots settling in predominately Catholic regions – Ireland among them. Courtesy of the Huguenot Library, University College, London.

Huguenot Nightmare (2), The Day of Okewas in Virginia, 22 March 1622: The bloody surprise attack by tribesmen of the Powhatan nations was widely publicized and certainly brought home to the Huguenots the parallels of St. Bartholomew's Day 50 years earlier, and the perils of settling in a foreign environment. Engraving by Theodor De Bry; courtesy of the Library of Congress: LC-USZ62-13459.

Huguenot Nightmare (3), The 1641 Rising in Ireland: The killing of Protestant settlers in 1641 was, as *Abstract of the Unnatural Rebellion* . . . indicates, well-remembered in 1689, nearly a half century later, and certainly raised apprehension in the minds of potential Huguenot immigrants to Ireland. Courtesy of the Queen's University Library, Belfast.

Huguenot Houses ("Dutch Billies"), Dublin: Gabled buildings with massive central smokestacks that were so much a part of Dublin's physical make-up from 1680 to 1750 came to be thought of (erroneously) as a Huguenot invention. Now, few are left, and those that are have been much-altered. The structure with two windows on the top floor, located on Molesworth Street is genuine, though it does not have its original gable (the present one was added later). The other, on Kevin Street, is a later reproduction but retains more faithfully the original appearances of these houses.

Friedrich Hermann, Duke of Schomberg (1615?–1690). Courtesy of the Huguenot Library, University College, London.

Henri Massue De Ruvigny, Earl of Galway (1648–1720). Courtesy of the Huguenot Library, University College, London.

St. Paul's (The French Church) at Portarlington, founded by the Earl of Galway. The church has been in existence since 1694 and was enlarged and remodelled in Victorian Gothic style in 1852. Courtesy of St. Paul's Canon, Leslie Stevenson.

La Lande House, Portarlington, built *c*. 1710: François Daulnis de La Lande was a Huguenot military pensioner who moved with his family to Portarlington prior to 1702. His daughter Henrietta ran a French School at this house during the 1720s. Courtesy of Mr. Ronnie Matthews, Portarlington.

Plaque commemorating the Cathedral of St Paul's in Portarlington.

Les Pseaumes de David (Dublin 1731): Dublin was, by far, the site of the largest Huguenot concentration in Ireland and there was always demand for new editions of French Psalters and Prayer Books. Courtesy of the Lisburn Historical Society.

Sermons sur divers texts de l'Ecritude Sainte (Dublin 1728): The author, Gaspard Caillard, was French minister at Dublin and (later) Portarlington and was noted for the eloquence and erudition of his pulpit sermons. Courtesy of the Lisburn Historical Society.

Dublin: Gallery to Archbishop Marsh's Library: From 1701 to 1719 the Library building was home to the eminent scholar, public official and clergyman Elie Bouhereau, who also served as the first librarian of this, the oldest operating library in Dublin. Courtesy of the Library Keeper, Mrs. Muriel McCarthy.

Title page and inside page of Louis Crommelin's *Essay towards the improving of the hempen and flaxen manufactures in the Kingdom of Ireland* (Dublin 1705). Courtesy of the Irish Linen Centre and Lisburn Museum.

Conjectural Map of Lisburn, *c*. 1700. Courtesy of the Irish Linen Center and Lisburn Museum.

"Printers at Work". From a Lisburn Museum publication. Copyright Lisburn Borough Council.

Louis Crommelin as found on gravestone.

Waterford: The Bishop's Palace on the Mall. It was completed under the auspices of the Huguenot prelate, Archbishop Richard Chenevix, a descendent of Williamite military veterans. Photograph courtesy of Mrs. Petra Coffey, Newtownmountkennedy, County Wicklow, Ireland.

Waterford: Tray of traditional "Blaas", a specialty of the region. It is believed that the Huguenots introduced the soft bread rolls that are unique to the Waterford area. Though the origin of the name is subject to debate, many attest that it derived from the French "blanc". Photograph courtesy of Mrs. Petra Coffey, Newtownmountkennedy, County Wicklow, Ireland.

Cork: Site of the French Cemetery: Located at Carey's Lane the lot enclosed behind this wall and as yet not publicly accessible is what remains of the French Church burial ground in use from 1733 to 1901. It is only one of two (the other being Merrion Row in Dublin) nonconformist Huguenot cemeteries in Europe and is the focus of energetic preservation efforts by the Friends of the Huguenot Cemetery, Cork. Photograph courtesy of Mrs. Petra Coffey, Newtownmountkennedy.

Holy Ghost Friary, Waterford: The Medieval Franciscan Friary (also known as "Greyfriars") housed the Huguenot community's French Church from 1693–1819. Photograph courtesy of Mrs. Petra Coffey, Newtownmountkennedy, County Wicklow, Ireland.

Maps

◈ PREFACE ◈

How did an individual of impeccably Catholic lineage on his mother's side, whose ancestral roots run deep into the De Guise heartland of Lorraine, and who once earnestly aspired to the priesthood, become involved with the Huguenots?

One factor was my grandmother, Madeleine Marchal, a lady of broad and tolerant perspective whose views transcended those of her generation. Quite early on in my life, it was she who immersed me in the history of France. The admiration that she expressed for these French Protestants could not help but impress a youngster such as myself, who was already firm in his conviction that there existed no more relevant and constructive of disciplines than the study of the past, and what that might portend for the present and future. And if the Huguenots inspired such esteem in a lady whose conscience and heroism had impelled her to save some 200 potential Holocaust victims during the Nazi Occupation of Paris, then they had to have been formidable individuals indeed. The more I learned about them, the more perfectly did the parallels fit between Holocaust rescuers like my grandmother, and the Huguenots themselves, who had so steadfastly defended their freedom of conscience, taken such terrible risks for themselves and for others, and had made such heart-rending sacrifices.

I stored her words in my mind . . .

When the time came for me to settle upon a viable topic for my Master's Thesis I was living in Bray, County Wicklow, Ireland in cramped, costly accommodations under financially strapped circumstances. I supported a family (augmented by three-year old twin sons) on a full-time work schedule as a petrol-station attendant, which was with some difficulty sandwiched around my graduate studies at University College, Dublin. I was set on the idea that my research would be on a topic related to Modern/Early Modern France, but my family could scarcely afford the time and expense for extensive research in areas too far afield. My graduate advisor, Dr. Hugh Gough, suggested the Huguenots in Ireland – a topic that was grossly under-researched, and where most of the material, much of which was in French, might be reasonably close at hand.

I recalled my grandmother's words . . .

* * * *

Like the master's and doctoral research I pursued for over a half-decade, this volume took on a life of its own and branched out in unforeseen directions. The more I progressed the more evident it became that there were certain areas that demanded greater attention than others. There had been no definitive monograph written on the Huguenots in Ireland since before World War II. Fortunately, two superlative volumes: *The Huguenot Settlements in Ireland* by Grace Lawless Lee (1936) and *L'Influence des Huguenots Français en Irlande au XVIIe et XVIIIe Siècles* by Albert Carré (1937), each with its own distinctive focus, paved the way for my endeavors.

Nothwithstanding the efforts of Lee, Carré, and a handful of others (notably Thomas Philip Le Fanu) the term "under-researched" proved all too appropriate. Subsequent experience has clearly demonstrated to the author that the problems confronted twenty years ago have not receded, and that different (flawed) perceptions regarding Ireland's Huguenot Refuge exist on both sides of the Atlantic.

In the Americas, the very notion of Huguenots seeking asylum from persecution in their native France by traveling to "Holy (Catholic) Ireland" seems to be, at face value, a total absurdity – a classic case of the cliché "out of the frying pan into the fire". Slaves fleeing from a Virginia plantation in the years before the American Civil War, for example, would hardly expect to make good their escape from bondage by running to Alabama or Mississippi. The primary task in this instance has been that of enlightening individuals about the complexities that made Ireland a less-unlikely haven for Huguenot men and women than might initially have been supposed.

In Ireland, the fact that Huguenots did dwell there is certainly well-known even to schoolchildren in the remotest areas. The problem there, and in Britain, lies in the misconceptions and embellishments that have been repeated so often and have gone unchallenged for so long that they now masquerade as truth. In fact this has worsened since the advent of the Internet, and it requires an effort to avoid falling into total despair over the sheer persistence of these mistaken notions. This has to some extent determined the thrust of this volume: in the first instance the

Ormondite Huguenots who reached Ireland between 1662 and1692 have been appallingly neglected and much space is devoted to partially redressing this deficiency; secondly, the intensity and persistence of the religious disagreement within the Huguenot refuge over the issue of Conformity has been so glossed over through the years that a fresh look at the issues and personalities involved is absolutely essential; and thirdly, the reality of a tremendous diversity that existed among those Huguenot families who made their way to Ireland needs to be further examined in order to counter the myths that would limit the scope and dimension of their contributions.

The subject has grown too large to be adequately covered in one volume; this author imagines that it would be difficult to claim to have composed a "definitive history". And as much as one would like to believe that this monograph states much of what needs to be brought out, there is a good deal more that remains to be said. In uncovering the record of history, there is no such thing as a "final word".

And like almost every other project that I have undertaken, the subject matter assumed its own direction and led the author down unforeseen byways, leaving certain areas of knowledge under-cultivated. Though much has been discovered about the Huguenots in Ireland, much more awaits examination, particularly the so-called and misnomered "minor settlements" (the colonies at Dublin and Portarlington so predominated the Huguenot Refuge as to overshadow the far-from-negligible role played by the less-populous centers); and the story of the assimilation of the French Protestant immigration into Irish society during the late 18th–early 19th centuries. Nothing short of another volume could adequately continue and conclude the saga of these remarkable individuals in their association with an adopted land so different from the environment whence they came.

The availability of records has similarly proved to be a stumbling block. Again, it is the two largest settlements of Dublin and Portarlington that have by far proven to be the best-documented of the Huguenot communities, and therefore figure most prominently in this book. Though the bane of all Irish historians – the Four Courts Débâcle of 1922 that decimated the Irish National Archives – certainly merits its share of the blame, I am convinced that much more that has been overlooked or set aside is there to be rediscovered and can, on an optimistic note, truly state that research on the Irish Huguenots is still pretty much in its stage of infancy.

But the most compelling purpose behind this book lies in making the attempt to touch the humanity of these elusive French exiles. Even as I was seated at a postage-stamp sized kitchen table in our cottage in Bray, fumbling with note cards on which I was trying to re-construct Huguenot families while my wife was keeping the toddlers at bay – both of us all the while voraciously sipping one cup of tea after another – I never allowed myself to stop thinking about the human beings behind the baptismal, marriage and burial entries, of the tears they shed, of the hopes they nurtured, nor of the debt I owed them and, which I hope, has been partially repaid in the following pages.

And speaking of debts . . .

☒ ACKNOWLEDGMENTS

One can never be too lavish in one's praise for all who have contributed to and inspired the making of this volume. The author first acknowledges an infinite debt to the Creator, then to his family; particularly his wife Mary Claire; sons Thomas, Sean, Joel and Matthew; his grandmother, Madeleine Marchal; his parents, Thomas Preston and Nicole DeVizcaya Hylton; Mary Claire's parents Alice Henrietta and Eric Hugh Whitrow; Mary Claire's aunt and uncle, Magda and Dr. Gerald Whitrow; siblings, nieces and nephews; and the Masson "cousins" in France.

Expressions of gratitude must also go to academic mentors/colleagues Dr. Hugh Gough, Dr. James McGuire, Professor C. E. J. Caldicott, Dr. F. Edward Lund, and Dr. Robin Gwynn; old friends Thomas Edward Otey, George C. Johnson, and Mrs. Walke; to the students who have never let me lose sight of the true purpose of scholarship; and to Mr. Anthony Grahame at Sussex Academic Press, and all the staff members who contributed to the shaping of *Unlikely Haven*.

RPH

❖ PROLOGUE ❖

Lines in Ink

Fifty-odd miles from Dublin, slightly off the Naas–Limerick Highway, the market town of Portarlington lies along the River Barrow, taking in land from both Counties Laois and Offaly. This is the heart of the Irish Midlands, bog-and-turf country. The region boasts an electrical power plant and, until recently, a major flour-processing mill. Portarlington seems anything but extraordinary to the casual glance, and there are very few signs of the oak, yew and elm forests which once dominated the area; but it enjoys a heritage unique among Irish towns.

Some yards from the old central square, the Victorian-Gothic (Anglican) Church of St. Paul houses a set of parish records, dating as far back as 3 June 1694, written in French. One of the shorter entries reads, in translation:

> "Burial: Wednesday 18th November 1713. On Tuesday the 17th day of this month between the hours of four and five o'clock in the evening there passed on, in the Lord's faith, and in the hope of the Glorious Resurrection, ———— Zaintonge, member of this congregation whose soul has gone to God, and whose body was interred today by Monsieur de Bonneval, minister of this church, in the adjacent cemetery."

Tersely-worded though these sentiments may be, the very simplicity and directness through which they are expressed conceal a deep poignancy. These brief strokes of the French clergyman's quill, adhering strictly to the "standard" formula for recording burials, are all that testify to the existence of this particular human being – one of six hundred or so refugees comprising Portarlington's once-flourishing Huguenot colony. Indeed, this may be all that will ever be known about this individual. Why Monsieur (Antoine Ligonier) de Bonneval neglected to inscribe a Christian name is a matter that one can only speculate upon; we are not even granted the knowledge as to whether Zaintonge was a man or woman; child, adolescent or adult; noble or commoner. The surname "Zaintonge" fails to appear in any other record in Ireland, and documentary associations with France have yet to be established. There seem to have been no relatives or descendents who bothered to perpetuate their ancestor's memory. If a gravestone for "Zaintonge" had even been erected in the old Huguenot burial ground behind the present church, and if perchance it has survived, the ravages of time and the elements have unfortunately long effaced the inscription.

This is certainly an intriguing entry – and all the more so because of the many unanswered questions it raises. In a larger sense this might generally be applied to the Huguenots of Ireland as a whole: they are difficult to know and, for every question that is resolved by scholars, many more are suggested, and endlessly debated. Certainly, the tales that this Zaintonge and other expatriated Huguenots might have related: of betrayal and brutalization at the hands of their neighbors and the government they had hitherto respected; of the perils of capture by royal dragoons and bounty-hunters; of excruciating choices between spiritual integrity and physical safety for themselves and those closest to them; of the privations of flight and the protracted pangs of exile – must remain forever unrecorded. The mysterious Zaintonge was only one of an estimated 10,000 French Protestants whose consciences compelled them to dwell in Ireland, and whose presence proved to be a significant source of blessings salvaged by their adopted land during an era otherwise marred by antagonism and unease.

For all of that, however, the story of these most constructive of immigrants has long been ill-documented, under-explored, and then obscured by folklore. The fireside legends that have become so engrained over the centuries often depict the Huguenots as builders of the "Dutch Billy" gabled townhouses; as inaugurators of the Irish linen industry; and as an industrious clan of weavers who – from the confines of their "ghetto" in Dublin's Liberties – waged a vicious feud with Catholic butchers and meted out vigilante justice to miscreants within their own bailiwick. The fact that so much is pure myth does not divert from the historical truth, which reveals a Huguenot presence infinitely more diverse and interesting than that which has hitherto been suspected.

The true chronicle of Ireland's Huguenots is, in opposition to the narrow misrepresentations of the past, one of extraordinary richness and variety, as befits an ethnic group whose influence permeated into every nook of Irish life and society. It is not simply a tale about internationally-known luminaries like Lord Justice Henri Massue de Ruvigny, Earl of Galway; Librarian-Bibliophile & Minister Élie Bouhéreau; Camisard warlord Jean Cavallier; the Latouche banking dynasty; or the architect James Gandon; but also the likes of Zaintonge; the Guionneau triplets;

grocer Jean Clamouse; "François the gardener"; Marie Gerrard, proprietress of the *Merry Shepherd* millinery shop on Dame Street, Dublin; and all the lesser-known refugees of conscience whose distinct and pervasive contributions have become an ineradicable element of Ireland and her cultural heritage.

◈ INTRODUCTION ◈

THE FRENCH NON-CONNECTION: PRE-ORMONDITE HUGUENOTS, c. 1569–1661

"Abolish out of that city that old heresy newly raised and invented, and namely Barnaby Daly and all them that be Huguenettes both men and women."
James Fitzmaurice of Desmond to the Mayor and Corporation of Cork,
12 July 1569

It was a matter of faith; it was a matter of politics: in terms of the Huguenots and their place in the grand historical scheme, it is immensely difficult to trace the dividing-line between the two. Political controversy would certainly dog the Huguenot movement from the time of its inception in France, and well into the years of exile. The primary motives behind the establishment of a Huguenot presence in Ireland were geopolitical in nature. Unlike Britain, which was a natural haven of refuge because of its proximity and a certain general measure of sympathy from the population towards foreign fellow-Protestants, Ireland offered – to say the least – very few attractions for persecuted French Calvinists. Inducements had to be artificially generated, and it was from Dublin Castle and Westminster that the necessary policies of incentive and support were put into place. The advent of some 10,000 Huguenots, pouring into Ireland in three distinct "waves" and establishing a permanent presence, testify to the success of the continuing schemes on the part of the Irish and British governments to buttress the "Protestant interest" against the Irish Catholic majority.

But it was not until 1662 – quite late on, comparatively speaking – that calculated administrative policies were initiated and carried through in earnest. Though individual Huguenots may have been present in Ireland as early as 1569, the existence of a Huguenot community simply did not occur until well into the Restoration period. Until this time, mutually negative perceptions of Huguenots and Irishmen towards each other substantially impeded all variety of interchange. In Ireland's case there was no John à Lasko to act upon the wishes and largesse of a King Edward VI and to exert leadership in securing favorable conditions for foreign Protestant immigration on a large scale, as in southern and eastern England. Whereas in Britain prior to 1662, identifiable Walloon/Dutch and Huguenot settlements had long existed in at least eleven separate sites (London, Canterbury, Dover, Southampton, Sandwich, Maidstone, Convey Island, Colchester, Yarmouth, Norwich and Sandtoft), Ireland had absolutely none. Geographical factors certainly contributed to making Ireland a less attractive destination for potential Protestant immigrants. Ireland was simply not as accessible to fugitives from France as the Low Countries, the Swiss Cantons, the German states, southern England and the Channel Islands. Very few refugees from France, it is fair to say, arrived in Ireland by a direct route. Of the three main paths of escape out of France: overland to the Low Countries in the northeast; through mountain passes into the Swiss cantons from Burgundy, Dauphine, Lyonnais, and Provence; and across the sea from Normandy, Brittany, Aunis and Saintonge – the last was at once the most perilous, and the only route over which fleeing Huguenots could enter Ireland directly. Ireland's situation on Europe's western fringe dictated that virtually all who sought haven there would invariably pass through Britain. More often than not, prior to even setting foot on the English coast, the refugees traveled via the United Provinces, Switzerland and/or Germany, with the free city of Frankfurt am Main functioning for a long time as a sort of center for assemblage and distribution.

Geography aside, Ireland was rendered all the less alluring by the political turbulence and confessional strife that were all-too well-publicized hallmarks of that island's 16th–17th century historical development. The perennial tribal upheavals; the Tyrone Wars and (perhaps most alarmingly in the mind of French Calvinists recalling the St. Bartholomew's Day Massacre of 24 August 1572 and the accompanying provincial bloodbaths that claimed thousands of their number); the horrendous reports of atrocities against Ulster Protestants in 1641 – all this did not act as a magnet. The fact that modern scholarship has revealed that the 1641 crimes attributed to Irish Catholic insurgents were grossly exaggerated (and even, in certain instances, fabricated) does not obscure the truism that often, what actually occurred counts for far less, in the immediate aftermath of an event, than what was popularly believed to have occurred. Luridly-illustrated accounts of atrocities were, in modern parlance, "hot copy"; as comparisons of 1641 literature might square with those current in the wake of the 1572 St. Bartholomew's Day débâcle and those relating the decimation of the Tidewater Virginia colony by Powhatan Indians on March 22, 1622 (the "First Day of Okewas"). The Huguenots would not have had to stretch their imaginations too far to have drawn their own parallels from these contemporary events. Thus Ireland largely lost out on the first two major periods of Huguenot dispersion experienced by England and many other continental Protestant-dominated states: that following the St. Bartholomew's Day events; and that arising from Cardinal Richelieu's reduction of the Huguenots as a military force in campaigns culminating in the Fall of La Rochelle and The Peace of Alais (27 June 1629).

Huguenot Origins

The English Channel may be only between 20–80 miles wide: this is the geographical reality. But in terms of an equally inflexible mental reality a totally different logic has often prevailed on either side. In France the Huguenots were very quickly defined in radical, anti-establishment, and even treacherous terms; while Catholics rapidly claimed the high ground as pillars of order, stability and responsibility. In Britain it was the Protestant element that assumed the garb of respectability; while English (and foreign) Catholics were marked as untrustworthy minions of a dangerous "Papist Internationale". Though this scenario was extremely simplistic (and in many cases unfair) in its characterization, it nonetheless reflected the conventional wisdom of the age.

The British equation of Protestantism with loyalty and Catholicism with treason date to even before the *Act of Supremacy* (1534) enshrined it into the legal code of the realm, and certainly the appearance of the names of: Thomas Bulleine & Jean Claregenette (vicarschoral to Leo Browne, first Anglican Archbishop of Dublin); Bernadin de Valoys (?),Martin Pierre (Pirry?) & Olivier d'Aubigné (respectively: master-gunner, under-treasurer, and controller of the Mint), might *possibly* indicate the presence of foreign Protestant households in Ireland during the reigns of Henry VIII and Edward VI. By no stretch, however, could these individuals be designated as "Huguenots" – as some sources have done. The term was not even in use prior to 1560.

Calvinism itself did not come into existence as a distinguishable, orga-nized sect of Christianity until John Calvin's recall from exile (in Strasbourg) to Geneva in September 1541, followed by the city council's adoption of the *Ordonnances Écclésiastiques* two months later. What was in effect a coup by Calvin's supporters led to the establishment of a theo-cratic state which served as a base for aggressive missionary work, and the dispatching of agents throughout Europe. Even then, it would not be until the 1550s that Calvin's religio-political movement, radiating from its Genevan bastion, began making appreciable inroads into the Reformation in France. Such Protestants as worshipped in France before the mid-16th century fell under diverse strains of inspiration: Lutheran; Erasmo-Humanist; Bucerite; Zwinglian. Pre-Calvinist French Protestant-ism was multi-focused, negligible as a political force (from the Calvinist point of view disorganized, even anarchic), and, especially after the Affair of the Placards in October of 1534, under persecution by the Valois monarchy. The assertion of Calvinism into the framework of the Protestantism in France to the point where the two were virtually synonymous, and the evolution of French Calvinism into a high-profile movement taking on the attributes of an influential political party, were both salient developments of the latter years of the reign of King Henry II (1547–59). Calvinism secured substantial converts among the urban mercantile and professional classes, most visibly in the Languedoc where a mass following was even achieved among the hearty peasant populations of the densely-wooded Cévennes and Vivarais regions. What was most ominous, however, was the new adherence to Calvinism by powerful aristocratic warlords, some of them sharing in the Blood Royal and entertaining claims to the throne itself. Such warlords brought in their wake retainers with significant military experience; members of the ancient *noblesse d'épée*. It was this minor or fringe-nobility anchored in the martial tradition, the écuyers, which was to provide the leadership and expertise for what was to become the Huguenot Movement and whose members much later on – into the years of exile in Ireland – were to set the tone for their transplanted congregations and communities. By 1560, a formidable network apparatus, knit together by locally-based armed forces recruited from congregations put together and led by écuyers (who very often held the balance of power in the individual consistories) and under the ultimate control of grandees like the Condés and Châttillons, had created a virtual rival state within France itself. The political implications inherent in the fact that the local, regional, national tiers of Huguenot organization were mildly republican in their structure and functioning was not lost even at the time on both foes and supporters of the reformed faith: it would later give rise to the Huguenots themselves being depicted as harbingers of liberal democracy.

The designation of "Huguenot" seems to have been applied to French Calvinist as a direct consequence of the Tumult of Amboise of 12 February 1560. On that date a hot-headed young Huguenot écuyer, Jean de Barry, Seigneur de la Renaudie, and a small force attempted to abduct or perhaps assassinate King François II near the Chateau of Amboise. This ill-conceived conspiracy, which many alleged that the Prince de Condé and upper echelons of the Calvinist leadership were aware of, was a total fiasco and shortly thereafter "Huguenot" was being hurled by Catholics as a term of derision against the Protestant partisans. The derivation of the term itself has given rise to elaborate and exhaustive theorizing but, in view of the circumstances prevailing in the aftermath of the Amboise Plot, was most probably adapted from the German *eidgenot,* denoting a subversive, or traitor. This conspiratorial taint was destined to besmirch the Huguenots themselves long afterwards and to engender feelings of suspicion against them that transcended national frontiers and altered circumstances.

While the term "Huguenette" was applied by James Fitzmaurice of Desmond to certain individuals in Cork City in 1569, and while they may genuinely have been French Calvinists, we just cannot be certain unless corroborating evidence can be unearthed. There is no further mention of Huguenots in Cork for another century after Fitzmaurice of Desmond's admonition to the city fathers to "abolish" heresy. Considering the pejorative nature of the term "Huguenot" it cannot be ruled out that this may have been employed as a blanket phrase encompassing all presumably-traitorous Protestants. Fitzmaurice of Desmond's usage here may be akin to the way that the term "Communist" was bandied about to define a variety of individuals and organizations in the United States during the "McCarthy Era" of the early 1950s. If so, this would only be the first of many myths and legends associated with Ireland and its French Calvinist immigrants.

Myth of the Rochelle Merchants

One of the earliest and most tenacious myths to arise concerning the Huguenots of Ireland was that of an alleged colony of French Protestant merchants who, originating mainly from La Rochelle and Bordeaux, had evidently established themselves in Dublin city early during the reign of Queen Elizabeth I. Many of these merchants were reputed to have owned their own ships and to have engaged in the importation of French wines into Irish ports. These foreigners supposedly inhabited the district from St. Nicholas Street to Cornmarket East and West "on the south side of the flesh shambles which in the reign of Queen Elizabeth was kept in High Street". One street in the vicinity of Christ Church Cathedral was known as "Rochel Lane", "Vicus Rupellae" of "Vicus de la Rochel", presumptively after the concentration of Rochellois Protestant merchants. In 1586 a statute enacted by the Irish Parliament required licensure from the Queen or the Lord Deputy for the discharge of all cargoes into Dublin and other entrepots, such as Cork and Waterford, and empowered the Lord Deputy, Lord Chancellor, two Chief Justices and the Chief Baron of the Exchequer to bid in concert to set wine prices. The Rochellois merchants' protests were in vain and the provisions aimed against trade by foreigners were strictly implemented. The Rochellois departed and their colony dwindled into extinction. During the reign of James I (before the year

1610 at least) the flesh shambles were moved from High Street and buildings were joined to those facing the north side of Rochel Lane, which consequently disappeared, the resulting thoroughfare being dubbed "Back Lane" as it ran along what had formerly been the back portion of houses. The name "Rochel Lane" lingered nostalgically in common and legal usage into the 18th century.

As nice as this legend is, considerable doubt is cast upon it; Rochel Lane definitely did not derive its name from Huguenot merchants or even from the town of La Rochelle. Manuscripts of Christ Church Cathedral refer to it as early as 1281, and MacCready speculates that it was laid out around 1185. The name's precise origin cannot be traced conclusively, but it was often spelled "Roche Strete" or "Roche Lane", which suggests a connection with the Roche family. Roche, as a surname, is probably of Norman derivation (sometimes written: "De la Roche"), and the first individuals of that name in Ireland are noted subsequent to the advent of Strongbow.

There is no real evidence for the existence of Huguenot residents in Dublin; there certainly exists an ambiguous reference to Sir William Fitzwilliam's highly-commended servant "Durant" at Dublin Castle in 1572. However, the odd domestic in the service of an English or Anglo-Irish noblemen cannot be genuinely classified as a colonist or settler.The only foreign Protestant colony to merit the name during the Elizabethan Age was set up under the auspices of Viceroy Sir Henry Sidney at Swords, County Dublin. It proved to be abortive and was not Huguenot at all, but Flemish.

Early Stuart Era

Throughout the reign of James I, and that of Charles I up to the Viceroyalty of Thomas Wentworth, Earl of Strafford (1633–41), traces of French Protestant immigration to Ireland are scant. Only five denizations of Frenchmen are recorded between 1601 and 1633: Jacques Fouchier, 16 June 1615; Simon Everard and Jacques Channeau, 21 November 1623; Henri Delaune, 9 January 1628; and Etienne Denis, merchant, 28 April 1628. A reputed resident of Dublin and second-generation Huguenot immigrant, Jean Thorius, was supposedly admitted as a Fellow of the Royal College of Physicians in 1627. What makes this story problematical is that no records of the original fraternity of the Royal College exists to the degree that we can be certain as to the total composition of its members. In the original manuscript the name "Thorius" is not listed though the door is left slightly ajar by an acknowledgment to physicians whose "names are lost".

On the surface it would appear that the Earl of Strafford did make a serious attempt to bring over foreign Protestants during the course of his eight-year stewardship in Ireland, though little seems to have come of it. This initiative was purportedly undertaken in conjunction with efforts at developing the Irish linen industry. By 1636, Strafford boasted of having imported spinning wheels and six looms, and to have planted craftsmen-from Languedoc and the Netherlands. How many Huguenot and/or Dutch-Flemish Calvinist craftsmen actually came to Ireland, and where they resided, has not been conclusively determined – though it is asserted that most of Strafford's manufactures were located in Ulster. The venture is commonly described as a failure. Strafford claimed that he invested and lost 3,000 pounds of his own money while accusers at his subsequent trial testified that the Earl had taken unfair advantage of the two proclamations regulating the size and production of cloth and yarn to fill his own looms with confiscated materials and so eliminate competition. No further mention of the foreign Protestant craftsmen is made by the time of Strafford's impeachment and, during his Vice-Regency only six denizations of Frenchmen are noted in the Patent Rolls: Jacques de Cocquiel, 17 July 1634; Philip Bigot, 10 June 1637; Theodore Rohart (of Lille), 4 November 1639; Daniel and Jean Desminières, 4 November 1639; and David Lomeron (of Chinon), 9 December 1639. Notwithstanding the ardent bit of lip-service that Strafford paid to the idea of providing incentives to French Protestants to dwell in Ireland, it would seem that, like his linen manufactory schemes, little was achieved of any significant effect.

In France: Subversion to Loyalism

It is not possible to understand the eventual emergence of an exilic French Calvinist community in Ireland without some knowledge of the tumultuous story of the Huguenot movement in its homeland from 1562 to 1629, and an appreciation of the depths of its transformation. Festering political rivalry among the great noble houses; deterioration of royal authority after the mortal wounding of King Henry II in a joust; and religious hatreds broke down into a drawn-out series of murderous clashes and depredations by fanatical armed mobs directed by local warlords who knew little and cared less for predestination and transubstantiation. This thirty-eight year raping of France and its resources has been termed the *Wars of Religion*. It began in 1562 with the burning alive in their own Temple of worship at Vassy in Champagne of Calvinist men, women and children by Catholic soldiers under command of François de Lorraine, Duke de Guise; and would only subside in 1598 as King Henry IV secured the final signatures to the Edict of Nantes.

When stripped of pretenses aimed at justifying the inexcusable, it boiled down to two factions interested in the acquisition of raw power: a loosely-coordinated collection of warlords choosing to galvanize Calvinist écuyers and consistories into a Huguenot Party; and equally-unsavory notables manipulating the Catholic elements of the realm into what was later to be dubbed the "Holy League". The degree of sheer butchery practiced by both sides, and the proportion of political assassinations and acts of terrorism in these conflicts, was remarkable even by 16th century standards. It was the Catholic partisans who proved to be a bit better at it; and when confronted by the shock of betrayal by the Royal House of Valois on that fateful St. Bartholomew's Day of 24 August 1572 the Huguenot intelligentsia and clergy found cause to openly justify rebellion against tyrants and the violent overthrow of oppressive regimes – and indeed the Huguenots became notorious throughout Europe as fomenters of subversion and insurrection. The brilliant Philippe de Mornay, Seigneur du Plessis-Marly was the most influential of these "zealots". A survivor of St. Bartholomew's Day, his most significant work, *Vindiciae Contra Tyrannos* (1579), asserted the concepts of government as a contract based on the monarch's respect for fundamental liberties, and the right of the people, through their "lesser magistrates" to resist – or even depose – constituted authority in the event of violation of this trust. In future years, Huguenots would sometimes experience great difficulty in shaking off this turbulent image.

When the Protestant Henry of Navarre came to grips with the fact that the majority of his potential subjects were not going to budge from the Catholicism of their ancestors his pragmatic conversion to the Papal faith in 1593 in effect secured his actual accession to the French throne as King Henry IV. However, he was not able to end the conflict that had ripped France apart until 1598, and only at the cost (to royal authority) of allowing the Huguenots to maintain their private armies and *places de sureté* and function as – to repeat the trite phrase – a "state within a state".

In a France where sentiment gravitated towards a strengthening and centralizing of governmental power, the free-wheeling partisan brand of Huguenotism gradually fell into disrepute as one grandee after another drifted back into the Roman fold. Even Mornay was anxious to distance himself from the sentiments of *Vindiciae Contra Tyrannos* and took pains to demonstrate his loyalty to King Louis XIII (though that did not prevent his deposition as governor of Saumur).

The outbreak of the Rohan War of 1621–29 gave Cardinal Richelieu the pretext to dismantle Calvinist strongholds and to forever break the Huguenot Party as a military/political threat. As an arch-Machiavellian Richelieu did not let his office as prince of the Roman Catholic Church intrude upon his political agenda and contented himself with that. The

Peace of Alais which he negotiated with the chastened Huguenot leadership confirmed, though in slightly altered form, the essential guarantees for worship as stated in the Edict of Nantes.

This pragmatic policy certainly earned Richelieu the enmity of the fanatically-Catholic dévot faction at court (which was never far from the King's ear), but it was to generate enormous advantages for the royalist cause in the decades to follow. The mass defection of the grandees and the eclipse of the Huguenot Party allowed the écuyers and the bourgeois elements to blossom as never before, and the French Calvinist community embarked on a quiet but steadfast attempt to assimilate into the mainstream of French society. Under different leadership Huguenotism (or the *Religion Pretendu Reforme* – RPR – as it was legally designated) shed much of its militant character and the majority of its worshippers assumed an attitude of pronounced, even painstaking loyalism *vis-à-vis* the Bourbon monarchy.

Cromwell & the Huguenots

On first glance, one might assume that Huguenots were only too glad to relocate to a nearby land where the religious and political leadership favored a creed so similar to to their own. Commonwealth and Protectorate England dominated by reformist Protestant ideology would seem to have favored the establishment of substantial numbers of French Calvinists in occupied Ireland, and the existence of such settlements is asserted by at least one source. It certainly is true that British Puritanism and French Calvinism held most basic religious tenets in common, and that Lord Protector Oliver Cromwell evinced great interest in trying to persuade foreign Protestants to come to Ireland. These included: New England Puritans; Bohemian refugees of various denominations; Dutch Reformists; and Huguenots. As an inducement the Cromwellian administration in Dublin held out letters patent of denization under the Great Seal of Ireland to individuals of any nation whatever, who professed Protestantism. These efforts and religious affinity notwithstanding, there is no evidence to indicate the existence of a Huguenot colony in Cromwellian Ireland; indeed, all signs point to the contrary.

Conditions in France itself militated against mass emigration. The Commonwealth and Protectorate period in England (1648–60) coincided almost perfectly with a sort of Indian Summer for the *RPR* in France when most of the Huguenot subjects of King Louis XIV basked in the favor of the powerful First Minister, Cardinal Mazarin. During the crisis years of the Fronde (1648–52), the French Calvinist population had displayed overwhelming solidarity in support of the youthful king and the Cardinal-

Minister, spurning nostalgic appeals from the Prince de Condé. The Huguenot écuyers, whose ancestors had formed the backbone of the armies of Coligny and Condé, distinguished themselves this time on the side of their Catholic monarch against the Frondist rebels. Isaac Dumont de Bostaquet from Normandy, future writer of *Mémoires* who was to become one of the notable Huguenot expatriates in Ireland, was among the armed participants in this conflict.

At court, the work of the *Députés-Générals*, who officially represented their Calvinist co-religionists to the king and his ministers, was instrumental in temporarily securing a more advantageous legal position for the Reformed faith. Beginning in 1649, the Marquis d'Arzelliers and his successor (1653) Henri Massue, Marquis de Ruvigny played upon this consistent demonstration of loyalty to bolster the legal position of the *RPR* under the framework of the Edict of Nantes. On 21 may 1652, d'Arzelliers succeeded in obtaining a Royal Declaration in favor of the Huguenots which expressly reconfirmed the Edict's safeguards and went as far as nullifying all judgments of Parlements and other sovereign courts which could be proven to be contrary to its spirit. The trend for the extension of limited favor at court for the realm's Huguenot minority continued under Député-Général Ruvigny but came to an ominous halt when the Royal Declaration of 18 July 1656 abrogated that of 21 May 1652 and left the *RPR* potentially open to parlementary attack, as it had been immediately after the Peace of Alais. Though the 1656 Declaration was to mark a point of departure, and thereafter the position of the Huguenots would gradually deteriorate, Mazarin's residual gratitude assured that their situation would not suffer a drastic downturn as long as he was alive. The Cardinal's well-known comment is nonetheless worth repeating: "I have nothing against the Little Flock, for though they graze on bad herbage, at least they do not stray".

Nor did similarities in worship translate into approval for Cromwellian policies. As early on as 1610 shocked reactions within the Reformed community to Henry IV's assassination by François Ravaillac indicated a shift away from endorsement of regicide. By 1649, this had developed into a mood of abhorrence when news of the execution of King Charles I by order of Parliament was received in France. One Huguenot proclamation denounced the beheading of the king as "the most horrid crime committed since the death of the Prince of Glory", and exalted through Biblical example (i.e.: that of David refraining from harming King Saul in 1st Samuel 26:9) the inviolable covenant between subject and sovereign. The Provincial Synod encompassing Aunis, Saintonge and Angoumois issued a strongly-worded admonition for all Reformed congregations to maintain complete obedience to the Crown. Cavalier expatriates were sheltered and generously assisted by a variety of sympathetic Huguenots, and in the case of one of these exiled Stuart supporters, James Butler, First Duke of Ormond, this experience was to translate into the first successful attempts at establishing French Calvinists in Ireland.

The loyalist posture taken by most Huguenots as personified by Ruvigny and his namesake son (the future Earl of Galway, who shared the office of *Député-Général* with his father from 1678) was often upheld at the expense of more zealot-minded co-religionists, and was to develop into a festering source of friction and recrimination during the years of exile.

Only one immigrant is recorded as having availed himself of the generous naturalization incentives offered up by the Cromwellians: Isaac Ablin from Caen in Normandy on 18 January 1656. Louis Desminieres, who received his letters on 11 December 1655, cannot truly be counted inasmuch as his family had resided in Dublin since at least 1639, and perhaps as early-on as 1631.

It may therefore be concluded, from the evidence as it now stands, that no Huguenot settlement of any reasonably distinct or permanent nature or of sufficient size to deserve this designation existed in Ireland prior to the Restoration era. It was only after 1660, when events in both France and Ireland conspired to inaugurate a drawn-out period of mass immigration of persecuted French Protestants, that Huguenot colonization became a reality.

References

Primary sources

British Library (London): Sloane Ms. 1008.
Calendar of State Papers (Domestic) 1660–85, p. 363.
Calendar of State Papers (Ireland) 1509–73, pp. 36, 45, 116, 119, 127–8.
Calendar of State Papers (Ireland) 1601–30, p. 629.
Calendar of State Papers (Ireland)1669–70, addenda 1625–70, p. 267.
Huguenot Society of London: Quarto Series, Vol. XVII.
Irish Statutes. Vol. I, 28 Elizabeth c. iv, pp. 410–15.
Royal College of Physicians (Dublin) Manuscript: List of Fellows.

Secondary sources

Barnard, T. C. *Cromwellian Ireland*, pp. 53, 57–58, 85–87.
Coonan, T. L. *The Irish Catholic Confederacy and the Puritan Revolution*, pp. 109–21.
Deyon, Solange. *Du Loyalisme au Refus*, pp. 9–10.
Dunlop, Robert. *Ireland Under the Commonwealth*, Vol. II, pp. 560, 582–83.
Gill, Conrad. *The Rise of the Irish Linen Industry*, p. 8.
Gimlette, Thomas. *The History of the Huguenot Settlers in Ireland*, pp. 109, 113, 129–30, 136, 179.
Kearney, Hugh F. *Strafford in Ireland, 1633–41*, pp. 155, 157, 159.

Kingdon, Robert M. *Geneva and the Coming of the Wars of Religion in France, 1555–1563*, p. 59.

Lee, Grace Lawless. *The Huguenot Settlements in Ireland*, pp. 4–5, 8.

Leonard, Emile G. *Histoire Generale du Protestantisme: I La Reformation*, pp. 261, 270–6. *II L'Etablissement*, pp. 82–6, 94–103, 332–3.

Ligou, Daniel. *Le Protestantisme en France de 1598 à 1715*, pp. 18, 118, 120, 171–6, 180, 194.

Lindley, Keith J. "The Impact of the 1641 Rebellion Upon England and Wales, 1641–45" in *Irish Historical Studies*, Vol. XVIII, 1972, pp. 143–8, 150, 152, 176.

Magdelaine, Michelle. "Le Refuge: le role de Francfort-sur-le-Main" in Caldicott, Edric, Gough, Hugh, and Pittion, Jean-Paul, *The Huguenots and Ireland: Anatomy of an Emigration*, pp. 151–9.

Miquel, Pierre. *Les Guerres de Religion*, pp. 211–13.

Mousnier, Roland. *L'Assassinat d'Henri IV*, pp. 245–46.

Parker, David in Hepburn, A. C. *Minorities in History*, pp. 17–18.

Rushworth, John. *The Tryal of the Earl of Strafford* p. 422.

Seymour, John D. *Oxford Historical and Literary Studies. Vol. XII: The Puritans in Ireland, 1647–1661*, p. 112.

Smiles, Samuel. *The Huguenots in England and Ireland*, p. 428.

Thompson, James Westfall. *The Wars of Religion in France, 1559–1576*, pp. 16–17.

❖ PART I ❖

The Ormondite Refuges

Change often occurs so rapidly and dramatically that history invariably leaves behind individuals or groups of individuals whose contribution, and even existence, are not acknowledged for centuries – if at all. Records may be so fragile and fragmentary that all that remains is, at best, oral recollection that is eventually garbled into lore and legend. The waves of Huguenot immigrants who arrived in Ireland during the 30-year span of the Restoration period are one such set of historical orphans. They were so subsumed by the Huguenots who came after 1691 that they have in effect lost their identity as the distinct phenomenon that they were.

Even the term "Ormondite" is admittedly, somewhat arbitrary. Though the First Duke of Ormond was the indispensable designer and catalyst of the French Protestant immigration, and by virtue of his two terms as Restoration Viceregent of Ireland (1662–9 and 1677–85), the most influential Irishman of his day, the Huguenot community that developed assumed an independent existence of its own. Despite the vicissitudes of the Jacobite/Williamite struggles for control of Ireland, this community survived to lay the basis for the more dominant influxes of French Calvinists that were to come.

◈ I ◈

THE EARLY ORMONDITE REFUGE,
1662–1680

"An Irish Roman Catholic doctor has threatened to have me burned. He says he knows I have come to hunt them (Irish Catholics) out and that I was a pernicious Huguenot of (La) Rochelle . . ."

Dr. Desfontaines-Voutron (Jacques du Brois de Fontaine?) to Joseph
Williamson, 18 January 1670

James Butler, First Duke of Ormond was an innovator. He was versatility personified; the "White Duke" had survived against all odds – his swashbuckling escapades had endowed him with legendary status. As a youth he had openly defied the formidable Strafford (far from retaliating, the Lord Deputy had been impressed enough with the young nobleman to become his friend and political mentor). He had walked a tight rope during the Confederation period, and – sneaking in and out of Britain in true cloak-and dagger fashion – had continually cheated the axeman by promoting the cause of Charles II under Cromwell's very nose. He and his family had subsisted – sometimes in straitened circumstances – as expatriates in France. Foremost among those who offered the Butlers succor and comfort were members of the Huguenot community: pastors, nobles, merchants, artisans and professionals. Unlike the Stuarts whom he served, particularly the newly-restored and repatriated King Charles II, Ormond was not inclined to forget or cast aside those who had stood by him in leaner times.

Ormond's years in exile had further refined his perspective from that of provincial grandee to that of a seasoned statesman capable of measuring his realm of Ireland in trans-national terms. During the most productive of his four tenures in office as Lord-Lieutenant of Ireland (1662–9), Ormond energetically fostered a policy that encouraged urbanization; economic growth and a more independent position for Ireland *vis-à-vis* inter-Britannic trade; patronage of the arts and humanities; the bolstering of the Anglican Protestant church; and the fashioning of a capital city worthy of functioning as a showcase, and anchored by an appropriately resplendent vice-regal court. One cornerstone upon which the Duke's modernization program was to rest was French Protestant colonization of Ireland. The seed for this idea may have germinated during the years of Ormond's apprenticeship under Strafford, for it maintained a distinctly commercial slant. However, the Duke's perceptions were undoubtedly deepened and expanded by the Huguenot contacts he had established in northern France in the course of his exile. Ormond grew to share the admiration of many of his contemporaries for the proverbial energy, integrity, competence, skills and business acumen that characterized Huguenot merchants, professionals, clergymen and artisans. The rather patronising expectation (expressed on more than one occasion) was that the example of these assiduous newcomers might inspire the general Irish population to habits of hard work, sobriety and thrift. But the consideration which seems to have weighed heaviest in the reckoning of an arch-loyalist like Ormond was degree to which the Huguenot community had expressed fidelity to the monarchial principle and had condemned Parliamentary and Protectorate policies against royal authority. Therefore, out of both principle and gratitude they could prove themselves to be towers of strength against future challenges to the restored Stuarts.

The 1662 Irish parliamentary *Act for Encouraging Protestant Strangers and Others To Establish themselves in Ireland* was crucial to the Duke's schemes. Under its provisions, valid for seven years, foreign Protestants – on subscribing to the Oaths of Allegiance and Supremacy – were to be automatically naturalized and further considered the same as natural-born subject of the Crown regarding rights under the law. Collective naturalization under this system was intended to give immigrants to Ireland some distinct advantage over those putting down roots in England, where the process of naturalization remained a cumbersome procedure and letters were granted on an individual basis – as a favor that was slow and difficult to come by. Foreign Protestants were further to be allowed the freedom of the city upon payment of twenty shillings, and entrance into most guilds and professional corporations without payment of fine.

Among the first French Calvinists to benefit from the 1662 statute were those who had accompanied Ormond out of exile and formed part of his cortege. These included: Jacques Hierome from Sedan, the Duke's personal chaplain; the youthful but promising Pierre Drelincourt (future Dean of Armagh Cathedral); Pierre de St. Pol; Miché Du Metz; and the brothers André and Pierre Le Moyne. Hierome (sometimes denoted as "Jerome"in certain records) undoubtedly exerted influence upon the Duke, and upon the direction taken by Early Ormondite colonization, and perhaps functioned initially as leader ofthe Irish Huguenot community –

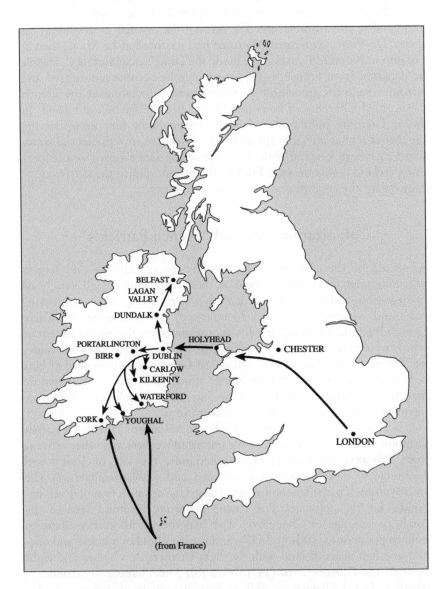

Major routes of Huguenot immigration into Ireland

such as it was. Hierome was an individual of considerable intellect, having been educated by the eminent Louis Cappel at the Seminary of Saumur, and gaining considerable note for the skill he evinced in defending his thesis, *De Voto Paupertatis*. Hierome had pastored at Le Mans, then at Fécamp in Normandy, where he made the Duke's acquaintance. Thence he departed from France to England where he became naturalized and adroitly made the transition to Anglicanism, officiating at the French Conformed Churches of Somerset House and the Savoy until 1662. In 1663, Hierome published a French prayer book for newly-arriving Huguenot immigrants. He also at times evinced an entrepreneurial strain which, while in keeping with the tenor of the Duke's own vision for a "new Ireland", was to work both to the benefit and to the detriment of projects for the re-settlement of his co-religionists.

Colonization sites and "French Patrick's"

As would be the case later, Dublin – as the capital city and largest urban/commercial center – served as the natural hub for all variety of immigration, and it was there that what was probably the most substantial (and certainly the best-documented) concentration of Early Ormondite Huguenots occurred. Other settlements, the establishment of which were masterminded at least in part by the Duke, Pastor Hierome, Sir William Temple and Colonel Richard Lawrence, experienced at best only transient success and included: Waterford (which was mainly mercantile); and Clonmel, Carrick-on-Suir, and Chapelizod (which were intended to be industrial/artisan concentrations).

It was at Chapelizod, then a far-western suburb of Dublin City, that Ormond's agent Sir William Temple imported weavers and other artisans from Brittany, Normandy, the Netherlands, the Isle of Jersey and Saintonge to establish a center for linen and wool manufacture. The viceroy himself provided looms and ordered the construction of dwelling-houses for the colonists. For Pastor Hierome, Ormond secured the Anglican vicarage of Chapelizod with a perpetual allowance of thirty pounds per annum (10 June 1667), and the leasehold of a house and one-and-one half acres of land with the right to graze two horses and eight cows in the Phoenix Park (14 July 1668). The Chapelizod settlement, which included Flemish as well as French immigrant weavers, had a promising debut. By 1669, Ormond and Temple had entrusted the administration of the linen and wool processing to the ambitious and controversial Colonel Richard Lawrence, at which date the enterprise appeared to be doing well. The Chapelizod works enjoyed a monopoly on supplying the army in Ireland with linen, and had received an advance of 1,900 pounds from government coffers. A bleach yard was authorized by the Irish Parliament, and subsequently set up at the site where there were allegedly 300 artisans employed in the production of cordage, sailcloth, tacking, linen cloth and diaper that was especially renowned; even blankets and friezes were manufactured with a fair degree of initial success. The Duke of Ormond himself introduced useful initiatives: Dutch spinning wheels; protective duties to bolster the linen traffic; and prizes for linen and flax cultivation – all of which proved much more successful than Strafford had been.

However, for reasons which are not entirely clear, and despite every apparent encouragement, and generous government subsidies, the enterprises at Chapelizod had foundered by 1677. Lawrence was out of the picture and the Huguenot/Flemish colony had passed into extinction. As for the enterprise itself, it seems to have been revived for a time in a much more modest scale; Alderman Christopher Lovett was granted the lease of the bleach yard by the government, in 1677, for the term of 21 years, together with stock (including looms) valued at 1,200 pounds. After Lovett's death his wife Frances managed the works. In 1690 Mrs. Lovett, supporting the claims to the throne of William III, refused to supply the French and Irish armies and consequently suffered the seizure of her goods and property, a Quaker named Broomfield assuming proprietorship. On 11 June 1692, acting on an appeal by Mrs. Lovett, Whitehall upheld her claim and she was released by letters patent from all constraint. After this, there is no further mention of linen works at Chapelizod – no trace of its existence in the early eighteenth century has been found, though some have sought in vain for it. The Huguenots had certainly long gone – perhaps even prior to the time that Lawrence's business had folded.

Grace Lawless Lee ventured that the Huguenots at Chapelizod were domiciled too near to Dublin to sustain a separate identity and, worshipping at the French Church which was established at St. Patrick's Cathedral, "became indistinguishable from the Dublin Huguenots". This is unlikely; one would ask why they would have been inclined to make the journey as far as St. Patrick's when chapels existed in and nearer to their village for that purpose. The same author uses a similar argument to hypothesize about the demise of the Huguenot colony at Wicklow Town during a later period; in view of the greater distance involved, this is rendered even less plausible. There is furthermore nothing to suggest that any weaver, or person of other trades related to linen or wool manufacturing processes who resided at Chapelizod, attended St. Patrick's. The only document that might remotely be construed as supportive of such a contention is the presence, in the Freeman's Rolls of the City of Dublin, of a French Protestant weaver named Jean Combs, who was admitted in Easter of 1678. The earliest pertinent reference in the Register of St. Patrick's mentions one

Jean Légeron, a wool-comber who arrived from Vouillé in Poitou along with his wife Adrienne Saran prior to 1685. Every circumstance, however, suggests that this family formed part of the Late Ormondite group of Huguenot immigrants and, as such, entered Ireland no earlier than 1681 – much after Lawrence and his workers had departed. Absolutely no evidence exists to even remotely support the contention that the colonists moved from Chapelizod to establish themselves in the Liberties of Dublin. Few details are known about the French Calvinist settlers who reached Ireland during the three years immediately following the 1662 Act, but there appears to have been a largely favourable response to the incentives held out by this piece of legislation, at least in Dublin. By late 1665 there were probably some 24 families comprising some 100-odd individuals. French Calvinists had by then become a sizable enough minority (and one that might potentially expand into an influential economic and political force) to arouse some measure of concern at Dublin Castle. Problems might be posed that required solutions to address the cultural, linguistic and religious isolation of the new arrivals.

The most vexing question centered around how to shepherd growing numbers of French Calvinists into the Anglican Church and prevent their making common cause with dangerous Presbyterian dissenters – for whom Ormond had a particular revulsion. Even at this stage, the seeds would be planted for the permanent, often-bitter, rift within the Huguenot dispersion in Ireland over the desirability of choosing Anglican Conformity (and security in an alien environment under Episcopal protection), as opposed to remaining steadfast in the ancestral Calvinist faith, for which so much had already been sacrificed. Upon arriving, the immigrants would tend to attempt to conserve most of what they had been familiar with in France, forms of religious practice included. However, the ethnic and language barriers coupled with their relatively small numbers worked to disorient and intimidate the new arrivals, and made it extremely difficult for congregations to meet living expenses for their pastor – let alone the cost of maintaining an independent church. Or, at least, this held true for the Early Ormondite group.

The Duke determined that the occasion was right for proposing that a specific meeting place be established for conducting services in French, where it could be assured that the worshippers would act in conformity with the Anglican communion, and thus not pose a potential threat. He began by addressing a formal letter on 30 November 1665 to Dr. Michael Boyle, Archbishop of Dublin, explaining the necessity for finding an appropriate lieu for French Protestants "and others who wished to join them" to worship in their native language under the rite and discipline of the Church of Ireland. The Archbishop suggested the Chapel of St. Mary's (commonly known as the Lady Chapel) within St. Patrick's Cathedral. On

23 December 1665, the Lady Chapel was formally granted to the newly-constituted French Conformist congregation, and would be renewed, as it proved, every twenty-one years, at the rent of one shilling, until 1817. Shortly thereafter a special delegation, which included four Huguenot members – Hierome, Élias de Ruinat, Jacques Du Brois de Fontaine, and Jean Hérault – was appointed by the Lord-Lieutenant to negotiate terms with the Cathedral Dean and Chapter. It was agreed to lease the Lady Chapel directly to the delegates, who would function as the French Congregation's Trustees, under condition that:

(1)   The French parishioners would themselves be responsible for the Chapel's upkeep;
(2)   French services would never interfere with those conducted in the choir of the Cathedral;
(3)   Burials in the Chapel were left in the hands of the Dean and Chapter;
(4)   The Chapel area might still be used for special meetings of the bishops: and
(5)   The French congregation must submit "in all manner" to the Anglican discipline.

The final provision would by far prove to be the most controversial.

Dr. Boyle agreed to Ormond's request that Jacques Hierome be named minister of what was to be formally styled the "French Conformed Church of St. Patrick's" (colloquially known as "French Patrick's"). The formal opening service was held on 29 April 1666 and duly attended by the Lord-Lieutenant, the Primate of the Church of Ireland, Dr. Boyle, and the Lord Mayor of Dublin. This particular Lord Mayor – the second individual to hold that distinction – was the Huguenot, Jean Desminiéres.

Troubles & Eclipse

Sparse though the records for the 1660s that reflect upon the Early Ormondite Huguenots may be, they nonetheless hint at steady unspectacular population growth from 1662–8; a sharp but short-lived influx from 1669–70; and a very drastic dwindling between the period 1671–9 to the point of the colony's virtual extinction.

The Duke of Ormond's fall from grace and removal from office in 1669 could not have had anything other than a dampening effect upon the new Huguenot residents, despite the fact that the Duke's dismissal was tied to his connection to the banished Earl of Clarendon and opposition to King Charles II's new pro-Catholic policies, and had no bearing on his colonization schemes. Ormond had after all been their patron and protector. Almost simultaneously, the generous provisions of the Act of 1662 lapsed. Perhaps, also the settlers had been somewhat mesmerized by "sales pitches" extolling the advantages they would derive from transplanting to Ireland, and experience had not borne out their expectations. If so, they would certainly not have been the only disillusioned group to resort to the phenomenon of return migration.

There is, in seeming contradiction, a curious letter from the Duke of Montague (then British Ambassador to France) to Lord Arlington, Principal Secretary of State, dated 9 November 1669 stating that at that date the number of Huguenots departing France to settle in Ireland was of sufficient proportion to have alarmed King Louis XIV. The King, in consequence, issued an order for all his subjects to return to France within six months' time. The King had no reason for alarm, because this seems to have been a strictly local migration, the extent of which reports had grossly exaggerated. There was a great deal of consternation in the city of Rouen, Normandy where in 1669 the Chambers of the Edict of Nantes were being suppressed. Rouen had a long-standing, substantial Huguenot population, though it had been in decline and under intermittent intimidation since the St. Bartholomew's Day Massacre. Mercantile families from Rouen had maintained strong connections to Dublin since at least the 1630s, and six additional families fitting this description registered as new arrivals in Dublin from 1669–70. This Rouenais impetus rapidly spent itself, and the number of incoming French immigrants reached a standstill.

Jean Carré credits this to a lessening of pressure on Protestants in France as a by-product of the Franco-British alliance against the Netherlands from 1672 to 1674. The influence of the *Caisse des Conversions* during this time must also be counted as a factor. Paul Pellison (1624–93) was an erstwhile Huguenot who converted to Catholicism in 1670 and was able to exert sufficient influence on the Louis XIV to receive royal authorization to utilize funds from vacant or moribund Catholic benefices that were at the Crown's disposal (initially, those properties in the possession of the Abbeys of Cluny and St. Germain-des-Près) to cajole and bribe Huguenots into abjuring their faith. This *Caisse des Conversions* became the semi-official organ for the gradual attainment of religious conformity. Any former Huguenot who could produce a certificate of acceptance into the Roman Catholic Church could qualify for a stipend. In the early 1680s it was felt that the returns in conversions were too few and proceeding too slowly in relation to expenditures, and the *Caisse* would be superseded in favour of a more repressive policy.

The Huguenots of the *Réligion Prétendu Réformé* who took the quiescent stance also found a ready and substantial champion in Jean Baptiste

Colbert (1619–83), Controller General of Finance for Louis XIV. Colbert's energetic mercantilist schemes and economic reforms, in the twenty years between 1661–81, reduced the French national debt by five-sixths. Colbert saw the hard-working Huguenot minority as an economic asset and generally favored them in his business and trade policy decisions. One of the cornerstones of Mercantilism was for a nation to strive for economic self-sufficiency and to minimize foreign imports. To this end he was particularly anxious to encourage the development of luxury-producing enterprises, notably: lace; textiles & linen; carpets & tapestries; draperies; silk; and leather products. The Huguenots were heavily (ungenerous souls even said disproportionately) involved in all of these. Colbert himself, and his family, remained staunchly Catholic (a brother and a cousin became bishops), but many of his less-pragmatic and more fanatical co-religionists were ready to use his policies against him and level the accusation that he was a crypto-Calvinist. Colbert was not able to stem the rising tide of petty legalistic harassment of Huguenots that began in the mid-1660s, and worsened as time went on. Even before his death, the Controller-General was losing his grip on power and was unable to effectively protect the Huguenots from the full rigors of state-sponsored persecution.

However, before this broke down, the Colbertian mania for practicality and the generally moderate measures of the 1660s–70s certainly had the effect of snuffing out the Huguenot immigration into Ireland. In 1672 a contemporary source revealed that, even in Dublin, only twelve French Protestant families could readily be found. Many factors might account for a decline – but how can one explain a decline so profound and so rapid? One point worth making is that the Early Ormondite influx, unlike those that followed, cannot be considered a "refugee" phenomenon. Certainly Huguenots experienced discrimination and some measure of harassment in their homeland during the 1660s–70s, but the situation had not deteriorated to the point where life was intolerable. And it is an irrefutable fact that, as long as this was so, no amount of incentives within the power of the Lord-Lieutenant or anyone else to offer could effectively induce French Protestants to leave all that they had grown to know and cherish to settle on an island on the fringes of Europe that was so alien to them in language and tradition. Only when faced with the unendurable did Huguenots arrive in sufficient numbers, at an adequately consistent rate to assure that any of their settlements had substantial basis for survival.

Nature of the Early Ormondite "Refuge"

Why not just use the term "Ormondite", and leave out the more fastidious qualifiers: "Early" and "Late"? This is because, notwithstanding the fact that these were all mainly Huguenots, two separate and opposing communities are being embraced. The Early Ormondite settlers (1662–80) were predominately mercantile, politically passive and largely composed of Huguenots from Northern French Provinces. The Later Ormondites (1681–92) were more socially diverse, less amenable to following authority and to religious conformity within the Anglican fold, and encompassed refugees who came mainly from Southern France.

Who were the Early Ormondites? Among the heads of families arriving in Dublin who were Huguenots (or in a few cases, Protestant strangers who identified themselves with the Huguenot community), the social status/occupation of 37 are known, and out of this 15 were definitely merchants (Cossart, Benoit, Le Moyne, De Langle, Dupin, D'Amour, Pain, Boyer, Choisin, Desminiéres, De St. Croix, Bazin, Michel, Laffarier, and Duchemain). As far may presently be determined, the social composition amongst the Early Ormondites, exclusive of mercantile families, breaks down to: three noblemen (Herault, St. Jean, De La Mézandière); one physician (Du Brois); three clergymen (Hierome, Viridet, Drelincourt); and one joiner (Comtesse); shoemaker (Cocheteux); "Dutch painter" (De Milly); ribbon-weaver (surname unknown); lapidary (also unknown); blacksmith (Destreé); goldsmith (La Roch); baker (Moule); glazier (Tonge); barber-surgeon (Lenere); weaver (Combs); serge weaver (Picard); tallow chandler (another Destreé); engraver (Destaches); and stationer (Sisson). A glance at the known provincial/regional origins of these families reveals that the majority formerly dwelled in areas north of the River Loire: 16 families as opposed to three from the south. Normandy had by far the most (7), with the preponderance of Norman settlers listed as being from Rouen. One is tempted to raise the question of the existence of a trading network or confraternity in which the Desminières, in view of their Norman and Dutch connections, and their positions of influence within the corporate elite of Dublin City, may possibly have had a guiding hand. Other merchants from Normandy who appear to have been in a class to themselves, were the Pereiras, Emanuell (alias Jacques Vandepeere) and François. They were the first to take advantage of the provisions of the 1662 Act for "Encouraging Protestant strangers *and others* . . . to settle and plant in Ireland" (emphasis mine). The Pereiras took the Oath of Supremacy and Allegiance on 3 October 1662, and Emanuell is recorded as having been admitted as a Freeman at Michaelmas of that same year. It would seem that the Pereiras were actually Jewish, though to what degree they maintained themselves so in faith, while paying lip-service to the Anglican Church, is a moot question (the possibility that they were converts cannot be totally ruled out, nor would they have been unique in capitalizing on legal loopholes as regards confessional matters). Huguenot families from other northern French provinces included: four from Ile de France; and one each from Flandre, Picardy, Anjou, Champagne and Burgundy.

The Robartes, Berkeley & Essex Years

The modernizing impetus did not grind to a halt upon Ormond's dismissal; in point of fact the Duke's three successors pushed urban expansion and property development to levels that he must himself have envied while having to relegate himself to an observer's role. Sir John (Second Baron) Robartes (1669); Lord Berkeley of Stratton (1669–72); and Arthur Capel First Earl of Essex (1672–7) presided over a substantial construction boom on the north side of the River Liffey. This was climaxed by the exploits of the flamboyant entrepreneur, politician, and one-time Lord Mayor, Sir Humphrey Jervis: the substantial Jervis Estate was subdivided and developed, and the Essex Bridge constructed to link its residents to the main part of Dublin across the Liffey.

The three viceroys who succeeded Ormond were much less committed to protecting the Anglican faith and only lukewarm to the notion of encouraging the immigration and settlement of Protestants from the Continent. There was a sea-change in Dublin Castle regarding religious policy: Dissenters were granted greater leeway (which tended to split the fledgling Huguenot community) and Catholics were allowed much more freedom of action, and even privileges. Though there was by no means even mild (and certainly not orchestrated) persecution of Huguenots, the atmosphere in Ireland after 1669 was decidedly less welcoming; and the favours visited on Catholics certainly emboldened them to the point where they were at times unabashed in expressing contempt for Protestants both native and foreign. If as sheltered an individual as Dr. Du Brois de Fontaine (attached as he was to the powers at Dublin Castle) was subject to abusive and threatening encounters with increasingly-assertive Irish Catholics, how much more unnerving must the atmosphere have been for his less-protected co-religionists (recall the epigraph at the beginning of this chapter).

A letter written in 1672 by Mr. George Blackall, later a Dublin alderman, to his cousin sheds light on what was probably the nadir of the Huguenot community in Ireland – what remained of it. Blackall indicated that he had been deliberately searching for French families resident in the capital and had discovered only 18 – of whom 6 had been found to be Catholics. What is even more revealing is that Blackall felt compelled to divide the twelve French Protestant households into "Anglicans" and "Presbyterians". It had not taken long for the problem of non-conformity to have broken through the veneer of the "French Patrick's" arrangement.

Significantly, half those unearthed by Mr. Blackall were classified as non-conformist "Presbyterians": a "Monsieur Le Roy"; Andre Boyer (a confectioner from Montpellier); Paul De Melly or Milly (described as a "Dutch painter" – which could conceivably mean a painter in the Dutch style); Jean Comtesse (a joiner from Amiens); an un-named lapidary; and an equally-anonymous ribbon-weaver. Those Huguenots termed "Anglicans" included: Du Brois de Fontaine (surgeon); Jean & Louis Desminières; Isaac John (sic?); and two who are not named (though one was undoubtedly David Cossart, a merchant from Rouen). There was evidently a problem over a friend of Mr. Blackall's cousin; this friend being a French minister in search of a flock – with a living to support himself. The general thrust of Blackall's letter indicated that the situation was unpromising.

In 1677, the Duke of Ormond returned to Dublin Castle for what was to be his ultimate term as viceroy. Even as he savored his vindication, events in France were being set into motion that would brush aside the Pellison system of cajolery and usher in a time of brutal persecution. Colbert's physical strength was on the wane, as was his moderating influence at Court. Louis XIV's second wife, Madame de Maintenon, whose Catholic piety spilled over into bigotry against her former co-religionists, missed no chance to play on her husband's natural preference for rapid and decisive solutions. Louis himself, having survived a dangerous operation, and reaching the age of forty, became ever-conscious of his own mortality, and therefore as fervently Catholic as his spouse. King Louis and Madame de Maintenon lost patience with Pellison's program (Pellison himself admitted that, at the rate conversions were being obtained, 900 years would be needed to eradicate French Calvinism). Sensing this shift in royal views, zealous officials and sycophantic justices of the parlements intensified the application of petty and gradually-restrictive measures on French protestants during the late 1670s. Many Huguenots, like Jews in Nazi Germany in the mid-1930s, considered this a passing inconvenience to be "waited out". Few were to know that it presaged a global crisis that would explode in 1681, with the Huguenots in the eye of the hurricane.

References

Primary works

Calendar of State Papers (Ireland) 1666–9, pp. 48–9, 88–9, 373–4, 628, 635–6; 1669–70.

Calendar of State Papers (Domestic) 1660–85; 1672; 1691–92.

Calendar of the Ancient Records of the City of Dublin. Vol. V, pp. 566–77.

Historic Manuscripts Commission Publications. Rep. 6, p. 742; Rep. 10; Rep. 14; Buccleuch and Queensbury Mss; Vol. III (New Series); Vol. IV (New Series).

Irish Statutes Vol. II, 14–15 Charles II c. xiii, pp. 498–502.
Parish Registers Society Publications: Volumes I, II, III, IX.
Proceedings of the Huguenot Society of London-Quarto Series. Vol. VII; XVIII.
National Library of Ireland Manuscripts: 76–9, 2675, 2678, 8007, 12, 122, 12, 131; Microfilm 7517.

Secondary works

Anonymous. *Call to Hugonites.*
Bagwell, Richard. *Ireland Under the Stuarts,* pp. 322–3.
Benedict, Philip. *Rouen During the Wars of Religion,* pp. 125–51.
André, Louis. *Michel Le Tellier et Louvois,* p. 484.
Burghclere, Lady. *The Life of James, First Duke of Ormonde, 1610–88,* pp. 131–2.
Carré, Albert. *L'Influence des Huguenots Français en Irlande,* pp. 5, 55–6, 114.
Carte, Thomas. *A History of the Life of James, Duke of Ormonde,* p. 202.
Combe, J. C. *Huguenots in the Ministry of the Church* of Ireland, Unpublished Doctoral Dissertation (Belfast, Queen's University, 1980) pp. 51–3.
Corish, Patrick J. *The Catholic Community in the 17th & 18th Centuries,* pp. 55–6.
Craig, Maurice. *Dublin 1660–1680,* pp. 3–4, 38.
Gerard, Frances. *Picturesque Dublin Old and New,* p. 124.
Gill, Conrad. *The Rise of the Irish Linen Industry,* pp. 8–9.
Gimlette, Thomas. *The History of the Huguenot Settlers in Ireland,* pp. 195, 232.
Kretzer, Hartmut. *Calvinismus und Franzosiche Monarchie in 17 Jahrhundert,* p. 431.
Laurence, Colonel Richard. *The Interest of Ireland in Its Trade and Wealth Stated.*
Le Fanu, T. P. in Lawlor, Hugh Jackson, *The Fasti of St. Patrick's,* p. 279.
Le Fanu, T. P. "The French Churches in Dublin" in *Proceedings of the Huguenot Society of London (hereafter referenced as: PHSL),* Vol. VIII, n. 1, p. 9.
Lee, Grace Lawless. *The Huguenot Settlements in Ireland,* pp. 10, 12, 202, 218–20.
Ligou, Daniel. *Le Protestantisme en France,* pp. 213–18, 224–5, 229.
MacCurtain, Margaret. *Tudor and Stuart Ireland,* p. 167.
Mours, Samuel & Robert, Daniel. *Le Protestantisme en France du XVIIIieme Siècle à nos Jours,* pp. 30–2.
Orcibal, Jean. *Louis XIV et les Protestants.* p. 65. Parker, David. in Hepburn, A. C. *Minorities in History,* p. 17.
Schickler, Baron F. de. *Les Eglise du Refuge en Angleterre.* Vol. II, pp. 203, 229.
Smiles, Samuel. *Huguenots in England and Ireland,* pp. 294–5.

2

THE LATE ORMONDITE REFUGE, 1681–1691

"Prisoners of La Rochelle . . . certify that we had to leave home (due to) violence and cruelty (suffered) under Monsieur Marillac . . . thirty-three of us without sustinence fled to the town of La Rochelle. Hoping to go to England we found a merchant who had a vessel. Just after embarking, we were discovered and apprehended. Without charity, we would have starved . . . slept two nights on the hard floor; some of us without much clothing . . . (our) only crime was not professing faith in the Roman Catholic Church . . . it is better to die than to abjure."

— Deposition of Poitevin Refugees, 4 November 1681

There are pivots around which the history of the world alters direction and turns, and the Dragonnades of Poitou are among the most overlooked of these singular events. The term "dragonnade" itself derives from the military personnel known as "dragoons", or musket-bearing cavalry. A "dragonnade" – the quartering of these troops upon a certain selected element of the civilian population for purposes of coercion and intimidation – was hardly an innovation of the 1680s. Huguenots had already suffered dragonnades on three prior occasions: 1615 (Chablais); 1627 (Aubenas); and 1660 (Montauban). Moreover, Huguenots had not been the sole victims: Breton peasants and Ultramontanes in the diocese of Pamiers had endured enforced billetings during the 1670s. What set the 1681 Dragonnades apart were their much more ambitious scope and the far-reaching chain of events that were their very success inspired.

The Dragonnades of Poitou were themselves seemingly the product of a misinterpretation of directives from Versailles on the part of René de Marillac, Intendent of Poitou, and the Marquis de Louvois. Marillac proposed the troop-quartering tactics to try to accelerate Protestant abjurations in letters to Louvois at the War Ministry dated the 5th and 12th May 1681. Louvois broached the idea to Louis XIV. The War Minister, misconstruing the King's rather hazy comments on the subject, assumed that a blank cheque approval had been given and replied to Marillac on 18 May authorizing the use of troops to implement his scheme.

It appears that Marillac's zeal far outstripped expectations; nor were the diplomatic repercussions adequately foreseen. International revulsion, spurred on by lurid reports of brutality leaking out of France, was especially sharp in Brandenburg (where the "Great Elector" Frederick William called the French ambassador Rebenac to a special audience for the purpose of personally expressing his displeasure); the United Provinces; and England. The ripples within the Court environment at Versailles were also such as could not – at least at that moment – be ignored. The Ruvignys interceded with the King and though their inquiries were initially met with evasion, the Députés-Général persisted, while Louvois covered himself through half-hearted and ineffectual protestations that the over-eager subordinate Marillac had misinterpreted his intent and that he should cease and desist. The combination of domestic and international protests ultimately worked towards a reversal in royal policy. Louvois, acting at Louis' behest, officially halted the dragonnade in August, transferring the troops to Bayonne on 26 November. On 6 February 1682, Marillac suffered the fate of a scapegoat: being disowned by Versailles and recalled in disgrace. There is ample evidence, however, that even if royal and provincial officialdom paid lip-service to the apparent easing of persecution, unofficial harassment/persecution of Huguenots continued in many cases into the Fall and early Winter. During the most intense weeks of the dragonnade the soldiers (who were in many instances under orders to behave as obnoxiously as possible) proceeded to inflict varied indignities on the Protestant households on which they were quartered. These included: furniture and china-smashing; drunken orgies in every room of the house; butchering livestock for "sport"; obscene language in front of the women; torturing the occupants by diverse means at hand (notably holding their bare feet in the fire); and all varieties of property vandalism. Not far away, a priest would be conveniently available to tend to any Huguenots who wished to abjure their faith and convert to Catholicism in order to be rid of their unwanted guests.

Nor would a mild respite prove to be any more than a transitory phase; the dragonnade had proven itself to have been far too successful from Louis XIV's vantage point. Naturally predisposed to uniformity; the King was now being nudged and flattered along towards an increasingly unbending religious policy. Colbert's effectiveness had been all but eclipsed and upon the Finance Minister's death in 1683 would evaporate altogether. No sooner was Colbert dead than he was conveniently saddled with the blame for whatever had rendered the Sun King's regime unpopular. So effective was this campaign that precautions had to be taken after his burial to assure that elements of the populace would not disinter and desecrate his body. Madame de Maintenon, furthermore, played upon the King's guilt at not perhaps having led the exemplary Catholic life, and the exaggerated Catholic piety with which he became infected led him to abandon the moderation of his earlier years in favor of further repression.

In Ireland

The Duke of Ormond had resumed the Viceroyalty of Ireland in 1677, after an eight-year hiatus. He had ridden out the crisis that had followed in the wake of Titus Oates' Popish Plot, and had done what was in his power to mitigate its effects in Ireland. Despite his earlier advocacy of the Huguenots, his administration was hesitant in its reactions to the Poitou Dragonnades Crisis. Ormond's actions in Ireland in this regard have been compared unfavorably to those of the British government.

As early as 28 July 1681, King Charles II and his Privy Council, acting upon a petition presented by the Huguenot Conformed Church of the Savoy only one week before, agreed to grant refugees: free denization; the right to practice the crafts and trades to which they were qualified on an equal par with native Englishmen; for their children to likewise be admitted to schools and universities; that their personal effects and any other items apart from specific merchandise be exempt from customs duties; for free passage to British ports and compensation to ship's captains for any expenses incurred; that debarkation procedures be expedited and transport provided from ports to ultimate destinations in Britain; that bishops organize relief collections for the destitute among the refugee population that the Privy Council designate one of its members as a "watchdog" and advise the King and Council on individual problems and petitions. Nor was this by any means the final action taken on the government's part. The September 1681 brief for the collection of funds for emergency refugee relief authorized by King Charles was unprecedentedly sweeping and thorough, specifying what steps needed to be taken at the neighborhood level, and placing the primary responsibility for collection and disbursement on the parish itself rather than on the bishop. The brief was extended for a two-years duration.

By contrast, Ormond simply proposed to the Irish Privy Council that funds be voted for refugee aid, making the initial donation by way of setting the example, and authorizing the Lord Mayor of Dublin to organize a door-to-door collection with the aid of prominent citizens. Then he seems to have been content to leave it at that until confronted with irrefutable evidence as to the magnitude of the crisis. This appears to have occurred in November 1681 – a considerable time-lag behind King Charles' actions in late July. It may well have been a case of living in denial. So harrowing and numerous were the atrocity reports in the letters and pamphlets emanating out of France that the Duke barely credited them with truth, expressing surprise that Louis XIV's basic good sense and humanity could have permitted the occurrence of such a sordid catastrophe. When the initial shock passed and the viceroy was confronted with personal depositions, and some greater measure of reality had set in, Ormond seemed for a time to have returned to his ideas for encouraging foreign Protestants into Ireland. He was able to so convince the Dublin Corporation of this that elaborate plans were drawn up to re-fortify the city, this time encompassing the suburbs which had grown up outside the old town walls since the Restoration. In this way refugees were offered the incentive of relocating to an area where they could be afforded at least relative protection from reprisals from France.

The Dragonnades of Poitou had an immediate, traceable effect in the capital at least. The French Protestant population of Dublin was at minimum, doubled from 50 to 100 individuals by the end of 1681. One source would have the number at closer to 170, but this source often based its information on hearsay and gossip; extant records do not at present substantiate the higher total. By the end of 1682 the number may have risen to some 240–50; to 380-odd in 1683; and in 1684 to at least 430. The discrepancy in the comparatively higher rate of growth of the Late Ormondite refuge as opposed to the anemic totals of the Early Ormondite immigrants is graphically illustrated in the fact that between 1662–80 only 21 Huguenots took advantage of the Corporation's sympathy and availed of the Freedom of the City, while in the year 1681, in and of itself, 34 newly-arrived refugees did so. In 1682, fifty-five obtained their Freeman's status; fourteen in 1683; twenty-seven in 1684; twelve in 1685; twelve in 1686; and six in 1687.

The Late Ormondite refuge in Dublin alone contained at least 24 families of Poitevin origin – the largest provincial grouping among all the French Protestants arriving between 1662–87. This is a unique situation for, as far as can be determined with any certainty, the Poitevins were in a pronounced minority of those immigrating to Dublin during every other epoch in that colony's history. This also holds true for the Huguenot community at Portarlington and, as far as may yet be ascertained, Cork, Lisburn Waterford or Belfast. Eleven of these 24 Poitevin families appeared in Ireland either during or shortly after Marillac's Dragonnade.

There is a signed deposition by Poitevin Huguenots in the Archbishop Marsh's Library papers of Abraham Tessereau which is dated 4 November 1681. The deponents alleged that they, their families and companions, to the number of thirty-three individuals, were unceremoniously driven out of their houses and forced to walk to La Rochelle where they at last found a merchant who was willing to transport them to England in his vessel. The ship had hardly embarked when it was pursued and they themselves were apprehended and held in prison. They were compelled to sleep on the naked stone floor and constantly harangued by Monks who attempted to make them abjure their faith. Outside intervention – perhaps from Ormond himself, or one of his lieutenants – was not long in coming and the prisoners were released, three of the deposition's signatories turning up in Ireland shortly thereafter. They were: Matthieu Moussault; Isaac Renard; and Jacques Cossoneau. Moussault is first noted on 28 January 1682, some twelve weeks later, as residing in Dublin. The privations and ill treatment in France, augmented by the rigours of the journey to Ireland, may have proved too great a strain on the health of his wife, Françoise, neé Brissault, for she died that same day. Moussault's son Jacques also passed away in July 1685. However, his daughter Marguerite married Abraham Tripier and was living in Dublin with her husband at least as late as 1698.

Isaac Renard and his wife Madelaine Faitou were certainly in Dublin by 3 January 1683, when their child Jeanne was born. Jacques Cossoneau and his wife, who had fled from their home at La Motte, Poitou, became the parents of a son who was baptized at St. Patrick's Cathedral on 11 August, 1686, though the couple had probably been residing in Dublin from late in 1681 – and their descendents remained in the capital for at least the next two generations. Of another 13 Poitevin families we cannot be certain as to whether they fled to Ireland as a consequence of the initial 1681 Dragonnade, or of a later dragonnade (1683) launched under the aegis of Marillac's successor, Lamoignon de Baville, the same Baville who afterwards gained such notoriety for his ruthlessness in suppressing Protestantism as Intendent for the Languedoc.

The years 1684–7 witnessed the high-water mark for the Late Ormondite Huguenot migration into Ireland. A flood-tide of Protestant families departing in the face of relentlessly escalating pressure (which encompassed the so-called "Great Dragonnade of the Midi" which lasted from May to September 1685, swept through Guyenne, Gascony, Languedoc and Provence, and spilled over as far as: Pays de Gex in Dauphine, Lyonnais, Aunis, Saintonge and Poitou, and yielded perhaps 300,000–400,000 lip-service conversions), accelerated the rate of immigration and swelled the refugee population to its greatest extent up to that time. The Revocation of the Edict of Nantes through Louis XIV's new Edict of Fontainebleau on 17 October 1685 was merely the crowning blow upon which culminated an endless series of incidents of judicial harassment; fiscal discrimination; outright thuggery; and a persistent chipping-away at the provisions of the 1598 pact between the monarch and the reformed churches within his realm. In 1685, new arrivals and births had bolstered the Huguenot element in Dublin itself to some 600 by year's end and, in 1686, up to 650-odd.

A Fluid Situation

Again the Butler family and their circle of retainers and allies extended their assistance to distressed Huguenot refugees, and this aid was sometimes even solicited by individual refugees who sought haven in Ireland and were aware of Ormond's past largess. A Monsieur Chaillé of La Rochelle, formerly Secretary to the Marquis de Montau, who was in the process of transferring property to Ireland, petitioned Ormond's son, the Earl of Arran, through Lord Preston, for his assistance and protection in the carrying out of this venture. Preston was also prevailed upon to intervene with Ormond on behalf of a Huguenot physician, Philippe Guide, who was indeed taken on in Ireland as one of the Duke's personal medical practitioners.

The problem of accommodating refugees was made even more acute by the presence of spies. In Ireland in 1683, the case of one Albert Sheldon, in particular, aroused a good deal of controversy and embarrassment in this regard. Feigning an allegiance to Protestantism, Sheldon contacted Ormond, further asserting that though he was English (his parents having both been bereft of that nationality) he had been persecuted as a Huguenot because of having been born in France. Actually, as an agent of the Marquis de Louvois, and having presumably been interviewed by Louis XIV in person, and acting in conjunction with another French agent, Jean de Luz, he abused of Ormond's compassion to enter Ireland and survey fortifications, and the size and deployment of military units. Disclosures of Sheldon's espionage led to royal directives aimed at reinforcing troops in Ireland in the event of invasion. A scandal such as the Sheldon Affair naturally reflected unfavourably upon incoming refugees, and only served to heighten the difficulties of settling them. Jealousy and fear were also kindled among the Irish themselves against these exotic refugees who seemed to be disembarking in swarms.

The balance of Huguenot refugees/immigrants to Ireland, always concentrated heavily in Dublin, was rendered increasingly so during the course of the 1680s. In any case, those French Protestants who had chosen to settle beyond the capital region and east coast of Ireland were, by 1685, departing in droves to colonize Pennsylvania. There was widespread fear that the long arm of Louis XIV could extend to apprehend them even in Ireland, where rumours of a French invasion abetted by Irish Catholics were widely circulated. Huguenots who ventured "beyond the Pale" could of course not be guaranteed the same measure of protection as those who resided within easy distance of Dublin.

One exception to this general rule occurred in Wexford town, where a serious attempt was made to establish a distinct, organized exilic community. The Wexford Huguenot colony which had emerged by 1684 enjoyed an interrelationship with that of Dublin. Due to a petition filed by the French Protestants of Wexford on 21 April of that year to Richard Butler, Earl of Arran, Lord Deputy-General of Ireland, the names of the heads of the ten families (comprising at least 42 individuals) of Huguenots at Wexford, and their occupations, have been documented. In hopes of securing the financially-strapped colonists on a firmer footing, the Earl of Arran, in concert with the then-Bishop of Ferns and Leighlin, Narcissus Marsh, granted them a French minister and the right to hold conformist services in French at St. Mary's Church in Wexford town. Antoine Nabes, who had briefly co-pastored at French Patrick's, left Dublin to minister to the Wexford Congregation. No further record of his pastorate has been found. Of those who attempted to relocate to Wexford, at least five families had resided in Dublin, those of: Pierre Baudouin, merchant; Abel & Michel Franc, ships' carpenters; Pierre L'Anglois, also a ships' carpenter by trade; and Charles Vallot, cooper. Despite the benevolent intentions and efforts of Arran and Bishop Marsh, the Wexford settlement was not a resounding success, at least three families soon returned to Dublin. Vallot was back in the capital little over a year later, when his wife passed away (25 June 1685). The family of Antoine Vareille, merchant, gravitated towards the city by 1706, and his descendents continued to worship mainly at the French Conformed Church of St. Patrick's. The tallow chandler Samuel Billon had quit Wexford for Dublin by 1702; dying there in 1707 at the age of sixty-five. The Huguenot colony at Wexford seems, by any evident approximation, to have been short-lived. It is true that two additional families – those of the merchant Pierre Tomeux, and of Jean Chadaine – were still in Ireland at least up to the year 1693, though it is unclear as to whether they were still resident in Wexford by this date. One can at present do little better than to confirm prior findings that the numbers of Huguenots in Wexford were never that great and that sources on this subject remain scanty.

By contrast, the rapidly-expanding numbers of refugees, and their greater social and provincial diversity (as compared to the Early Ormondite community) placed added pressure upon the Irish government. In geographic terms, whereas the Early Ormondites had originated for the most part in French provinces north of the Loire, the larger number of these Late Ormondites were southerners: 24 families from Poitou; 10 from Aunis & Saintonge; 2 from Guyenne; 2 from Languedoc; and one from Lyonnais. This total of 39 Southern provincial households contrasts markedly to the nine northern families appearing during these same years: 7 from Normandy; and one each from Ile de France and Flandre.

The merchant Daniel Hays, or Hais, who sometimes anglicized his surname to "Hayes", and who became an alderman and a substantial property-owner in Dublin, may well have been of Poitevin origin, or some of his family members may have resided in Poitou, though he is listed as being from Calais. A Huguenot of the same surname is mentioned as being from Poitou in the Tessereau deposition of 1681, and as it was not uncommon to mistakenly write down the place through which a refugee either departed from France or where he/she temporarily resided before reaching Ireland rather than the actual region of origin, this might possibly have occurred in this case. This seems certainly to have been so with other refugees who arrived during this period: Eleonore Bitré Claset (listed as being from Clandé, near Liège); Jean de Cassel (London); and Le Geé (Mannheim). In their social breakdown, the late Ormondites also differed markedly from their predominately mercantile predecessors of 1662–80. There was a much wider range of situations and occupations, and merchants did not dominate as before. To be sure, 15 new mercantile families did arrive during the years 1681–7, but they were more than offset by 3 nobles, 3 ministers, 3 surgeons, 2 physicians, one apothecary, 2 pewterers, 2 goldsmiths, 4 cobblers, 3 cordwainers, 5 tailors, 2 stationers, one innkeeper, 4 wool combers, one tallow chandler, 4 carpenters, one paumier (whose specialty it was to make tennis racquets), 2 wood sculptors & one stuccodore (the brothers Tabary), 2 saddlers, one personal secretary (Paul Chaillé, for the Marquis de Montau), 3 joiners, one mason, 8 sergeweavers, one dyer, 2 linen weavers, 3 silkweavers, 2 vinegar makers, 2 distillers, 2 watch makers, 6 coopers, 4 ships'carpenters, 6 perriwig makers, 3 tanners, 7 chandlers, one shearman, one smith, one schoolmaster, one gunsmith, 2 plasterers, 6 sailors, 7 curriers, one blacksmith, one engraver, 2 braziers, 2 confectioners, 2 watchcase makers, 3 wine coopers, 3 butchers, one coachman, one worsted weaver, one hatter, one fan maker, one brewer, one narrow weaver, one button maker, 2 notaries public, 6 barber surgeons, one malster, one baker, 3 glaziers, one locksmith, one huckster, one felt maker, 2 glover, and one sail maker.

Ferment, Repression, & The Roussels

The new predominance of southerners and reduced proportion of northern merchants produced a much more restive, less manageable element in the refugee population. It must be borne in mind that the situation was unprecedented; that Ireland had never before witnessed an immigrant crisis of this magnitude, and it was inevitable that problems would arise. The difficulties associated with refugee relief: accommodation; provisioning; acclimatization; employment; the potential for negative reactions from the indigenous population would have been challenging – in and of themselves – but the controversies pitting French Calvinists against Anglican Conformity came openly to the fore. The massive, rapid influx and a change in the complexion of the refugee community created an extremely difficult situation for Hierome's successor as pastor of French Patrick's, the genial Moses Viridet. In was on 22 June 1678 that Viridet took the oaths required by statute to begin officiating in Dublin. The pastor was a native of Normandy who first ministered at Grosmenil in that province, then as an expatriate at Threadneedle Street in London, becoming Ormond's chaplain in 1675.

By 1683 many Huguenot immigrants who favoured the zealot-apocalyptic point of view had poured into Dublin and ignited a situation that went beyond Viridet's control. A non-Conformist minister was able to organize a large part of the St. Patrick's congregation behind him and to convene dissenting conventicles which made common cause with Anglophone Presbyterians. Realizing his helplessness, Viridet went to Ormond's son Arran, who was deputizing at Dublin Castle while his father was in London. The government suppressed the conventicles in a stern business-like manner and, although there appears to have been no bloodshed, a sense of resentment and sullen acquiescence split the French Community under the surface. Viridet seems to have lost much of his spirit, and perhaps some of his health as a result of this crisis, which was somewhat tied in to the Rye House Conspiracy in Britain. The increased burden of officiating to such an unpredictably expanding and volatile congregation taxed his energies and it became necessary for the Irish government to disburse special funds for auxiliary ministers: Jean Majou in 1683; Anthoine Nabes from 1683–4; and from 1684, Josué Roussel, who succeeded Viridet as chief pastor on 16 June 1685. The latter's final public act was to intervene with the Lords of the Treasury on behalf of colonizing French Protestants, petitioning that they be allowed to import their own clothes, domestic effects, professional equipment and utensils into Ireland free of charge. Weary of his situation in Dublin, which told on his basically easy-going disposition, Viridet resigned to become Rector of Arklow, and died there in February of 1688.

As minister of the French Patrick's congregation Roussel represented a new type of leadership. He was the first Huguenot of the zealot-apocalyptic strain to make an impact in Ireland; and in his person was embodied resistance and martyrdom. There were hard-liners among French Calvinists who advocated meeting persecution by more energetic means (at least with open ardour and passive resistance) and who were linked with apocalypticism and often (though not in the case of Roussel) with dissent. The zealots were involved in an eternal antagonism with their more passive or accomodationist brethren who followed the lead of the Ruvignys. This mutual resentment created severe strains both within the homeland Huguenot community and within the international *Corps du Réfuge* (as it came to be called). The resulting rifts were permanent and at times intense.

The zealot-accomodationist fissure ran along broad geographic and social lines. The uneven distribution of the Calvinist minority within France itself lay at the heart of the problem. North of the Loire, Huguenot congregations tended to be quite small, scattered and vulnerable – islands in a sea of Catholicism. A great many Temples depended on the whim of the local seigneur for their very existence. Such a situation naturally dictated a diplomatic stance *vis-à-vis* a secular authority which was often more sympathetic to a powerful, competing denomination. In many northern reformed communities the philosophy for survival had been, since at least the time of the St.Bartholomew's Day débâcle, one of subdued loyalism to the crown (perhaps followed in succeeding generations by loyalism of a more sincere variety). Mercantile interests likewise played a strong role in fashioning the attitudes of Northern French Calvinism, as evidenced in the carry-over into the Irish Huguenot Refuge up to 1681. It was only logical that a merchant or trader, who was dependent (particularly in a foreign land such as Ireland) on the good will of royal, municipal and ecclesiastical authorities and other Anglican neighbors for his very commercial subsistence, should not wish to jeopardize his enterprise by unnecessarily creating a stir.

By contrast, Huguenots whose provincial origins lay south of the Loire enjoyed the advantages of numerical concentration and in some areas of Poitou, Aunis, Saintonge, Guyenne, Dauphiné, and the Languedoc (especially in the rugged Cévennes & Vivarais regions), even predominated. There was therefore greater scope and opportunity to foment resistance. Indeed, the situation would ignite into violence that would culminate in the uncompromising guerrilla struggle of the Camisards that raged through the Cévennes from 1702 to 1705. The social composition of the Huguenot communities of the south (as reflected in the Late Ormondite colony) included a stronger admixture of artisans, small shopholders, and peasants. Indeed, the wooded Cevennes Mountains was one of the few areas where Calvinism had penetrated into the ranks of the peasantry to an appreciable extent, obliterating both the pre-Christian rural folkways and the veneer of Roman Catholicism.

Josué Roussel was in many respects a personification of southern French Calvinism; his outspoken personality contrasted to that of his placid predecessors at French Patrick's. Roussel came from the Dauphiné and was called successively to serve as pastor at: Anduze (1662–7); St. Christol

(1667–8); and Le Vigan (1668–84). He was conspicuous for the part he played in siding with Claude Brousson and other zealots such as Pierre Jurieu and Fontaine des Lozes in advocating a vigorous show of defiance to confront the surge of official harassment of members of their faith. Ministers from Dauphine, Vivarais, Cévennes, Upper & Lower Languedoc, Guyenne, Saintonge, and Poitou held an inaugural assembly at Brousson's house in Toulouse on 7 May 1683 and drew up plans for a campaign of passive resistance. These schemes would crumble in the face of selective repression executed by regiments under Marshal (Charles Chalmont, Marquis de) St. Ruth in the summer of 1684. Roussel had by this time become a marked man. With the assistance of his son Charles, who had been minister at Aveze from 1681, he had served as the elected Moderator of the General Assembly of the Churches of the Cévennes and Gevaudan, which was held in Colognac. Fleeing from their impending condemnation, both father and son had reached Dublin by 25 June 1684. The Roussels were tried *in absentia* at Nimes for their association with Brousson in preaching in prohibited districts. On 3 July 1684 the elder Roussel was sentenced to be broken on the wheel and his son to be hanged (the sentences were carried out in effigy), and both to have their property confiscated.

Josué Roussel would prove to be a unique personage among members of the Huguenot Diaspora in Ireland. He combined the respect of martyrdom, personal presence and charisma, credentials of zealotry, and an ability to knit together disparate elements within the refugee community. The choice of Roussel first as Viridet's vicar, then as minister in his own right – seconded by his son – bears the hallmarks of a deliberate policy decision. Roussel possessed the unique advantage of being both a proven zealot *and* amenable to Conformity within the Church of Ireland. Hence from the vantage point of Dublin Castle and Armagh Cathedral he would have seemed the ideal person to bridge the gap within the refugee community occasioned by the suppression of Huguenot non-conformity in 1683. Leadership proved to be an elusive quality as far as Ireland's Huguenot settlers were concerned, but in Roussel – for a fleeting instance – lay the best chance that was to occur for a bona fide *Corps du Réfuge*, unified in a single community of interests.

Time was running out once again for the Duke of Ormond. King Charles was set to replace him once again as viceroy, and he only managed a short reprieve because of the "Merrie Monarch's" death as a result of a stroke on 6 February 1685. Charles' younger brother and successor James II, as an ardent Roman Catholic, was uneasy at the thought of such a redoubtable champion of Anglicanism as Ormond remaining in at the crucial post of Lord Lieutenant of Ireland, and ultimately replaced him (after an interim stint by Lord Justices (Archbishop Michael Boyle of

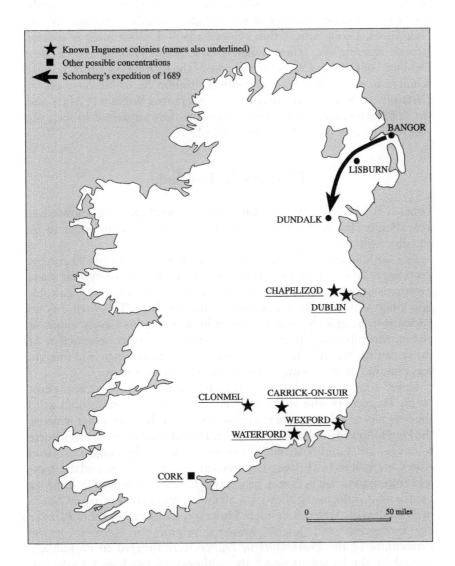

★ Known Huguenot colonies (names also underlined)
■ Other possible concentrations
◀ Schomberg's expedition of 1689

BANGOR

LISBURN

DUNDALK

CHAPELIZOD ★ ★
DUBLIN

CLONMEL ★   CARRICK-ON-SUIR ★

WEXFORD ★
WATERFORD ★

CORK ■

0   50 miles

The Ormondite Colonies and Schomberg's route

Armagh and Arthur Forbes, Earl of Granard) with the more malleable Henry Hyde, Second Earl of Clarendon, who had no natural power base on the western side of the Irish Sea. Clarendon proved less fervently Anglican and more moderate in his attitudes towards Protestant dissent. Huguenots, among others, thus enjoyed a period (albeit brief) of greater latitude than before. James Butler, First Duke of Ormond, demised in October 1688 at age 69, on the very eve of the Revolution Crisis, leading scholars to speculate on what political position he would have taken. Certainly, if the influential magnate had supported William & Mary and the 1689 Settlement (as a revered colleague once suggested to me), the course of history would have been altered.

The Jacobite Interlude

James II is a paradox who continues to confound the most knowledge-able of scholars, and a king whose contemporaries considered to be equally baffling.

As a Catholic monarch whose English subjects were roughly 94 percent Protestant, he was to demonstrate such a lack of sensitivity that some historians have been inclined to doubt his sanity – or at the very least, his grip on reality. Solidly supported by the Anglican Tory majority in Parliament, he quickly turned on them in favour of his largely impotent and numerically insignificant (save in Ireland) Catholic co-religionists. At the same time his attitude towards dissenters, both domestic and foreign, was ambivalent and he was never able to obtain their trust.

James' accession in February of 1685 had, at first, no appreciable effect on the Huguenots who settled in Ireland, despite initial misgivings as to the new sovereign's ultimate intentions. In this, as in many other matters, the king followed an ambivalent policy. He did open his own privy purse to refugee relief and renewed the privileges received by Huguenots from King Charles II in 1681 (free passports, letters of denization, and the duty-free importation of personal property). He even extended a hand to French non-conformists, allowing Calvinist services at the refugee Church of Threadneedle Street in London. However, Claude's book *Les Plaintes des Protestants* and Joseph Reyner's volume *An Account of the Persecution of the Protestants in France* were ordered to be publicly burned by the hangman under the authority of the King's Orders in Council; and the renewal of a virulent persecution waged against Scottish Covenanters when James had still been Duke of York was viewed with trepidation by all variety of Calvinists.

The death of Charles II in February 1685 and the promulgation of the Edict of Fontainebleau in October of that same year did leave a gap of eight months, which would have given ample time for French Protestants to gauge King James' true inclinations and the degree to which his regime posed a threat to their well-being before deciding to settle in his dominions. An additionally compelling fact is that there were other places closer at hand (i.e.: the Netherlands, Brandenburg, the Swiss cantons) with sympathetic Protestant regimes, so that Great Britain and Ireland need not have been factored in at all if James had truly been the bigoted monster of legend. We are, in effect, placed in the ironic situation of witnessing Huguenot immigration and settlement in the British Isles not only flourishing but attaining what was up to that time it zenith in terms of numbers, under a Catholic ruler.

In Ireland, the influx continued through 1686 and into 1687, according to even unsympathetic contemporary accounts – notably that of Louis XIV's chief spy in London, Monsieur de Bonrepaus. Once they had arrived in Ireland the Huguenot refugees seemed content enough to stay. Clarendon's moderate administration offset any misgivings that a Catholic monarch, enthroned hundreds of miles away, might have inspired. The only notable exceptions to the trend of planting roots in Ireland were Jacques and Jean Benest, former servants of Pierre Le Moyne who, on 15 July 1685, embarked from the port of Dublin on board the ship *Margaret* bound for the Carolinas in North America.

It was actually the rise to power of one of Ormond's erstwhile political rivals, Richard Talbot, Earl (later Duke) of Tyrconnel, that marked the true point of departure. Talbot, a fervent Catholic, had been a rising star on the horizon as soon as James ascended to the throne. In January of 1687 his strivings were crowned with the ultimate success that he had long coveted: the vice-royalty of Ireland. Even though Tyrconnel was disappointed in having had what was technically a lesser title of Lord Deputy conferred upon him rather than that of Lord Lieutenant, as his Protestant predecessors had been conferred, he held what in effect was overwhelming power. Though Clarendon had held the vice-regency, it had been Tyrconnel who had been retained as commander-in-chief of the army in Ireland. The Duke was certainly forthright in his intentions to decimate the "Protestant Interest" in Ireland and to pack the courts; corporations and the army with Catholics. Jacobites. Ireland under Tyrconnel was to prove to be the last revival of the "Old English" establishment. In what was to be proposed as the new order of things, the Huguenots had no place.

The Glorious Revolution

In Ireland, as elsewhere in the British Isles, the three-odd years from 1688 to 1691 witnessed sweeping, dramatic change. In England, the smouldering crisis coming out of King James II's Catholicism and absolutist policy leanings, and the birth of Prince James Edward Stuart in July of 1688, came to a climax.

From the beginning, all that King James did seemed calculated to destroy the very power-base that his brother had skillfully built up during the early 1680s. Seldom has a sovereign so quickly frittered away such an advantage. It had been the establishmentarian Tories, particularly the High Church stalwarts among the gentry and clergy, that had rallied around the person of the monarch during the Exclusion and Rye House Crises and had decimated the Whigs. James, as his brother's beneficiary, had thus inherited such a solid local support that the Duke of Monmouth's appeal for a Protestant uprising had fallen on largely deaf ears. The overwhelmingly Tory Parliament of 1685 seemed prepared to grant King James all the financial assistance that he could have asked, but the issue of religion would drive the first wedge between the King and his supporters. The Commons demurred at the King's rather prematurely-conceived insistence on a relaxation of the Test Acts and other disabilities on Catholics, whereupon James lost patience and dissolved Parliament. In the months that followed the Stuart monarch would employ dubiously-legal (even extra-legal) methods to insinuate Catholics into positions of influence. He sought to offset the erosion of Tory support by reversing his initial policy and opening opportunities to Protestant Dissenters. The Declaration of Indulgence of 1687, which was designed to benefit both Dissenters and Catholics by suspending the penal laws against them, did not have the desired effect. Dissenters (including Huguenot expatriates) were far too suspicious of James' motives and of the ultimate conse-quences of admitting Catholicism to such a level of legal respectability. When it came down to a choice, Dissenters and Anglicans preferred to bury their differences and make common cause against the Popish threat – which was seen as by far the most frightening. Images of St. Bartholomew's; 1641; the Inquisition; and the Dragonnades were only too readily available to remind all Protestants and drive them into alliances of convenience, if nothing else.

Thus the events of late 1688 unfolded with the resident Huguenots either lying low or in certain cases providing discreet intelligence to adver-saries of the government. King William III disembarked at Torbay on 5 November 1688 with a force which included Huguenot soldiery and, after making a final pathetic reversal on the religious issue by appealing for help from the Tory Anglicans that he had left in the lurch, James completely lost his nerve and fled, abandoning his realm, and handing William III and Mary II, and the Whig-Tory coalition in Parliament aligned against him an incredibly easy victory. The coup placing William III and Mary II on the throne as joint-sovereigns, under certain strictures negotiated between

Parliament and the newly-minted monarchs can thus indeed be classed, taking the criteria of ease and lack of bloodshed, as a "Glorious Revolution".

While the Revolution Settlement, as it was called, was readily accepted in England Wales – and after the death of Robert Graham of Claverhouse, Viscount Dundee at the battle of Killecrankie, the Jacobite cause in Scotland was temporarily eclipsed – Tyrconnel lost no time in securing Ireland for the exiled James II. James would sally forth from his makeshift court at St. Germain with the blessing and support of King Louis XIV, with an ambassador from Versailles and military advisors, landing at Kinsale in March of 1689. In response to this and to the Jacobite onslaught that had overwhelmed every Williamite garrison in Ireland except for Derry and Enniskillen, King William organized a multi-national force which included English, Dutch, Danish and Huguenot units, and was commanded by a Huguenot, Frederick Hermann, Duke of Schomberg.

The Huguenot Regiments

Of all the spectres that would haunt Louis XIV in the latter part of his reign, none returned more swiftly and devastatingly than the defection of thousands of Huguenot military and naval personnel from his realm. Robin Gwynn's theory of Huguenot military refugees contributing decisively to the frustration on the *Roi Solleille's* international designs in the Wars of the League of Augsburg and the Spanish Succession would seem to be borne out by the evidence. As was the case in the sixteenth century Wars of Religion, it was the traditionally military-service oriented *noblesse d'epeé*, the *écuyers,* that formed the sinew and muscle of the Huguenot Party during the years that it contested for political power. The *écuyers* formed a natural nucleus for leadership, as they had in the Feudal Age long predating the Reformation. It was thus only a matter of course that the *écuyer* class should continue to be looked upon – even into exile – as a core around which their fellow-refugees might feel some measure of security and direction. Tradition would have been very important to a displaced population thrust into unfamiliar topography, and living in hope of return to what they had once known; and the petty nobility to whom they had always deferred could to some extent have fulfilled these wishes. Sieur Jean Faurel, for example, might have dwelled in Portarlington on scanty means in a room measuring only fifteen feet in length, but as an *écuyer* he would ineradicably be considered an object of the utmost respect by even the likes of his contemporary, Isaac Vauteau, a prosperous leather-tawer who owned or developed at least twelve separate properties in Dublin City.

Following the final destruction of their Party by Richelieu as a result of the Huguenot War of 1621–9, the *écuyers*, this time as loyalists, gravitated into the royal army and navy, and became a valued element of the officer corps. Huguenot officers seem to have formed an a significant part of the engineering branch. Their value as trained cogs in what was acknowledged to be the Europe's most efficient military machine was recognized by Protestant powers like the Electorate of Brandenburg, and the United Provinces of the Netherlands. In Brandenburg, Frederick William of Hohenzollern, the "Great Elector" expeditiously proclaimed the Edict of Potsdam (1686) to counter the Edict of Fontainebleau and broadcast that he was prepared to receive refugee Huguenots with open arms – especially those who could bring military expertise. The French officers were instrumental in imbuing the Brandenburg, and later Prussian, army with a level of training and discipline which was the envy of all Europe; and could arguably be said to have set into place the German military force whose dominance was not shattered until 1945. Prince William III of Orange, as Stadtholder of the United Provinces, had barely survived the French army's onslaught during the Dutch War of 1672–6, and was more than eager to employ the veterans who had been forced to defect from Louis XIV's juggernaut. William was forced to employ them into his personal forces and pay them from his own pocket as the States-General of the United Provinces rejected the Stadtholder's request for a state stipend. While in the Netherlands, Huguenot veterans were not placed into distinct units but integrated within existing ones: the Red Dragoons; Blue Dragoons; and the Prince's Own Guards. Prior to the Torbay Invasion of November 1688, William III contacted Frederick Herman, Duke of Schomberg (1615–90). Though not strictly-speaking a Huguenot, Schomberg was a German Calvinist, born in Heidelberg, and had been in the military for 56 years, serving in the Netherlands, Sweden, Portugal and France. It was Louis XIV, under whose command he remained from 1652–85 who conferred upon Schomberg his dukedom and marshal's baton. When he left the French King's service in 1685 in disgust over the Edict of Fontainebleau, he was considered one of the most accomplished warriors in Europe. Schomberg was enticed out of retirement in 1687 by Frederick William "The Great Elector" of Brandenburg. William III, on a diplomatic mission to the Electoral Court, was able to persuade Schomberg to become second-in-command of the expedition to Great Britain. Because of James II's baffling refusal to engage the invading force, followed by his breakdown, the Huguenots saw little, if any, action and were in the process of disbandment by early 1689. However, Ireland's declaration for the Jacobite cause and Tyrconnel's military buildup necessitated their hasty recall. William placed Schomberg in charge of a reconstituted expeditionary force: the Huguenot veterans now being organized into distinct units. Three infantry regiments were formed: Du Cambon's; La Melonière's; and La Caillemotte's. Schomberg himself commanded the one Huguenot cavalry squadron ("Schomberg's Horse"). Among those most instrumental in organizing the units was the Ruvigny family. The Marquis de Ruvigny and his eldest son Henri, who were the last Huguenot Députés-Général at the Court of Versailles, had departed for exile to Britain, despite enjoying a special dispensation from the King, who was willing to permit them the right of private practice of their faith and their estates within the realm, entreating them in vain to stay. The Ruvignys were fortunate in having an influential English connection, Lady Rachel, widow of the Whig martyr Lord William Russell. She was the daughter of the Marquis' sister, Rachel Massue de Ruvigny Wriothesley, Countess of Southampton. The Marquis, his two sons Henri and Pierre, Sieur de La Caillemotte, were given a residence at the Royal palace in Greenwich,where they quickly established a sort of Huguenot headquarters-in-exile. Henri, who would succeed to the title of Marquis upon his father's death later in 1689, remained for the time being in London, while his younger brother Pierre left with Schomberg's forces as colonel of the infantry unit that initially bore his name: "La Caillemotte's Foot".

Schomberg's ill-fated 1689 expeditionary force to Ireland consisted of Huguenot; English and Anglo-Irish levies – at first the outlook seemed promising. The siege of Derry was lifted and Enniskillen held out. Shortly thereafter, Schomberg's forces successfully invested Carrickfergus, which surrendered within a week. Schomberg then ordered a march southward, which culminated in the disastrous encampment at Dundalk, County Louth, which came close to destroying the Williamite army. To be fair, many factors have to be borne in mind when assessing responsibility for the Dundalk Débâcle during the winter of 1689–90, but the inescapable fact remains that Marshal Schomberg must shoulder the bulk of it. The aged commander had never been fully tested during his long and distin- guished career, and now lacked the grasp and audacity to take advantage of the initial success of his landings in Ulster. Slowed down by "scorched earth" tactics by Irish forces, Schomberg set up camp on exposed marshy terrain outside of Dundalk and refused to do battle with the Jacobites troops, now led by King James II himself. Schomberg's unexpected timid- ity destroyed Williamite morale, as severe outbreaks of what was probably several epidemics led to thousands of men (one estimate asserts up to half the Williamite army) being lost to disease and desertion. Dysentery and pulmonary complaints were the most common symptoms; at one stage Schomberg himself was afflicted by a severe chest disorder. Supply and victual problems, arrears in the men's receiving their pay and Schomberg's open favoritism towards the Huguenots and contempt for the English and Anglo-Irish troops under his command further fueled dissention within the ranks. The Huguenots had benefited from their prior professional training, it is true, constructing shelters which were far more adequate than those of their Anglophone counterparts, and suffering far fewer casualties from disease and exposure. This may, however, have only increased their unpopularity among their colleagues, who perceived the French as being aloof, arrogant, and all too ready to seize more than their fair share of booty and contraband. This deplorable situation was made all the worse with the discovery that some of the French troopers were not Huguenots at all, but French Catholics masquerading as such, and thus functioning as agents for espionage or, at best, the further erosion of morale.

Seeing his forces bogged down and disintegrating, and most of Ireland still in the enemy's hands, King William angrily took matters into his own hands. He never forgave Marshal Schomberg for the disaster at Dundalk. The King had to thus divert more allied forces to Northern Ireland, including substantial additional contingents of Danish, Dutch and Huguenot veterans; and had to journey from England to Carrickfergus to assume personal command of the Allied forces. Schomberg maintained his titles, and his position as colonel of the Huguenot cavalry squadron, but was otherwise shunted aside and studiously ignored.

On the eve of the Battle of the Boyne William's continuing anger may have led him to reject advice by Schomberg which could have materially lessened the casualties his army subsequently absorbed; some sources assert that William's typically cold manner towards all who displeased him may have personally effected the old Marshal to the point of recklessness, and contributed to his death. His was one of two fatalities that would impact upon the future formation of French refugee settlements in Ireland. Schomberg's fall has been dramatically recounted to the point where it has taken on a folklorish quality. While trying to ford the River Boyne near Oldbridge, Du Cambon's and La Caillemotte's Foot were heavily engaged by Irish cavalry, and in danger of wavering. Old Schomberg is said to have ridden down to them and attempted a rally, uttering: "*Allons, mes amis rappelez votre courage et vos ressentiments, voila vos persécuteurs*". Shortly thereafter he was killed, perhaps by "friendly fire", though some accounts depict him as being surrounded by enemy cavalry and brutally cut down. Prior to this, the debonair Colonel Pierre De La Caillemotte had also perished in spectacular fashion. Mortally wounded by Irish horsemen, he is reported to have called out" "*En avant mes enfants, en avant: à la gloire, à la gloire*" as he was being led away to die. His was the other battlefield death that would tie in directly to future efforts to bring substantial numbers of Huguenots into Ireland, for it opened the door for his influential elder brother Henri – now Marquis De Ruvigny – to intervene decisively in the ongoing conflict.

Genesis of a Legend

The events of 1 July 1690 along the River Boyne and the subsequent conduct of the War of the Two Kings, as the Williamite vs. Jacobite conflict in Ireland is sometimes called, left Henri Massue de Ruvigny with a difficult decision. Upon the death of his younger brother Pierre he felt some sense of obligation to join the Williamite forces. This course of action, however, might completely alienate his former sovereign Louis XIV, and surely result in the confiscation of the Ruvigny estates in France. The conduct of the campaign after the victory at the Boyne seems to have played a role in his ultimate choice of options. After Dublin and Leinster had fallen into their hands William's army had absorbed a devastating setback at the First Siege of Limerick City. A suicidal attack on the Jacobite position at St. John's Gate in the city, held by the French Catholic Marquis de Boisseleau, and Patrick Sarsfield's daring raid on King William's supply wagons, seemed to turn the whole course of the campaign. The assault at St. John's Gate exacted a particularly high toll on the Huguenots: 71 out of 77 officers in Du Cambon's Foot were either killed or injured. Another standstill ensued and in 1691 Ruvigny placed himself under the command of the Dutch General Godert van Reede de Ginkel as colonel of the Huguenot cavalry formerly commander by Schomberg. His brother La Caillemotte's infantry unit was now under Pierre Belcastel.

The defining moment in Henri Massue de Ruvigny's career would occur on 12 July 1691 at the pivotal battle of Aughrim. Jacobite forces, under the command of Marshal St. Ruth, whose dragoons had chased the Roussels from France, held a strong position on Kilcommadan Hill and having heavily repelled Ginkel's frontal attack, appeared to be on the way to victory. St. Ruth was riding to assess a threat to his left flank by Williamite cavalry when a chance shot from a cannonball decapitated him. What he would have noticed had he arrived safely at his destination was Ruvigny advancing with his horsemen. St. Ruth's death gave the Huguenot cavalry a clear opening. Ruvigny's charge would roll up the Jacobite left and centre and prove so instrumental in turning a potential disaster into an overwhelming triumph that Ginkel embraced him on the spot. Ruvigny was granted the title Viscount Galway and (in 1697) Earl of Galway; and, after his performance at Aughrim he rose high in

King William's favor. The legend of the Earl of Galway as a great military leader – which has been called into some question in view of his setbacks in the War of the Spanish Succession – was born out of the charge of Ruvigny's Horse on that summer afternoon in July of 1691.

The Huguenots in Jacobite Hands

It is certain that all variety of Protestants in Ireland, with the exception of Quakers faced discouragement and even intimidation. As far as the Huguenots were concerned, one example of outright persecution did occur. Protestants, both establishmentarian and dissenter, fled to Britain in droves. Among the English dissenters who left Dublin at this time of apparent danger was the noted Dr. Daniel Williams whose generosity launched the founding of the library on Gordon Square in London that bears his name. His connection with the Huguenots is uncertain and at this stage conjectural but there are hints that he enjoyed more than a passing acquaintance with the congregation of French Patrick's. One estimate places the number of Protestant families that abandoned their homes in Dublin alone at 1,500. Thus far it can be determined that this total included at least some 280 Huguenots who left Dublin between 1687 and 1690, and never apparently returned.

In June 1689 Josue Roussel and "several other" French Protestants were arrested by Jacobite authorities and imprisoned at the instance of the French Ambassador to King James II's court, Jean Antoine de Marmes, Comte d'Avaux. Roussel himself was presumably to be later transported to France, as a condemned fugitive from his native land. However, as some accounts would have it, the Williamite liberation of the Irish capital after the Battle of the Boyne interrupted this design before it could be carried out; Roussel and his companions were freed. There are some doubts, however, surrounding this scenario. This was more likely to have been the handiwork of Tyrconnell (as part of a precautionary measure against potential Williamite agents and fifth-columnists within the Irish Protestant population) rather than D'Avaux. Though fear of deportation to France undoubtedly existed, it remained more spectral than real. The fact is that, if this had truly been the intention, there was an ample window of opportunity (over one year) between the time of Roussel's arrest and the clash at the Boyne for the transportation to France to have been effected. It is certain that D'Avaux wielded a great influence on the Jacobite government's policy and could have arranged for deportation at any time if he had so desired, if Louis XIV had really been that hell-bent on making an example of a well-known felon. Given the opportunity that had presented itself, the evidence for an insatiably vindictive French campaign to reach out and apprehend its expatriates is simply not there – though this is not to say that King Louis was above being petty in individual cases. The relentless persecuting nemesis painted by propagandists and in some instances perpetuated to this day just does not fit the record. Carrying out a plan of revenge against refugee Huguenots for Louis XIV does not seem to have been part of D'Avaux's larger mission, which was more focused in this instance on influencing King James to favor his Catholic Irish subjects as being the only loyal element in the nation; selective acts of vengeance would have been a wasteful expenditure of time and resource and out of keeping with D'Avaux's shrewd and calculating methods. Anglophone protestants who were much more numerous and far wealthier posed a greater threat as potential allies for William and Mary in the aftermath of the Glorious Revolution. It was only as a portion of this larger grouping of "disloyal Protestant" that individual Huguenots might fall under official scrutiny. Josue Roussel's militant past certainly might have made him a prime suspect – a candidate for detention as a potential security risk. The presence of Huguenot supporters in the entourage of William III and, especially, the deployment of Huguenot regiments in the Williamite army certainly added to the likelihood that Roussel and some of his compatriots might be Williamite sympathizers with the connections and capacity for transmitting information to the enemy. Certainly William King, the then Dean of St. Patrick's Cathedral, was incarcerated for that very reason. One is tempted to speculate on what links could have existed between the pastor of French Patrick's and Dean King, with whom he was surely well-acquainted. However, no documentary evidence has yet established this. D'Avaux was eventually recalled as a result of political manouveuring by an opponent, the Antonin Nompar de Caumont, Comte de Lauzun. De Lauzun arrived from France at the head of an expeditionary force of 6,666 troops and would brook no rival on this highly-delicate mission. D'Avaux departed from Cork without incident and there was no mention of Roussel or his purported deportation. As for Roussel's son Charles, he is conspicuously not mentioned, though he would have been almost as sought-after by the authorities as his father. It is possible that the younger Roussel may have succeeded in going into hiding; whether he was part of a resistance/intelligence network or not is a matter for speculation.

Seen in this context, the imprisonment of Roussel and his co-religionists may be seen as more of a selective blow than a vehicle for vengeance. Certain more prominent (or militant) Huguenots might serve as exemplary lessons for others. These prisoners were perhaps intended to further act as hostages to ensure the good behavior of their community. While names are not given, one may surmise that one of those imprisoned could well have been Pierre Vatable, a vinegar-maker who arrived in Dublin around 1682, prospered financially, and later, as an intimate of the Earl of Galway's circle, became a pillar of the Williamite establishment. Other probable targets of Tyrconnel's "round-up" operations, whose philanthropy towards destitute fellow-refugees marked them as community leaders, were: Pierre Mariel and David Cossart. Daniel Hays, a Dublin alderman, is known to have evaded Tyrconnel's net, for he had joined his half-brother Claude in London in 1688. Thereafter, he can be much more closely identified with the London Refugee Community, serving for a while as a Threadneedle Street elder and becoming involved, as an assistant to the Royal African Company, in the Transatlantic Slave Trade.

It is indicative of this atmosphere of suspicion that Royal Proclamations were issued by King James ordering all Protestants living outside of Dublin to leave the city immediately and, conversely, that those who were legally resident in Dublin were commanded to remain within its confines. There were also the ceaseless "atrocity" reports that filtered out of Ireland, augmented and embroidered to a great extent by families fleeing an anticipated Catholic Jacobite terror. Even wealthy Protestants were asserted to have been reduced to starvation (there is no evidence for this), and more wandering aimlessly in fear of their lives and property. Protestant refugees from Ireland crowded into the town of Chester. Among them were: Thomas Sisson, stationer, and Charles and Gedeon Delaune, Dublin Huguenots who had eight children between them.

An assessment of the history of the Huguenots in Ireland during the years 1687–91 is no easy task: it is rather akin to driving through a tunnel where there are only a few stray shafts of light to illuminate the darkness.

French services at the Lady Chapel had resumed after Williamite forces entered Dublin. The fallen Schomberg's army, including the four Huguenot regiments, marched into the city on 6 July 1690 and immediately thereafter the captive Protestants were released. A service of thanksgiving was held in the nave of St. Patrick's Cathedral and the sermon was delivered, fittingly enough, by Dean William King. Narcissus Marsh did not suffer unduly. While in exile from Ireland he had secured a position of canon of St. Asaph's in Wales, and would in 1691 be elevated to the Archbishopric of Cashel; in 1694 to that of Dublin (he would be succeeded by William King); and in 1703 to the See of Armagh.

Schomberg's body had been embalmed and transported from the Boyne to be interred inside St. Patrick's Cathedral, just adjacent to the Lady Chapel. Although it had been intended that the remains would be transported for re-interment at Westminster Abbey, this plan was never acted upon. The old Huguenot Marshal was soon forgotten and it was left to an indignant Dean Jonathan Swift to direct the erection and inscribing of a marble slab to mark the burial place in 1731. It is there to this day and the words, as personally dictated by the Dean, are a superb example of Swiftian literary vitriol. He taxed Schomberg's heirs with ingratitude for neglecting to erect a suitable monument to their illustrious forbear's memory.

When the firebrand Josué Roussel died in March 1692, to be followed to the grave three days later by his wife Marguerite de Cahours, the Late Ormondite colony which hein many ways had come to personify was already fading. Even before he passed on a new wave of refugees was beginning to trickle into Ireland – a trickle that would rapidly surge into a flood. Though some of these new immigrants would settle into pre-existing communities, many engaged in surveying the hinterland for promising colonization sites. The military veterans, disbanded from the victorious Williamite army; the dispossessed aristocrats and merchants seeking a likely spot from whence to recoup their fortunes; the labourers and artisans looking for a peaceful ambiance in which to practice their trades and rear their families; the widows and heiresses in search of protection; and the artists and domestics wishing to re-establish sources of patronage – all loomed on the horizon to account for the most massive influx of French Protestants, in terms of numbers, social diversity, and influence, in Irish history.

References

Primary sources

Archbishop Narcissus Marsh's Library (Dublin): Tesscreau Ms. Z.2.2.9–10.
British Library Additional Ms. 7718; Additional Ms. 38,143; Harleian Ms. 7194.
Calendar of State Papers (Domestic) 1684–85.
Dublin City Archives, p. 474.
Dublin Registry of Deeds (King's Inn) Ms. 20–291–10655.
Historic Manuscripts Commission Publications. Rep. 7, pt. 1; Rep. 14; Rep. 15; Vol. II; Downshire Ms., Vol. 1, pt. 1; Finch Ms., Vol. II; 1920 (New Series). National Library of Ireland Manuscripts: 76–9, 670, 803, 1619, 1793, 2675, 3719, 8007.
Proceedings of the Huguenot Society of London-Quarto Series. Vols. VII, XVIII, XLI.
Royal Irish Academy: Dumont Ms., McSwiney Ms.

Books/pamphlets

Anonymous. *An Apology for the Protestants of Ireland.*
Anonymous. *Call to Hugonites.*
Cavallier, Jean. *Memoires of the Wars of the Cevennes*

Secondary sources

Andre, Louis. *Michel Le Tellier et Louvois*, pp. 485–7.

Aydelotte, James Ernest. *The Duke of Ormond and the English Government of Ireland, 1677–1685*, pp. 17–25.

Black Eileen and Maguire, W. A. *Kings in Conflict: Ireland in the 1690's*, pp. 33–7, 71–6, 151–65, 173–4, 222–3.

Carre, Albert. *L'Influence des Huguenots Francais en Irlande*, pp. 6, 9.

Chambrier, Baronne de. "Projet de Colonisation" in *PHSL*, Vol. VI, pp. 390–1.

Bagwell, Richard. *Ireland Under the Stuarts*, p. 306.

Benedict, Philip. *Rouen During the Wars of Religion*, pp. 125–51.

Carpenter, Andrew. "William King and the threat to the Church of Ireland during the reign of James II" in *Irish Historical Studies, Vol. 18 (1972–73)*, p. 23.

De la Force, Duc. *Lauzun*, p. 176.

Deyon, Solange. *Du Loyalisme au Refus*, p. 147.

Gimlette, Thomas. *The History of the Huguenot Settlers in Ireland*, p. 273.

Gwynn, Robin. *Huguenot Heritage*, pp. 144–59.

Gwynn, Robin. "Government Policy toward Huguenot Immigration and Settlement in England and Ireland" in Caldicott, Edric, Gough, Hugh, and Pittion, Jean-Paul. *Huguenots and Ireland: Anatomy of an Emigration*, pp. 205–22.

Gwynn, Robin. "The Huguenots in Britain, the 'Protestant International' and the Defeat of Louis XIV" in Vigne, Randolph, and Littleton, Charles. *From Strangers to Citizens: The Integration of Immigrant communities in Britain, Ireland, and Colonial America, 1560–1750*, pp. 412–24.

Le Fanu, T. P. in Lawlor, Hugh Jackson. *Fasti*, p. 286.

Le Fanu, T. P. in *PHSL*, Vol. VIII, pt. 1, p. 16; and in *PHSL* Vol. XII, No. 4.

Lee, Grace Lawless. *The Huguenot Settlements in Ireland*, pp. 14, 26–68, 114, 178–90, 196–200.

Leroy Ladurie, Emmanuel. *Les Paysans de Languedoc*, p. 328.

Ligou, Daniel. *Le Protestantisme en France de 1598 à 1715*, pp. 231–3, 236–8, 241. McGuire, James. "James II and Ireland" in Maguire, W. A. *Kings in Conflict: The Revolutionary War in Ireland and its Aftermath, 1689–1750*, pp. 45–57.

Miller, John. "The immediate impact of the Revocation in England" in Caldicott, Gough and Pittion. *The Huguenots and Ireland*, pp. 161–71.

Miller, John. "The Glorious Revolution" in Maguire, *Kings in Conflict*, pp. 29–44.

Mousnier, Roland. "*L'Edit de Nantes*" in Caldicott, Gough and Pittion. *The Huguenots and Ireland*, pp. 17–33.

Murtagh, Harman. "Huguenot involvement in the Irish Jacobite War, 1689–1691" in Caldicott, Gough and Pittion. *The Huguenots and Ireland*, pp. 225–35.

Murtagh, Harman. "The War in Ireland, 1689–1691" in Maguire. *Kings in Conflict*, pp. 61–91. Orcibal, Jean. *Louis XIV et les Protestants*, p. 65.

Parker, David in Hepburn, T. C. *Minorities*, pp. 14, 23.

Petrie, Sir Charles. *The Great Tyrconnel*, pp. 145, 153.

Schickler, Baron F. de. *Les Eglises du Refuge, Vol. II*, p. 268.
Smiles, Samuel. *Huguenots in England and Ireland*, pp. 193–5, 292.
Speck, W. A. *James II*, pp. 51–83, 101–15.
Stoye, John. *Europe Unfolding, 1648–1688*, p. 763.
Thomas, Roger. *Daniel Williams, "Presbyterian Bishop"*, pp. 3–6.
Vigne, Randolph. "The Good Lord Galway" in *Proceedings of the Huguenot Society of Great Britain and Ireland (PHSGBI)* Vol. XXIV, no. 6, pp. 534–5.

3

THE ORMONDITE YEARS IN PERSPECTIVE, 1662–1691

"The Corporation orders churchwardens in each parish, taking with them two or more persons appointed by their Board to make collection from house to house for the relief of French Protestants fleeing with their families on account of their religion to this Kingdom for protection".

— Waterford, 19 June 1682

Who were they, these Ormondite Huguenot settlers? Though scattered references may be found in earlier works on the Huguenots over the past century-and-half, there has been no real attempt to address the question. These individuals remain relatively unknown to us. It is therefore quite an understatement to assert that the Ormondite Refuge in Ireland has been an unsung chapter in history. Both the Early and Late Ormondite immigrations have perhaps suffered in comparison to the sheer weight in numbers and spectacular success of those of their co-religionists who arrived after 1691, and who have been labeled the Ruvignac (or Galway) Group. And yet these were the Huguenots who laid the foundation upon which Massue de Ruvigny, Bouhéreau, La Touche, Belrieu De Virazel, Crommelin, and others would build. And a remnant of at least 300 Ormondite settlers had endured despite the turmoil of the Tyrconnell era to welcome the new arrivals. It is only right to begin redressing centuries of omission to render due credit and to delve into what the documents might reveal as to the identity and contributions of these neglected "Protestant Strangers".

"Dutch Billies" & Other Legends

Fairly assessing something as intangible as the influence of the French Protestant Dispersion during those pivotal decades of unprecedented urban expansion and political turmoil is fraught with pitfalls. Not the least of these are the myths and fables which grew up concerning the alleged role of the Huguenots as propagators of the weaving industry; inhabitants of the Liberties of Dublin; a docile, one-sided minority; and originators of a revolutionary style of architecture. Beginning, however, with what can be broadly stated as fact, the Huguenot influx into Ireland coincided with a period of never-before witnessed expansion, building and modernization, particularly in Dublin City, which established itself as a true capital, in the modern European sense of the term. From being the hub around which revolved a cluster of medieval garrison towns anchoring English control over a turbulent hinterland, Dublin was transformed at least into Ormond's interpretation of the Continental showcase: a centralizing magnet for government, trade, industry and art. The quarter century of the Restoration, rather than the Georgian Age, witnessed the earliest, most significant strides in the construction of imposing buildings and monuments; and the designing of more spacious and harmoniously laid-out streets studded with brick dwelling and shops to replace the ramshackle wattle-and-timber relics of the Tudor and Jacobean Age which were squeezed miserably up against each other within the medieval town walls of pre-Restoration Dublin.

The Irish capital did experience a phenomenal upsurge in population: from some 9,000 in 1659; to 45,000 by 1685; and continuing well past the Restoration years to some 62,000 by 1706, 92,000 by 1728, and 112,000 by 1744. The physical restructuring which accompanied these demographic advances was equally spectacular.

It is appropriate here to dispose of the "Liberties" legend – at least insofar as the Ormondite Huguenots are concerned. Very simply, there is absolutely no documentary evidence to connect Huguenot immigrants of the 1660s–'90s with the Liberties of Dublin to the extent that the existence of a French community there can be considered, so lack of evidence alone rules out any such contention. The possibility of a post-1690s presence in that section of Dublin will be addressed further on.

One of the more endearing myths surrounding the Huguenots is their reputed linkage to the late 17th–early 18th century gabled style of building construction knownas the "Dutch Billy" or "Huguenot House" style. The most spectacular feature of this style is the ornamental gabling: either straight or curvilinear; the simpler pre-Georgian sunburst design on the doors; and the gigantic communal chimney stack, which was so designed because of the fact that all the fireplaces (of necessity corner fireplaces) in a pair of semi-detached buildings would feed into it. The introduction of the style did apparently coincide with the arrival of the Late Ormondite refugees because the earliest example we have of this type of building in Dublin is a contemporary drawing that dates to 1681. The

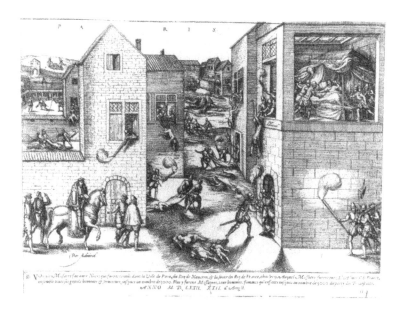

Huguenot Nightmare (1), St. Bartholomew's Day in Paris: The royally-sanctioned slaughter of some 10,000 Huguenot men, women & children in on 24 August 1572 ran deep into the ancestral memory of Huguenots settling in predominately Catholic regions – Ireland among them. Courtesy of the Huguenot Library, University College, London.

Huguenot Nightmare (2), The Day of Okewas in Virginia, 22 March 1622: The bloody surprise attack by tribesmen of the Powhatan nations was widely publicized and certainly brought home to the Huguenots the parallels of St. Bartholomew's Day 50 years earlier, and the perils of settling in a foreign environment. Engraving by Theodor De Bry; courtesy of the Library of Congress: LC-USZ62-13459.

AN

ABSTRACT

OF THE

Unnatural REBELLION,

AND

𝕭𝖆𝖗𝖇𝖆𝖗𝖔𝖚𝖘 𝕸𝖆𝖘𝖘𝖆𝖈𝖗𝖊

OF THE

PROTESTANTS.

In the KINGDOM of

IRELAND,

In the Year 1641.

Collected from the moſt Authentick Copies.

LONDON,

Printed, and are to be Sold by *Richard Janeway* in *Queens-head-alley* in *Pater-noſter-Rowe*, 1689.

Huguenot Nightmare (3), The 1641 Rising in Ireland: The killing of Protestant settlers in 1641 was, as *Abstract of the Unnatural Rebellion* . . . indicates, well-remembered in 1689, nearly a half century later, and certainly raised apprehension in the minds of potential Huguenot immigrants to Ireland. Courtesy of the Queen's University Library, Belfast.

(Above and Right) Huguenot Houses ("Dutch Billies"), Dublin: Gabled buildings with massive central smokestacks that were so much a part of Dublin's physical make-up from 1680–1750 came to be thought of (erroneously) as a Huguenot invention. Now, few are left, and those that are have been much-altered. The structure with two windows on the top floor, located on Molesworth Street is genuine, though it does not have its original gable (the present one was added later). The other, on Kevin Street, is a later reproduction but retains more faithfully the original appearances of these houses.

(Left) Friedrich Hermann, Duke of Schomberg (1615?–1690). Courtesy of the Huguenot Library, University College, London.

(Right) Henri Massue De Ruvigny, Earl of Galway (1648–1720). Courtesy of the Huguenot Library, University College, London.

traditional story has been that these gabled buildings originated in France and/or Holland and that French protestant architects and carpenters imported the style so that their co-religionists who were engaged in weaving might have a dwelling place/workshop, with additional space in the loft for the storage of looms. None of this stands up to closer scrutiny; there is really no evidence there to justify the idea of either French or Dutch architects having had a hand in the designing of these houses (though it certainly cannot be totally proven or disproven that individual Huguenot masons or carpenters might not have worked on some of these gabled buildings).

The straight gables, such as existed on Weaver Square or Chambers Street, had long been a feature of English architecture and more than likely derived from this less exotic source. The curvilinear gable, such as found in dwellings on Longford Street, may possibly have drawn on continental influence and it is more than conceivable that the advent of such gabled buildings coinciding as they did with the great influx of French Protestant fugitives inaugurated by Marillac's Dragonnade may have caused the two phenomena to blend and combine in the public imagination. The other architectural features of these buildings: the doors designs; string courses; and corner fireplaces (which are sometimes known as "Quaker" fire-places) feeding into the massive smokestack. apparently owe nothing to French influence. It is of course reasonable to state that, regardless of the fact that the Huguenots did not introduce "Huguenot Houses" into Ireland, some of them did indeed dwell in "Huguenot Houses". This is because the so-called "Huguenot" or "Dutch Billy" style, which initiated the first large-scale employment of brick as a building material in Ireland, continued to be the dominant architectural design into the mid-1700s, covering the city of Dublin from Leeson Street on the southeast; Marlborough Street, Dorset Street, and Montpellier Hill at its northern extremities; and into the westerly reaches of the Liberties (Marrowbone Lane, South Brown Street). Nor was this form of construction confined to Dublin: Waterford City, for example, had some fine examples of terraced and semi-detached "Dutch Billies" near the Holy Ghost Friary until the early 20th century.

Families & Individuals

Though their names are rarely remembered, Huguenots had quite adroitly infiltrated the social, commercial and artistic life of their adopted land from the very beginning; a harbinger of what they would accomplish to a much greater degree during the 1690s. Far from being negligible, their contributions were as diverse as the immigrants themselves.

Two Huguenot merchants – Jean De La Court of Baburican, County Cork and Jean Fontaine of Middleton, County Wexford – secured licenses to trade in staple commodities in 1667 and 1684–6, respectively. One Thomas Michel was active in the Irish wool trade, having been granted a trading license in 1679. At least one refugee is recorded as having parlayed his native language into a means of earning money. Early in 1687 Lady Katharine Perceval, who had already donated towards the relief of Huguenot immigrants in Dublin, employed a "Monsieur Rennadant" to give her French instructions every day for a half hour – for which he received a guinea per month. One individual at least was eager to leave Ireland as soon as he had arrived. Louis Beauval of La Rochelle wasted no time petitioning the Duke of Ormond (1681) to find employment for him in England as soon as possible. On this occasion the Duke's exertions (if it is to be assumed that he did act in Beauval's behalf) were of little avail – Monsieur Beauval was still in Dublin four years later.

Rene De La Mézandière was a nobleman who seemed to enjoy having a finger in many different projects; but whose entrepreneurial ambitions either outstripped his resources or foundered through his miscalculation of the business climate in Ireland. De La Mézandière first appeared in Cork in 1664, when the Duke of Ormond granted him the sinecure status of Customer of the City. On 19 January 1665, De La Mézandière successfully petitioned the Lord-Lieutenant to be licensed to operate hackneycoaches and sedan chairs in Dublin. Two years later he was given a monopoly in the running of public transport within the capital limits and shortly thereafter sought to extend his mandate to include inter-town services throughout the whole of Ireland. However, De La Mézandière was unsuccessful; his enterprise probably never realistically operated beyond the confines of Dublin and Ringsend. The country roads were in too deplorable a state and infested with too many footpads and highwaymen to justify the perils and expenses of maintaining regular coach services. Dublin itself was at this time was realistically accessible by sea only through the port of Ringsend, where coaches would await to transport disembarking passengers into town. De La Mézandière's monopoly expired in 1681 but it is probable that he gave it up of himself long prior to that date. In 1684 we have a final glimpse of this apparently well-connected Huguenot aristocrat; when he was admitted as Supernumerary Sergeant of the Poultry, by royal authority. His family conformed and worshipped at French Patrick's, though there is no record of them there after 1669 when his daughter or sister stood as Godmother to Jacques, son of Jean Comtesse and Juliane Pitart. De La Mézandière became embroiled in a 10-month controversy with two of Ormond's gentlemen of the bedchamber over unexplained "fees of honor" which he claimed were due to him and which, on 6 April 1668, he was awarded by the Duke's express order.

Huguenots were, in proportion to their numbers, well-represented in the capital's municipal administrative circles. The most outstanding office-holders were members of a pre-Ormondite Huguenot family, the Desminières. This family is illustrative of the connections of Northern Provincial Huguenot merchant houses with the United Provinces, and reciprocal networks by Dutch merchants in French ports. Though somewhat haltingly referred to by Blackall as "Dutch", their surname had originated in Poitou. Jean and Daniel Desminières had established themselves in Ireland as early as the reign of King Charles I; their main continental base appears to have been Rouen. However, the Desminieres' commercial links with the Netherlands were strong and one branch of the family did reside at Amersfoort in Utrecht Province. Louis Desminières was born at Amersfoort but was ultimately naturalized in Ireland by acts of 1655 and 1662. Jean Desminières gained the confidence and favour of Henry Cromwell through his overseas business contacts (which proved invaluable to a Protectorate regime experiencing economic woes), thus launching his family into its long involvement in civic affairs. Jean became a Dublin alderman and his political star reached its zenith when he became the second individual to hold the distinction of Lord Mayor of Dublin (1666). The family had rapidly assimilated itself into the Anglo-Irish milieu and were reportedly quite anglicized in speech and outlook by the 1670s. Louis served as alderman and Lord Mayor in his turn (1669).

As in the case of many public figures, the careers of the Desminières were stalked by controversy. During the mayoralties of both there were disputes over delays in the payment of bills allegedly owed for goods and services rendered. The complainant in both instances was one John Price who claimed that Jean and Louis, in their capacities as Lords Mayor, had ordered deliveries of candles respectively valued at fourteen pounds, nine pence and twenty pounds, eighteen shillings and five pence. Price was not paid until he petitioned Dublin Corporation on 22 January 1674.

Jean Desminières, when he was Lord Mayor, dwelled at the sign of *The Sugar Loaf* on Bridge Street. It is not known if he engaged in the lucrative enterprise of malting and brewing – his kinsman Louis certainly did. From 1680 to 1686 Louis paid out a six pounds, ten shillings water supply fine for malting and brewing; one pound, ten shillings water fine for "common horse and stabling"; and five pounds water fine for "ground in Oxmantown adjacent to his small house".

Urban expansion and property development were by-words during the Restoration years; indeed the Duke of Ormond's encouragement of development-oriented projects coincided with the Corporation's necessity for a more adequate tax base than the old town centre which was plagued with decrepit timber-framed edifices and narrow alleyways, and stood sorely in need of revitalization. In 1664, the Corporation launched the inaugural phase of an unprecedented program to open waste and/or common ground to private ownership (thereby creating additional rents-revenue for the city exchequer). The speculators who acquired these open lands at nominal cost would, it was hoped, not only plough rents and rates back into the coffers of the Corporation, but might be encouraged to further develop their holdings and thus foster the creation of wealthier residential areas, which in turn would attract more financially substantial townsmen to bolster the tax base. The first area to be so opened was to the southeast of the town centre and would be called St. Stephen's Green. The Green was subdivided into 89 numbered plots running north, east, south and west, which were allocated by the drawing of lots from a list of acceptable proprietors. The chosen property owner paid one penny per frontage foot for lots on the north, east and west sides, but the southern rim was assessed at a "country rate" of one halfpenny per frontage foot; plus a ten shillings fine for each twelve pence ground rent. Furthermore, to preserve the Green itself as a public amenity, the proprietors were obliged to plant six sycamore trees, pay for the street paving, and to see to the building and maintenance of that portion of the wall enclosing the park which lay opposite his property. Lot # 7 on the east side fell to Jean Desminières, and lot # 16 on the south to Louis Desminières. The western edge, latter to be dubbed "French Walk" because of the number of Huguenots who were later to dwell and hold property there had, in 1664 at least, neither Huguenot inhabitants nor Huguenot proprietors.

Again, in 1665, when Oxmantown Green on the North side of the River Liffey was opened to private speculators on the same basis as the St. Stephen's Green project of the preceding year, Jean Desminières was placed in charge of the lottery and he and Louis were again the recipient of parcels of land. Nineteen years later, when the strip of territory known as "The Strand", which ran from "Mabbott's Hill to the Furlong of Clontarf", was parceled-out, the Desminières obtained the rights to two lots. Two other Foreign Protestants, Germain Bazin and Charles Reniertz, who had attained the status of Commoners of the Municipality, also received plots of ground. Jean Desminières would not be the last Huguenot to invest and speculate in urban property, and he certainly would not do so in as daring or constructive a manner as would David Digues Latouche, Senior some 40 years later. He seems rather to have brought up dilapidated tenements in the older sections of the city, and to have acted as a slum landlord. He was certainly involved in his share of litigation. In 1667, for example, Desminières was brought to court by a Dublin merchant named Thomas Cook over the sale of a vessel called *The Sacrifice of Abraham* in Galway port. Another case in which he was enmeshed involved one of his sidelines: rent collecting on behalf of absentee land-lords. In 1681 one of these landlords, a certain Richard Barrots, contested Desminières' claim to a one hundred pounds per annum salary, contend-ing that no agreement had been entered into to that effect. In the event, four years were to elapse before a jury awarded Desminières a fifty pounds per annum salary. To Sir John Perceval, landlord for a decayed piece of property in Bridge Street, Desminières answered complaints over a decline in returns with a statement that could sound almost contemporary: "trade being all gone to new parts of the city by reasons of the markets being moved thither, so that all rents here have fallen".

Jean's son Henry entered the ministry of the Church of Ireland and held prebendaries in the dioceses of Ossory, Emly and Kildare. In a proclama-tion of 4 September 1689, Samuel Desminières of "Comb Walk" and Louis Desminières of "City Walk" are among those brewers who were permitted to retain two horses apiece, that were not to be commandeered by Jacobite officers but were reserved as being essential for their trade. Jean and Louis held their aldermanic positions consistently during the comparatively tranquil Restoration years but in 1689 both were expelled from City Council as part of a Jacobite-engineered purge. Jean returned under the Williamite regime, but Louis did not, nor apparently did Samuel, who had been a commoner of the municipality. From this point, the Desminières connections with the Huguenot Community are rare. "Peter"and "Jane" Desminières, who were naturalized in January and February 1692 respectively, may have been relatives who had chosen to remain in France until grimmer realities of persecution and the perma-nence of the measures following on the heels of the Edict of Fontainebleau had made their situation untenable. In the Registers of the Non-Conformed French Church at Peter Street, August Desminières is mentioned as Godfather to Elizabeth Dufay D'Exoudun on 29 July 1726, though this conveys little as far as establishing an ancestral identification as it was not unheard of at this time for certain Huguenot infants to be given godparents from outside the narrowly-defined French Protestant Community.

David Cossart, one of the ubiquitous merchants of Rouen, first appeared in Dublin on 5 February 1670, along with his wife Marguerite Conguaval and two relatives, Isaac and Judith Cossart. Anne Cossart, in all probability either a daughter or niece of David, married the widower Lieutenant Pierre Goullin from Lourmarin in the Provence, in 1693, and resided for a time in Dublin. The couple had at least two sons: Abraham and David, who each died in infancy. The Goullins had moved to Monasterevan, County Kildare by 1697 and were counted as worshippers at the French Church of the Huguenot settlement at Portarlington. Some Goullins remained at Monasterevan until at least 1770. Grace Lawless

Lee postulates that the elder David Cossart removed to Cork, but there is nothing at present to substantiate this. It seems apparent though that a branch of the family did relocate: one Pierre Cossart obtained the Freedom of Cork City in 1725 and commission as a Cornet in the Regiment of Horse of the City Militia. Members of the family, Pierre'sson John, and a certain Peter Cossart held the office of sheriff in 1753 and 1770, respectively. By way of irony, another John Cossart, the son of Sheriff Peter, moved to Dublin where he was established as a merchant by 1813. Some members of the Cossart family did at least continue to hold property and perhaps reside in the capital prior to this time, however. Transcripts of deeds indicate that they possessed houses and lots at James Street & Sheppey's Lane; Mill Lane; Jervis Street and Santry Street in the early half of the eighteenth century.

Daniel Hays (see Chapter 2), who is listed as being a merchant from Calais (though perhaps originally from Poitou) arrived in Dublin by 13 January, 1682, shortly after Marillac's Dragonnade, though it was not until January of 1690 that he took the oaths for naturalization. He was among those Huguenots who fled during the Tyrconnel Regime and in 1691 he was reimbursed 50 pounds on account of his prior dismissal by the Jacobites from the post of sheriff. Shortly thereafter he was sworn in as City Alderman. However, he never appears to have returned to Dublin for any appreciable length of time and increasingly identified himself with the English Huguenot dispersion. It was also in 1691 that Hays was embroiled in a curious incident which sheds light on the probable existence of a mercantile network between certain prominent Huguenots in London and Dublin, which could act to pull strings on each others' behalf. The *St. Stephen,* a ship laden with a cargo of wine & brandy and sailing out of San Sebastian in the Spanish Basque country, was driven by a storm to the Isle of Man and there seized and confiscated. The *St. Stephen's* owners were prosperous London Huguenots, Hillaire & Pierre Reneu, who contacted Hays. Hays enjoyed favour in high places (perhaps as a result of service to the Williamite cause) because he was able to gain the support of General Godert de Ginkel, First Earl of Athlone, who on 29 April 1691 tried to persuade the Comptroller of the Isle of Man to release the vessel. A Queen's Order was even later secured to that effect. Although a challenge was filed that the *St. Stephen,* which had been built in New England and berthed in Bordeaux, had engaged in smuggling, it must have proven to have been unfounded insomuch as Hillaire Reneu was commended by the British government as late as 20 April 1698 for "promoting the manufacture of alamodes and lustrings and discovering the fraudulent importation thereof".

One of the best-placed of the French Protestants was Dr. Jacques Du Brois Desfontaines-Voutron, whose exact title was Physician-General of the Army in Ireland. This exalted post did not prevent him from being menaced by at least one irate colleague, though he seems to have emerged from this confrontation reasonably unruffled (refer to the epigraph at the beginning of chapter 2). The Doctor was proactive in propagating some of the Duke of Ormond's colonization schemes, negotiating the passage and settlement of several merchants and tradesmen at Carrick-on-Suir in 1671.

Even if they might have had little to do with "Dutch Billy" architecture, the Ormondite Huguenots contributed their share to the artistic life of Ireland. Some were enrolled in the Guild of St. Luke the Evangelist, which was composed of cutlers, painters, stainers, and stationers and chartered by King Charles II in 1670. That same year charter member Paul De Melle (or De Milly, or De Melly) was made a freeman of Dublin. De Melle had previously resided in The Hague and there learned portrait-painting. He is numbered by Blackall as being among the French Protestants in Dublin; though it is unclear as to whether he was a Frenchman who learned to paint in the Dutch style or a Dutchman who associated himself – as some others did – with the French Patrick's congregation. De Melle is known to have painted, upon the Guild's foundation, a portrait of its first master, Samuel Cotton, cutler. The portrait is said to have hung in the Guildhall in Capel Street, Dublin, to whence the Guild had moved from its original meeting-place at the Common Hall in St. Audeon's Arch. Unfortunately, neither Cotton's portrait nor other works by De Melle's hands are known to be extant. De Melle was elected Guild Warden from 1674–6, but by early 1685, had passed away. The stationer Thomas Sisson was also a charter member and is listed among those Protestants who took refuge in Chester England in 1689. Pierre Surville was a later arrival in Dublin; he resided in Chequer Lane and first turned up in Guild Records as a painter in August of 1684, on which occasion he presented a full-length portrait of King Charles II. In 1689 the Dublin City Fathers commissioned Surville to paint a portrait of King James II, to hang in the Tholsel on High Street, for which he was compensated 24 pounds.

The artistic work of the three Tabary Brothers is extant and readily visible, for they did the wood and plaster work for the Chapel of the Royal Hospital at Kilmainham. Jacques Tabary, woodcarver, was made a freeman of Dublin City at Michaelmas, 1682 and his brothers Jean (sculptor) and Louis (also a carver) achieved that same distinction three years later. The Hospital itself is one of the few remaining architectural gems of the Restoration period and was chartered in 1683 under the name of "The Hospital of King Charles II for ancient and maimed soldiers of the Army of Ireland". It was designed by the noted architect William Robinson. Little is known of the subsequent career of the Tabarys, though Jacques at least was still living in Dublin as late as 1698.

What clearly emerges out of these and other examples is that the Ormondite community was certainly not so much obliterated as submerged after 1692; in fact the remaining families and individuals thoroughly leavened themselves into the larger refugee community that followed in their paths. There are hints that certain Ormondites proved invaluable in easing the transition of the far-more-numerous later arrivals and in laying the foundations for the Ruvignac *Corps du Rèfuge*.

One of these was certainly a man named Gendron, who by 1692 owned a Dublin hostelry in Copper Alley which catered to pensioned Huguenot military officers, among others. It is to be hoped that his inn was of better quality than the usual run of such establishments in 17th century Ireland, where accommodation was often barely tolerable and the food notoriously unpalatable. This innkeeper is very likely Marc Gendron, a member of the French Patrick's congregation who was admitted to the Freedom of the City as a wine cooper in 1685. Individuals bearing the surname Gendrin or Jendrin, who worshipped at French Patrick between 1693 and 1702, may have been relatives, though a conclusive link has yet to be established.

Joseph Archer is first mentioned as a Huguenot in Dublin in 1685, and was still therein 1700. Pierre Arché, perhaps a son, was in 1709 established as a merchant in Portarlington. Samuel Barré also arrived in 1685 and though deceased by 1699, had at least one (namesake) son. The Barré family endured as members of the French Conformed congregations up till 1807, by which time the French spelling had been superseded and anglicized to "Barry". Paul Bonnafon, who arrived in Ireland in 1687, became an elder at French Patrick's and later a *lecteur* (scripture-reader) at the breakaway French Conformed Church that met at the Chapter House of St. Mary's Abbey from 1701 to 1740 (it was popularly dubbed "French Mary's"). He passed on while still serving in that capacity on 23 January 1735.

Of the Ormondite families who elected to retain Ireland as their abode beyond 1692, the Vatables were perhaps the most fortunate. Pierre Vatable, "vinegar maker", arrived in Dublin in 1683 with his wife Marie Brevet. His subsequent close ties with the coterie that revolved around the Earl of Galway hints that he may have been a person of much higher consequence and far vaster resources than was apparent. His influence might possibly derive in part from substantial assistance that he might have rendered the Williamite cause as a covert sympathizer. Vatable's daughter Catherine married Daniel, son of Jacques de Belrieu, Baron de Virazel, one of Galway's closest associates and an influential landowner at Portarlington and Dublin. At the time, it was exceedingly rare for exiled members of the Huguenot nobility – even of the écuyer class – to marry outside their social stratum, let alone for a peer like Virazel to admit of such a union. Pierre Vatable was, in any case, surely far more than just a "vinegar maker".

Louis Leroux, merchant from Lyons, had established himself in Dublin by 1691, and married Elizabeth Cassel from Calais, who was eleven years his senior. The Lerouxs had a daughter, Anne, born in Dublin when her mother was 46, and who married the merchant François Claris on Christmas Day, 1707. Leroux became an elder at French Patrick's and died on 6 December 1716 at the age of 66, his wife having predeceased him by 12 years. Leroux is credited, whether rightly or wrongly is open to debate, for establishing one of the earliest silk manufactures in Ireland.

Pierre Caceau was 34 years of age in 1683 when he and his wife Marie Fontanelle escaped Daze in Poitou and disembarked in Dublin. Rearing a family of at least four children, Pierre ended his days as porter at the Lady Chapel and died 28 April 1713.

Where does one draw the line?

" . . . French Protestants, and others . . . " But who were the "others"? This is a problem that one encounters when studying the Huguenots. It exists acutely in the English Refuge where Walloon individuals and settlements have been inextricably intermingled with the Huguenots. In the Irish Refuge the problem is not as daunting but nonetheless the line between "Huguenot" and "other Protestant stranger" is sometimes difficult to sketch. "Others" did in fact worship at French Patrick's alongside those more readily identifiable as French. At times it is hard to tell if this is a subgroup operating within the Huguenot minority or individuals loosely identifying themselves with a larger group in order to derive a sense of belonging and protection. Just how are the few Dutch, Swiss, Germans and Alsatians to be classed. It is perhaps just as well not to split hairs and to accept the term "Protestant stranger" in the larger sense that was originally intended.

The Dutch were targeted for harassment and abuse not only because of their adherence to a Reformed faith nearly identical to that of the Huguenots but because of international politics. William III's attempts at forestalling Louis XIV's schemes for expanding the frontiers of his realm did not sit well with the *Grand Monarque*, whose so-called Dutch War of 1672–8 had been aimed primarily at forever eliminating this source of annoyance. This had developed into personal animosity and reached the point where the diplomatic, dynastic, confessional and ego-related elements were hopelessly entangled in a bloody rivalry that would at least in part give rise to two global conflicts. Both the Huguenots and the Dutch would be sucked into this conflagration as pawns.

There had been interchange between the Dutch and the Huguenots since the 16th century. Admiral Gaspard de Coligny's plan for a pre-emptive strike by the French army into the Spanish Netherlands in order to assist the Dutch "Sea Beggars" Rebellion against Philip II's suppressive regime was one of the factors that precipitated the the St. Batholomew's Day Massacre. Queen Mother Catherine de Medici feared that Coligny, who had gained an ascendancy over her unstable son, King Charles IX, would soon persuade him to undertake what she was convinced would be a suicidal military expedition against the vastly superior forces of the Spanish Duke of Alva (very likely it would have been). Anxiety over the future of her adopted country and – probably more to the point – the Valois Dynasty impelled Catherine to browbeat her son into authorizing a mass assassination of the Huguenot leadership and to employ the Catholic De Guises (whom she roundly detested) to carry out this scheme. What she had not foreseen was that popular elements would then get out of control and indiscriminately butcher an estimated 10,000 French Protestants of all classes and age groups in the days following 24 August 1572.

These tragic circumstances notwithstanding, Dutch and Huguenots continued to render mutual aid, comfort and protection. Dutch mercan-tile communities existed in many French port cities (including Rouen) where they lived side-by-side and associated most frequently with the Huguenot mercantile/professional classes. Several Huguenot families who eventually came to Ireland first resided in the Dutch Netherlands. There was also a communality as regards persecution. In the 1680s Dutch expatriates living in France were subjected to abominable treatment, and forced to leave.

Certain families of more or less obviously Dutch or German surnames do occur in the rolls of the French Conformed Church at St. Patrick's. In general persons of such surnames that can be traced in the 1680s tended to interact among themselves and to adhere to a subgroup within the larger Huguenot community. There is evidence of several such fam-ilies arriving in Ireland *en bloc*. Hendrik Van Kruys Kerk (or "Cross Church", as his name was already being anglicized) and his wife Catherine De Staar; his wife's parents Isaac De Staar the elder and his wife; and their sons Esaye and Isaac; along with Isaac the younger's wife Joachine Elisor and her brother Jacques Elisor – all converged on the Irish capital at the same time, in 1685. Others within the orbit of this subgroup seem to have included: Charles Reniertz; Joseph Wessencrof; and Guillaume (Willem?) Van Marque. Bartholomew Van Homrigh and Jacob Silvius, who had probably come to Ireland earlier and indepen-dently of the Huguenots, were nonetheless in association with the refugee community and at least occasionally attended services at French

Patrick's. Van Marque, a tailor, left Rouen to start afresh in Dublin in 1681, and was evidently successful. He married Susanne Le Geé (or Lesse), who had arrived in Ireland from the city of Mannheim in the Palatinate. This couple is recorded as having one daughter, Judith Susanne, who was born in 1684 and apparently died on 28 January 1686. Van Marque seems to have remarried for after his death at the age of 45 on 15 March 1694 his widow Susanne Seel married (12 May 1695) to Jean Augereau, another tailor. Joseph Wessencrof, a goldsmith, arrived in Ireland by 1685 and the German physician Jacob Silvius had two of his children baptized at French Patrick's: his son Lambert (December 1683); and an unnamed daughter (February 1685).

Batholomew Van Homrigh is easily the most intriguing of these individuals. His family must have been Dutch in origin, though one source states his birth place as the city of Danzig. O'Hart postulated that the Van Homrigh family had already established themselves in Dublin during the reign of King James I, though this does not seem to square with Bartholomew's only being naturalized in 1689. Van Homrigh, along with his daughter Esther (who was the mysterious "Vanessa" associated with Dean Swift) was admitted as a Freeman in 1688. An ardent champion of William III, Prince of Orange Van Homrigh would rise in favour and wax in honors during the years of his reign. He became: commissioner-general for the Williamite army; M.P. for Derry City; governor of the King's Hospital at Oxmantown (Blue Coat School); fellow of the Dublin Philosophical Society; and Lord Mayor of Dublin (1697). Though not strictly speaking a Huguenot, Van Homrigh seems to have worshipped often at French Patrick's and to have had correspondence with the French community prior to 1692. We may never be able to know the full extent, if any, of his possible communications with the Refugee communities in Ireland during the War of the Two Kings – but it is interesting to speculate that the Jacobite suspicion of "Fifth Columnism" on the part of the Huguenots and other foreign Protestants might have some basis in fact, and that Van Homrigh may perhaps hold one of the "keys" to such speculation.

Hints from the record

The unsettled nature of the Ormondite Communities' history, where turn-abouts in government attitudes and unpredictable spasms of persecution made it difficult to tell who was coming or going, rules out any truly effective family reconstruction. As if this were not trouble enough, limitations in the records we have render it impossible to compile complete demographic tables denoting infant and adult mortality; the ratio of births &

stillbirths per family; age at marriage; incidences of miscarriage; comparative longevity within gender or social groups; etc.

Church registries have always been a keystone for researchers, and Pastor Jacques Hierome was certainly not very thorough in his record-keeping (it was probably a rare enough occasion when he did personally officiate at French Patrick's). For those years (1681–6) on which the Conformed Church Register provides the most complete information we may only derive some tantalizing figures. In 1681, 4 births are recorded as occurring (2 male & 2 female) , and 7 deaths, including 4 infants & juveniles evenly divided by gender. In 1682 there were 12 births (5 male, 6 female, 1 unspecified), and 6 deaths, including that of an infant female. In 1683 the total had risen to 20 births (10 male, 10 female) and 23 deaths, including that of 9 infants (6 male, 3 female). The year 1684 saw 10 births (2 male, 8 female), and 6 deaths, 4 of which were those of infants (1 male, 3 female). In 1685 there were 31 births (13 male, 16 female, 2 unspecified), counterbalanced by 34 deaths, including 22 infants (13 male, 9 female). The year 1686 bore witness to 12 births (8 male, 3 female, 1 unspecified) and 15 deaths, including 6 infants (3 of either sex). The total proportion of infant death was 46 out of 87, or 52.87 percent. Even given the fragmentary records and the very rapid and drastic changes which took place during those same years in the wake of the Dragonnades and Revocation, what leaps out are the horrific figures relating to infant mortality, statistics which bear out the general trend for Early Modern Europe. The mortality statistics for multiple-birth deliveries are again consistent with those in other studies, revealing an even grimmer picture. There are five instances of multiple births, four of twins and one of triplets. Multiple births were more often than not lethal to both newborns and to the mother; in the case of our Late Ormondite Huguenots, 8 multiple babies died and only 2, perhaps 3, survived. A boy and a girl born to François Guintaval and Jeanne Bonnet died within three days of each other (22–25 May 1681). Twin girls of Elie Rambert's were buried together on 4 January 1685. A twin daughter of Jacob Riorteau and Elizabeth Allaire died on 12 October 1685, and her brother two days later. Twins were born posthumously to Pierre Moreau from La Rochelle, by his wife Susanne Audran on 15 January 1683. The late Monsieur Moreau seems to have been reasonably esteemed during his brief time of residence in Ireland, for standing as godparents at the baptism of his son Pierre (one of the twins) were Pierre Drelincourt, Alderman George Blackall, and the wife of Alderman John Ryder. Regretably, little Pierre died on 24 January 1683. It is unclear as to whether his twin sister was Marie Moreau, who died on 10 October 1683 or Anne Moreau, who survived into the Ruvignac years to marry Jean Beaume on 12 June 1699. Triplets were born in January 1685 to Jacques Guionneau and his wife.

The couple had previously lost an older son on 2 January of that same year. One of the triplets, Anne, died on 15 August 1685, but the son, Louis, and another daughter, Jeanne, apparently survived infancy.

The "Hidden" Refugees?

Regardless of the position of French Patrick's as the sanctioned church for the Huguenots of Dublin, and the only one known to exist for their specific use in Ireland at that time (and even at that, it was only in a chapel located within the greater Cathedral complex), not all Huguenots worshipped there. Many Huguenots certainly preferred nonconformity as being more compatible to their practice in France. However, the existence of a permanent French non-conformist congregation has not been established. There is a persistent assertion that such a congregation did assemble at the home of Lady Ossory, though her husband's family were on the whole unsympathetic to the whole notion of dissent. To the extent that this supposition appears only in a source that was written two hundred years later, and is supported by no original source that would have been contemporary to the events, it may well be totally apocryphal.

What is much more certain, however, is that some Huguenots drifted – even at this early stage – to establishing their center for worship at Anglophone Anglican Churches. We are on much more unsteady ground in trying to locate these "hidden" worshippers and to piece together their story. Some immigrants, it would so appear, desired to assimilate into their host population quite rapidly. In the case of others, the difficulty lies in the fact that certain names that might seem to be French may actually be otherwise. In some cases we can only conditionally state what we have discovered in hopes that future research might remove the qualifications that must be put in place.

In Dublin City, perhaps 8 families and 44 individuals worshipped at St. John's Church on Fishamble Street. The surnames include: Bouchard, Camplison, Minet, Que (a hatter), Verdon, and the more dudious ones of Vontandelow, Sechecivenall, and Anion. A branch of the Desminières family attended St. Audeon's; a certain Jacques Gimeriell married Jeanne Desminieres on 5 May 1687. At St. Bride's Church on 20 April 1684, Charles Lapparier married Jeanne Muniene; and on 23 April 1687, Charles Tresseé and Elizabeth Davise were united in wedlock. The wife of surgeon-general Du Brois de Fontaine was interred there on 1 March 1690. At St. Andrew's Church, Abraham Le Double married Marie Garin (27 January 1687). At St. Michan's near Oxmantown there are as many as 22 surnames that may indicate Huguenot families. Of these, eight may be perhaps classed as Early Ormondites, the rest as Late Ormondites. These comprised six gentlemen; a silkweaver; a glazier; a goldsmith; a felt-maker; a coachman; two merchants; a butcher; a winecooper; a weaver; a gunsmith; a maltster; a clothier; the rest indeterminate. The goldsmith, Daniel Zouche, and his wife Elizabeth, attended St. Michan's between 1684 and 1692. There has been some question about a possible connection with the Desouches family, but such does not seem to have existed. The Desouches, a long-enduring Irish Huguenot family, seem to have descended from Claude Desouches, a tanner and currier from Poitou. Guillaume Tonge, glazier, had arrived in Dublin and been issued the Freedom of the City by Michaelmas 1678. By1683 at least he resided in St. Michan Parish; his two sons Jean and Joseph, and his wife Jeanne, are buried in the church.

French Protestant families also seem to have concentrated around the St. Peter's and St. Kevin's Parishes on the south side of the City, where 12 probable surnames can be identified. Germain Bazin and his wife Alice dwelled in Aungier Street, where their sons Jean, Guillaume and Thomas, and their daughter Hester, were born between 1669–77. The joiner Jean Comtesse and his wife Juliane resided at Stephen Street from at least 1670 to 1684. Charles and Madeleine Le Maistre were among the earlier inhabitants of St. Stephen's Green (1674); Saul and Elinor Rezin lived on Whitefriar Lane; William (Guillaume?) and Elizabeth Garrard on St. George's Lane and Guillaume and Catherine Sarazon at Clarendon Market.

The most heart-wrenching case was that of Thomas Missal, a newly-arrived refugee who must have undergone great hardship to arrive in Ireland, only to die suddenly, possibly alone, on 8 April 1686 in rented quarters at the Robin Hood Inn on Stephen Street.

Early Instances of Assimilation

The signs of the French Protestants beginning to blend into their surroundings are, even at this point in time, unmistakable. There are of course the above-mentioned families who chose to gather for worship services at Anglophonic established churches when services in French were being offered at the Lady Chapel. It is true that the incidence of so many Huguenot families at St. Michan's might be partially explained by the geographical situation of Oxmantown on the City's extreme north-east. Those families inhabiting the north bank of the River Liffey would have found it inconvenient in some cases (and perhaps an added expense) to negotiate the passage across the river by bridge or ferry, and would have avoided so if they could. The danger factor was certainly not negligible, there was a paucity of bridges spanning the river at this juncture in time, and there could be considerable hazard in traveling through some of the rougher quayside sections of the city because of cutpurses and assorted rogues and ruffians. However, no such explanation suffices in the face of substantial numbers of French worshippers in the Anglophone Churches of St. Kevin's and St. Peter's parishes on the south side of the Liffey, where French Patrick's was within easy walking distance. This alone may indicate that the assimilatory tendency was asserting itself at quite an early stage. This blending-in process was apparently far-advanced as far as those remaining Pre-Ormondite Huguenot families, such as the Delaunes and the Desminières, were concerned. Furthermore, there are at least 33 families who never seem to have attended French Patrick's, but blended immediately into regular Church of Ireland congregations: the Onges, Wilmotts; Bazins; Rezins; Tonges; Brossier de Beaulieus; Pains; Le Doubles; La Marchants; Garrards and Harabins being among the most noteworthy.

Instances of marriage unions between Huguenots and Anglophone Protestants similarly provides some indication. During the Ormondite era, seven (possibly nine) examples of exogamous marriage may be discerned: the Delaune, Desminieres, Boyer, La Marchant, Cerines and Harabin families are involved.

Though the Ormondite refuges pale in comparison to the spectacular Ruvignac colony, the extant evidence would bear out the contention that its impact was none the less, in the context of variety and intensity, anything but negligible.

References

Primary sources

British Library (London): Additional Ms. 15, pp. 636–7; Harleian Ms. 7194.
Calendar of the Ancient Records of the City of Dublin. Gilbert, John T., ed. Vol. IV, pp. 295, 297–9, 303, 305, 307, 326–35: Vol. V, pp. 28–9, 419, 497–8, 500, 634.
Calendar of State Papers (Domestic) XXVIII, addenda 1660–1685, pp. 363–4.
Calendar of State Papers (Ireland) 1669–70, addenda 1625–70, p. 527.
Council Book of the Corporation of Cork.
Caulfield, Richard, ed., pp. 603, 613.
Dublin City Archives Ms. pp. 405–6, 419, 421, 429, 438, 467–9.
Dublin Registry of Deeds. Mss. 7–381–2722, 21–54812460, 92–198–50375.
Historic Manuscripts Commission Publications. Rep. 6; Rep. 10; Rep. 11, App. 2; Rep. 14, App. 4, 7; Vol. VII; Vol. 1 (New Series); Vol. IV (New Series); Egmont Ms., Vol. II; Dartmouth Ms., Rep. 11.
Huguenot Society of London-Quarto Series. Vol. VII, VIII, IX, XI, XIII, XIV, XVI, XVIII, XIX, XXIII.National Library of Ireland Manuscripts: 16–19, 100, 104, 1793, 2030, 2675, 10,991–A, 12,121–2, Microfilm n. 7517, pp. 751–7.

Proceedings of the Parish Registers Society of Ireland. Vol. II, III, V, XI, XII.
Trinity College Dublin Archives, Ms. 7.4.3.

Books/pamphlets

Drelincourt, Pierre. *Speech to His Grace the Duke of Ormond . . . to return humble thanks of French Protestants . . .* (Dublin 1682).

Secondary sources

Bagwell, Richard. *Ireland Under the Stuarts*, pp. 35–8.
Barnard, T. C. *Cromwellian Ireland*, pp. 57, 85–6.
Carré, Albert. *L'Influence des Huguenots Francais*, p. 88.
Combe, J. C. *The Huguenots in the Ministry of the Church of Ireland*, pp. 53, 56–9.
Craig, Maurice. *Dublin, 1660–1860*, pp. 3–5, 18, 62, 86.
Falkiner, Frederick. *The Foundations of the Hospital of King Charles II*, pp. 10–29.
Gerard Frances. *Picturesque Dublin*, p. 148.
Gill, Conrad. *The Rise of the Irish Linen Industry*, p. 16.
Gimlette, Thomas. *The History of the Huguenot Settlers in Ireland*, pp. 192, 273.
Gwynn, Robin. *Huguenot Heritage*, p. 152.
Haag, Eugene & E. M. *La France Protestante, Vol. IV*, p. 265.
Lebrun, François. *Les Hommes et la Mort en Anjou au 17 et 18 Siècles*, p. 180.
Lee, Grace Lawless. *The Huguenot Settlements in Ireland*, pp. 62, 221.
McLysaght, Edward. *Irish Life in the Seventeenth Century*, pp. 183–5, 207, 244–6, 251, 264.
Maxwell, Constantia. *Dublin Under the Georges*, p. 67.
O'Dwyer, Frederick. *Lost Dublin*, p. 108.
Simms, J. G. "The Restoration, 1660–1685" in Moody, T. W., Martin, F. X., & Byrne, F. J., *A New History of Ireland, Vol. III*, p. 449.
Skelton, Philip. *Complete Works, Vol. III*, p. 380 (Lynam, Robert, ed.).
Smiles, Samuel. *Huguenots in England and Ireland*, p. 294.
Strickland, Walter George. *A Dictionary of Irish Artists, Vol. I*, pp. 274, 418.
Walsh, John Edward. *Rakes and Ruffians*, pp. 10–11, 66–7.
Walsh, Peter. "Dutch Billies in the Liberties" in Gillespie, Elgy, *The Liberties*, pp. 61–2.

❖ PART II ❖
The Ruvignac Refuges

It was the waves of Huguenot immigrants who arrived in Ireland during the reigns of William III and Mary II, Anne, and well into that of George I, who defined what the Huguenot presence in and impact on Ireland would be. Indeed, they framed the image of the Huguenot settlers for succeeding generations. It is within the course of this thirty-year period (*c.* 1692–1722) that most of the estimated 10,000-odd French Protestant immigrants would set foot in Ireland. The ten thousand figure has held up reasonably well, and in the end will probably prove to be close to the actual tally – the only time the author mustered the courage to count individuals, albeit in a rough manner, he was able to verify a total of 7,990.

Again, these refugees have been rather conveniently labeled after a leading political figure of the day – in this particular instance, one of their own. Henri Massue (Marquis) de Ruvigny, Baron Portarlington, Viscount and Earl of Galway was Lord Justice of Ireland from 1697 to 1701 and between 1715 and 1717. However, as was the case with the Ormondite communities, this Huguenot immigration would soon transcend any individual, regardless of how influential he happened to be, and would extend even beyond the royal agenda. What had been primarily conceived in terms of political and military strategy became something far more all-encompassing, permanent, and, ultimately, enriching.

4

"FORTRESS IRELAND" – THE *LINCHPIN*: PORTARLINGTON'S SAGA, 1692–1720

"My assets consist only of a ramshackle cottage on a half acre of land of indifferent quality. I further possess a cow and two donkeys".

— Statement of Jacques Beauchant, retired corporal in Galway's Horse, and Portarlington resident, 30 January 1714 (later to become Portarlington's leading shopkeeper, and French Church elder)

It was certainly a victory, but a most precarious one. It took over two years of hard fighting, casualties; disease and suffering to lead to the Treaty of Limerick. Even when it was at its most secure, the Williamite regime was a fragile plant reposing on untested foundations. Its permanent success was never preordained; nor was the Glorious Revolution the truly unmitigated triumph later exalted by the Whig Legend. Like the American Revolution a century later, it was the government of France, the Continent's dominant superpower, that had swayed events. Its very success had hinged upon either, in the case of the Torbay Expedition, deliberate French non-involvement or, in the case of the War of the Two Kings, the calculated decision of the *Grand Monarch's* government that, in the overriding scheme of things, Ireland was of very low priority. If Louis XIV had exerted genuine effort to win the Irish Campaign, it is intriguing to speculate that the Boyne Triumph and myth surrounding it would never have occurred, Orangeism would have been stillborn, and Partition would not have become an issue. This had been one of those "close run" affairs that may delight historians and novelists, but whose consequences have become a fact of contemporary existence. If, in retrospect, it is no longer appreciated how insecure the "Revolution Settlement" actually was, the supporters of the New (Williamite) Order were under no such illusion. The legality of William & Mary's accession to the throne was widely questioned, and their regime was never popular. Its strongest basis of support was a negative one: that of being comparatively less undesirable than government under the deposed King James II. That even the likes of Lieutenant-General John Churchill, Earl of Marlborough (regardless of the questionable sincerity of his motives), should give lip service to Jacobite pretensions, resounded ominously.

If Ireland's Catholic majority assured that it would be a sullen portion of the realm, the Williamites were facing increasing difficulties in Scotland as well. The clumsy handling of the MacDonalds of Glencoe and transparent government connivance in the Massacre of 40 of their men, women and children had brought international condemnation and embarrassment on King William's head. The Scots would be further estranged from the regime over the Darien Fiasco, where nearly 2,000 Scots lost their lives in an ill-starred financial cum military venture to settle and trade on the isthmus of Panama, after having been led to believe that they could count on King William's support, only to see the government abruptly disown the scheme. The Scottish economy was in a shambles and there are those who attest to this day that without the failure of the Darien Venture, the Union of the Scottish and English crowns would not have been effected in 1707. Though allegations of deliberate intent on the part of Westminster to see the Darien Project fail in order to bring the Union about remain unproven, they enjoyed widespread currency in the 18th century, and have refused to go away completely. Jacobite sentiment in King William's Scottish realm would consequently fester for decades to come.

In England itself, King William was barely tolerated, and had always been considered an unavoidable appendage to his English-born wife, Mary II. Many would have been content to have relegated him to Prince-consort, if Mary had insisted that she would never accept the crown unless her husband were legally designated as co-monarch. His cold, off-putting manner irritated his English subjects, as did his perceived favoritism towards the foreign entourage that he had carried over in the wake of revolution and war. If, as Daniel Defoe pointed out, much of this animosity towards William over his foreign favourites, was unfair insomuch as most English courtiers had disdained him from the beginning and proved reluctant (and even uncooperative) when it came to rendering the government reliable advice assistance, the popular view that he relied "too much, on foreigners – Germans, Huguenots, and Dutch" – was fixed in the popular mentality, and took on a life of its own as the "conventional wisdom" of the time.

As a corollary, individuals like Ginkel, Bentinck, Schomburg, and Ruvigny (who would become Viscount, then Earl of, Galway) – influential foreigners who were seen to have benefited from William's largesse – became objects of suspicion: at best they were spongers who were milking the exchequer; at worst they could potentially become over-mighty

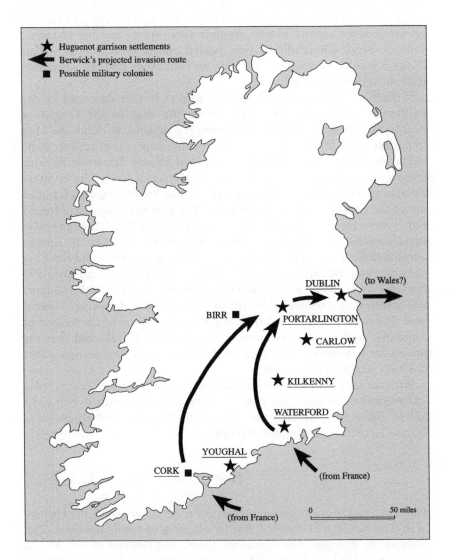

Legend:
★ Huguenot garrison settlements
← Berwick's projected invasion route
■ Possible military colonies

DUBLIN ★ → ★ (to Wales?) →

BIRR ■

★ PORTARLINGTON

★ CARLOW

★ KILKENNY

WATERFORD ★

YOUGHAL ★

CORK ■

(from France)

(from France)

0   50 miles

Berwick's invasion scheme and Galway's colonies

subjects bent on carving out their personal domains. Mary II's untimely death from smallpox on 28 December 1694 removed the last buffer that could moderate the animosity between King and subject – at least Mary, though she had not enjoyed overwhelming popularity, had been one of "their own". In effect, even prior to Mary's demise, a rival court had been set up centered around Mary's younger sister Anne, and her retainers, John & Sarah Churchill. As time passed and it became evident that William would not remarry and have an heir, Anne and the Churchills took on added importance.

William's effectiveness and credibility were further damaged by the indifferent progress of the Allies during the War of the League of Augsburg. Personal and political differences weighed in to decide the King to neglect using Marlborough, his ablest commander, as effectively as he might have; in Flanders the Allies absorbed bloody defeats at Fleurus, Steenkerke and Landen; and the loss at Marsaglia led to the eventual collapse of the Savoy Front in 1696, when Duke Victor Amadeus II pulled out of the Grand Alliance against Louis XIV that the League had forged eight years earlier. The resulting Peace of Ryswick of 1697, though sometimes depicted as a truce of exhaustion was, in the main, of greater advantage for Louis. The Alliance had not clung together, and the King of France emphatically reaffirmed his policy against the Huguenots. For the latter, it would be a bitter and lasting blow: most French Protestants still dreamed of a triumphal return to a chastened and repentant homeland. Many had thus pinned their hopes on the efforts of the League of Augsburg, and the disappointing terms at Ryswick indicated that the prayed-for redemption of France would not occur in their lifetimes, that this exile might be permanent.

With the advent of a rather disquieting and malcontented peace, political pressure on William and criticism of his regime intensified. Nor did a lull in the actual warfare put an end to the very real threat of a Franco/Jacobite incursion into Ireland.

1692

The year 1692 is one of those forks in the road, down which the History of Ireland turned and traveled, forever effecting its future direction. The Marquis de Ruvigny was appointed Lieutenant-General of the Armed Forces in Ireland, making the former Versailles courtier, potentially at least, the most powerful individual on the island. The "Penal Era" began as the triumphant Anglo-Irish Ascendancy set into motion restrictions on Catholics which would poison inter-denominational relations far beyond the ninety-odd years that it was in full force. The Huguenots have been traditionally placed in a bizarre situation as regards popular memory of the Penal Years. While the most prominent and powerful of the Huguenots in Ireland has long been unjustly castigated as a major instigator of penal measures against Catholic, his lesser co-religionists are warmly remembered as beneficial contributors and, despite having been part-and-parcel of the very Ascendancy that has been so despised, are esteemed as role-models. Huguenot ancestry is prized by both Protestants and Catholics to the present day; a variety of people would take pride in such a connection, if it were discovered in their lineage (during the course of this author's research, it was even inquired of him whether or not the surname "O'Reilly" was of Huguenot origin).

It was during this year, when the subjugation of Ireland was at least momentarily assured, the substantive plans for settling Huguenots in an Irish Haven of exile took shape. Through hearsay, concrete promises, but mainly – one would imagine – on hope, hundreds of French Calvinists poured into Ireland. How much of this Huguenot immigration was spontaneous, and predicated on individual initiative, is difficult to ascertain. However, planning and direction were deemed essential if one were to preserve a distinctive, and politically effective and coherent Huguenot community. The opportunities for proselytizing by example: for the Protestant virtues of work, thrift, self-restraint, sobriety and integrity believed to be inherent in the Huguenot lifestyle to hopefully "rub off" on the undisciplined Catholic Irish, was not lost on the Planners. Already the situation on the ground began to outpace the leadership's strategy and deliberations. The influx of individual and refugee families in Dublin, for example, had been so rapid and unanticipated that the newcomers soon far outnumbered the remnants of the Ormondite colony; composition of the refugee population had been radically altered, and the resources of French Patrick's, now drastically outstripped,could not immediately cope with the situation.

The majority of these new immigrants had in fact taken the initiative to form non-Conformist meeting groups, which would soon coalesce into a large congregation, thus precipitating severe confessional tensions within the refugee community. And it was worsening: religious differences over Conformity versus Non-Conformity were escalating to crisis levels, and refugee families were fanning willy-nilly outwards from the capital, under no apparent direction. The obvious directing voice, perhaps the only one capable of maintaining the integrity of the Huguenot emigration in Ireland and bending it to the overarching purpose of salvaging the "Protestant Interest", was the Marquis de Ruvigny.

The Threat

The lingering sense of peril and unease following in the wake of the Limerick Settlement fostered more than just simply legislation to bolster the Protestant foothold and disable Catholic participation in the governance of the country, but with it a fresh enunciation of state encouragement to French Calvinists, with much more sweeping concessions and incentives to families and individuals as were willing to dwell in Ireland than had yet been offered.

The passage by the Irish Parliament of the 1692 Act *"For Encouraging Protestant Strangers and Others to settle and plant in Ireland"* maps out this fresh approach. In a superficial sense only, could this statute be viewed as a continuation or re-statement of the similarly-entitled Act of 1662. It marks a genuinely new departure. The Act of 1692 went leagues further than Ormond's prior enactment in two significant respects, which lent it the potential of becoming a vehicle for innovative policy. The first had to do with a statement of official toleration for Protestant worship outside the Anglican communion, which not only facilitated the rise of dissent within the French Protestant Community but encouraged Anglophonic non-conformist groups like Quakers, Presbyterians, Baptists, Congregationalists, Independents – and even Jews. The second factor lay in the connection between the generous provisions of the 1692 Act and in the unprecedentedly massive inflow of French Protestants entering the country. The nature of the Huguenot Diaspora in Ireland was now irretrievably altered, and now this new face, to the delight and relief of both the British and Irish governments, was more markedly military, and aggressively colonial.

In the minds of Williamite supporters, Ireland was in fear and peril of French invasion, which would undoubtedly be abetted by a Jacobite "fifth column, and even atrocities on the loyalist Protestant population were not out of the question. There were further ranging implications – once Ireland fell, Britain could be accessible via the "back door". This was an age that accepted, as axiomatic, the cliché: "He that would England win, must in Ireland begin". This has, it may be added, never proven out to be true, no would-be invader, from Lambert Simnel on down, has ever succeeded through that route. However, the conventional thinking of the times tended to magnify the threat to Britain from the western approaches.

There were invasion scares in 1692 and 1696; the last of these coinciding with two assassination plots against King William, that of Sir George Barclay, and one involving the hired Italian nobleman-cum-assassin Count Bouselli, who was alleged to have been in the pay of King Louis XIV himself. What was known for certain is that one of the most imposing of the Jacobite generals had drawn up a grand scheme to recapture Ireland for the monarchs he served. What made this all the more credible was the fact that the general in question was James Fitzjames, Duke of Berwick, King James II's illegitmate son by Lady Arabella Churchill – a man who furthermore stood high in King Louis XIV's favor.

Berwick's Plan/Ruvigny's Counter-Plan

The invasion plan designed by the Duke of Berwick, with the imprimatur of Louis XIV was a most badly-kept secret, perhaps deliberately so. It called for semi-coordinated landings of French and Jacobite troops at Cork and at Waterford. From thence there would be a rapid two-pronged advance towards the north and northeast, with both forces hopefully taking on recruits and gaining momentum. Then a junction of armies would be effected in the Irish Midlands in the vicinity of the River Barrow. This united force would then press quickly across County Kildare to invest or, preferably seize, Dublin in short order before Williamite reinforcements could be dispatched from Scotland or Wales. The territory through which the French and their allies were to pass was considered a "soft underbelly", and it was believed that sentiment in the South and West was overwhelmingly slanted towards the Jacobite side. Berwick's strategy was patently obvious and direct, but the problem of how to stop it remained to be resolved. A major part of the solution lay in taking advantage of the military expertise and leadership skills of the Huguenot veterans. No other troops in the Allied/Williamite camp knew Louis XIV's forces as they did; few could match their incentive for retribution. Concentrating settlements of military personnel would further several desirable goals: certainly they would form a core of defense that would surely hamper and delay and, with reinforcements, stop Berwick's advance. Their presence would deter the Irish Catholic population from forming an active partisan resistance, or engaging in espionage; and the pensioned veterans and their families would be provided for in a place other than England where anti-refugee manifestations threatened to escalate. This would reap the further dividend of easing some of the pressure on King William and in some measure allay popular fears over the alleged favoring of foreign-born advisors and retainers over the native English. As the Huguenot leader, Ruvigny was the prime mover in this "Fortress Ireland" scheme that would have to rest on a core area (Dublin, of necessity); a strategic hinge around which defensive measures might be coordinated (ultimately, Portarlington); and defensive perimeters near the proposed landing areas (Cork, Waterford and Youghal).

The Linchpin: Portarlington

The key to Ruvigny's counter strategy was the putative junction area in the Midlands. If the Barrow River Valley and region around it in present-day Counties Laois and Offaly could be transformed by a strong Huguenot presence into a viable base of operations (one which an invading force could not afford to ignore) Berwick's march might at least be impeded, and the delay would buy valuable time – hopefully ample time for reinforcements from Dublin, and from Britain itself. As will be seen, the Marquis' plans for placing a Huguenot bastion in the interior encompassed commercial schemes along the lines of the First Duke of Ormond and Colonel Lawrence, but it would be the military idea, and the Huguenot veterans themselves, that would define what was to be Ireland's second-largest concentration of French Calvinists.

The Portarlington Project

Of all the colonization projects for transplanting Huguenots into (more or less) strategic towns and regions, the most successful was the Irish Midlands enclave of Portarlington. As the largest ultimate concentration of Huguenots in Ireland after that of Dublin, Portarlington would preserve significant vestiges of its distinct language, culture and heritage long after French Calvinist communities in the rest of Ireland had been absorbed into the larger Anglo-Irish Protestant element.

In part, Portarlington's uniqueness stems from being virtually an artificial creation; French Protestant settlers were placed into an environment where they far outnumbered what insignificant indigenous population there was, and where there was – at least by the time they arrived (probably in 1692) – no viable pre-existing town into which they could move.

What became the town was two sparsely-populated locales alongside a wedge-shaped bend in the River Barrow. One of the locales or "townlands" was situated north of the river in County Offaly and was known as Kilmalogue, and the one south of the Barrow in County Laois was Cooltedoora or "woody nook". The land was flat plain, subject to intermittent flooding and encircled by forest and bogland. It had been part of the O'Dempsey holdings until the title-holder Lewis O'Dempsey, Viscount Clanmalire fled Ireland after having taken part in the 1641 Uprising and Confederation War. A bill of attainder for treason rendered his lands forfeit and they were finally conveyed by letters patent to the courtier Henry Bennet, Earl of Arlington (27 July 1666). Arlington's title-name has been indirectly memorialized by virtue of his inclusion in the notorious, original CABAL which dominated British politics after the fall of the First Earl of Clarendon. For a time Arlington diligently devoted his energies to his namesake town (which received its prefix "port" either from a small riverside quay or from the Irish for "fort", from the existence of Lea Castle half a mile away). Streets were laid out into a crossroads, property parceled into lots; and the proposed settlement chartered as a parliamentary borough, enrolled in chancery as a deed of incorporation (3 August 1667). It was probably shortly thereafter that Bennet drained the land and began planting English colonists. As an incorporated borough Portarlington was presided over by twelve burgesses who elected one of their number as sovereign during the "sovereign court" session held every year on the first Monday after the Feast of St. John the Baptist (June 24). Of Bennet's English settlement, all that survived the War of the Two Kings was the Borough government. Not much is known about the original Portarlington community, but curiously, there was one Huguenot among its residents. Ananias De Hennezel had immigrated from Lorraine (most likely from the region of Metz) and established a glass manufacture at Portarlington prior to 1670. Very likely Hennezel was induced to come to the region by the De Bigault family, also from Lorraine, who had been running glassworks near Birr, County Offaly since 1623. Hennezel married into the De Bigault family, and an English branch of his family seems to have been active in the glassware industry at Newcastle-on-Tyne into the early nineteenth century. At Portarlington, however, all trace of Hennezel and his enterprise had vanished by 1691. Descendants though, under the name "De Bigault Henzel" may be traced in Dublin as late as 1820.

The reasons for the glassworks' probable demise, and much else at Portarlington, can be traced to the devastation that occurred in the area during the Williamite reduction. After the Earl of Arlington's death his holdings were acquired by Sir Patrick Trant, who supported the Jacobite cause, fled to France, and was in his turned attainted as a traitor. Violence and destruction took place on Trant's holdings to the extent that most, if not all of the structures of Bennet's Portarlington were unfit for use or habitation.

Marquis Henri Massue de Ruvigny's decision to take his slain brother La Caillemotte's place in the Williamite army impelled an indignant Louis XIV to confiscate the family holdings, which up to then had remained intact despite the Ruvignys' decision to go into exile. Partially as compensation for this loss, and partially as part of William III's overall policy of transferring forfeited land to supporters, the King granted Ruvigny the Trant estate. Ruvigny was conferred with the titles of Baron Portarlington and Viscount Galway on 2 March 1691; appointed Lieutenant-General of all royal forces in Ireland on 27 February 1692; and placed in charge of implementing what was foreseen as a massive Huguenot immigration into, and colonization of, Ireland.

Ruvigny is better known as the Earl of Galway, though that title was not conferred until 12 May 1697. For the purposes of this work, he will henceforth be referred to under the title of "Galway" rather than "Ruvigny".

Galway's plans for settling foreign Protestants in the Irish Midlands were articulated as early as 9 February 1692. What was at first planned-for was a commercial/industrial center to not only encompass Galway's new holdings in Laois and Offaly, but to eventually to exploit the lands of the Trant forfeiture in its entirety – and the 36,148 acreage also included territory in Kerry and Kildare. However, the emerging realities of the situation soon altered this plan. The logistical difficulties involved in transporting so many new arrivals into the Midlands with little or no economic resources to maintain them would have been overcome only at tremendous cost. And as the Jacobite threat became more menacing, the need for a substantial garrison settlement in the Midlands changed the character of the proposed colony.

At his own request, Galway was at first granted the forfeiture on an "in custodiam" basis (1693), and only three years later, on 26 June 1696, was it permanently conferred. However, the fact that the first leases were drawn in 1692 indicates that Galway already held the (de facto) fee to the Trant holdings.

The town's basic plan carried over the Earl of Arlington's 1666 layout, with a central market square at the intersection of four roads: King's Street; Queen's Street; Bennet Street; and James Street. The town/borough meeting-hall was at the center of the square (it has since been made into a garage); many of the buildings had been destroyed or damaged and Galway was obliged to construct or repair some 150 dwellings. This seems to have taken quite a while, and some of Galway's settlers had to be lodged in rented accommodations in the outlying hamlets/towns of Lea, Cloneygowan, Monasterevan, and Doolagh as late as 1698. The leases were for the term of three individual lifetimes, and renewable in perpe-tuity. Of necessity, rents were quite nominal, many veterans had no assets other than their pensions, perhaps a horse, and meager personal effects. Land income was set aside to fund the construction of a French church (present-day St. Paul's),a French school and a classical school. At a some-what later date the English church of St.Michael's was built along the market square. The property allotments were not changed appreciably from the Earl of Arlington's original plan. In many cases only the names were transferred: (John) Donnelly's parcel went to the Joly family; (John) Bignon's to the De Choisy's; Warburton's to the Dumont de Bostaquets;

and Arlington's to the d'Ully (Viscounts) De Laval, Camelins, and Du Clousys.

The Settling of Portarlington, 1692–1698

Apart from those who came on purely individual initiative, there were three groups of colonists who established a permanent French community. The first of these were the pensioned veterans of Huguenot units in the Williamite army, who had been retired to half pay after the Treaty of Limerick. These Limerick pensioners were mainly the older officers, and those who had been wounded or disabled. Thirty-nine of these officers (and one non-commissioned) arrived at Portarlington during the first few months of its settlement. They included six ensigns; one cornet; sixteen lieutenants, twelve captains; one lieutenant-colonel; two of undisclosed rank; and Corporal/Quartermaster Pierre Le Maignan of Galway's regiment of cavalry. Fourteen of the Limerick veterans were designated as being wounded/disabled, and an additional eight as aged or sickly – eight are specifically stated to have sustained injuries at the First Battle of Limerick.

Included among the first wave of Portarlington settlers was the Huguenot leader, Jacques Belrieu, Seigneur de St. Laurens, Baron de Virazel, a member of the Galway's inner circle. The Baron de Virazel, despite having seen no military service, was also pensioned on the Irish Establishment at the rate of 100 pounds per annum (which in itself marked him as privileged among the other pensioners, whose stipends were on a daily rate). His eminence as a jurist, lengthy term of imprisonment, and near-martyrdom in France may well have occasioned special consideration. A member of a noble house from Guyenne Province, Virazel served as counselor to the Parlement at Bordeaux and was noted by Elie Benoit for his skill and integrity as a Magistrate. Conspicuous as a Protestant community leader, he was seized, taken to Paris,and incarcerated at the King's pleasure in the Bastille from 14 March 1686 to 12 May 1687. Virazel married Marie de Gaumont in 1651 and had at least three children: their eldest son Daniel accompanied his parents to Britain and Ireland, after the Baron's release, but his brother Charles and sister Marie Anne stayed in France. As one of the wealthiest borough landowners, and an intimate in the Earl of Galway's clique, Virazel played a significant role in the Portarlington colony's establishment and early development.

Those pensions, which were calculated on a per diem basis, based primarily upon rank, were authorized in London; dispatched by boat across the Irish Sea to Dublin; and disbursed by Galway's secretary Elie Bouhereau, who often worked through intermediaries such as Virazel;

Daniel Le Grand Du Petit Bosc; and Jacques de Crosat, Seigneur des Pruniers to convey them to the individual veterans. Another influx of refugees who found their way to Portarlington in the 1690s were those from a professional or agricultural background who had seeped across the French border from Provence, Dauphiné and Burgundy to seek refuge in the Swiss Cantons. So many Huguenots arrived in the cantons in so short a span of time that the situation threatened to deteriorate into a humanitarian crisis. The indigent refugees could not long be accommodated, though Lord Galway was able to press some of the men into service with the Allied armed forces operating in the Piedmont Theater.

By January of 1693, some 400 Huguenots had been specifically selected for settlemen tat Portarlington. In this too, the efforts of Virazel, Charles de Sailly, Jean David Boyer,and Jean Nicholas as members of Galway's Irish Committee for Refugee Settlement proved invaluable. De Sailly had been dispatched to reconnoiter Ireland in March 1693 and journeyed from Dublin to Cork to locate and report on potential sites for Huguenot colonization. Though he undoubtedly took an active role in the formative stages of the Portarlington scheme he appears not, unlike Virazel, Boyer, and Nicolas, to have made a substantial personal investment in the venture. In 1700 the by-then Lord Justice Galway placed him in charge of the expedition of Huguenot settlers to Virginia which founded the Manakintown colony.

Jean Nicolas was born in 1663, a native of Jonsac in Saintonge, and would retire at half pay on a captain's wages following the War of the Spanish Succession after having served under Galway's command in Ireland, the Piedmont, Flanders and Portugal. He was one of the better-endowed Portarlington refugees, leasing some 2,000 acres around Lea Castle and paying Galway 150 pounds per annum on a stone house and farm near Clonygowan – and seems to have held substantial property in Dublin.

Lieutenant Jean David Boyer, born at Civry in Poitou in 1655, was so proactive as a member of the Huguenot Earl's elite circle that he was dubbed "Galway's steward". After four years in King William's service in Holland and Ireland, Boyer's military career was cut short when he sustained a serious wound before the walls of Limerick. Making a remarkable recovery, he seems to have taken charge of the day-to-day, onsite tasks of setting the colony on a viable footing; leaving the financial considerations and political/diplomatic niceties to Virazel, de Sailly, and Nicolas. He held the leasehold to a cabin on 88 acres in the neighborhood of the Kilmalogue townland.

A rather optimistic target date of April/May 1693 was set forward for the transit of at least some of the families to Ireland and King William asked for the States-General of the United Provinces and the Protestant princes of Germany to contribute towards this effort. When Parliament failed to pass a refugee subsidy bill, the Treasurer, Sidney Godolphin, assured Lord Galway that funds would be made available and, acting on that assumption, the project went forward. In the event, however, the promised monies were diverted towards military operations, though Virazel and other agents were able to funnel some of the monies to certain families bound for Portarlington.

It is hard to determine how many of these settlers reached the Midlands colony, and who they were. The *French Church Register* constitute our major (in many cases, sole) authority for the years prior to 1726. The Portarlington *French Church Register* is unique in that it is the only one that still exists in the original. The Four Courts Fire of 1922 destroyed the original records of the Huguenot congregations in Dublin, and perhaps those of other French Protestant congregations. Fortunately, the Dublin Conformed Records had been edited by J. J. Digges Latouche in 1893; and the Non-Conformist Registers by T. P. LeFanu in 1908. The Portalington records would have suffered the same fate if it had not been for the grace of sheer bureaucratic inertia which thankfully delayed their transfer to the Irish Public Records Office sufficiently to insure their survival. Perhaps there is some small virtue in the decentralization of archives. The first *Register* entry, recording the baptism of François César Meray by Pastor Jacques Gillet, is dated 3 June 1694. Gillet and his successors kept their entries solely in French until 1817. Though they are not without their limitations, the *Register* entries have opened some windows on this early, pioneering period. Documentary proof exists for the presence of at least thirteen of these families: Freau; Vincent; Poussete; Bonin; Champ; Pastre; Comte; David; Esperiat; Ouly; Marthe; and Vuilly, comprising, at minimum, 32 adult individuals by 1700. The first seven of these families were of Dauphinois origin;the Comtes and Davids originated in "Pont de Vele en Bresse" in Burgundy; the Esperiats in Provence; while the Oulys, Marthes, and Vuillys are simply listed as being "Swiss".There is strong, though admittedly inconclusive evidence for the presence of six additional Dauphinois families: Liotard; Bonnet; Neuache; Jordan; Serre; and Guiot.

This group was entirely non-noble. The Comtes, Freaus, Pastres and Esperiats arespecifically referred to as "laboureurs". From clues pertaining to instances of intermarriage and limited literacy it would seem that the Bonins, Champs, Davids, Marthes, Vuillys, and Oulys also fit under this classification. Daniel Esperiat, who married Anne Marthe, is additionally listed as "cordonnier". The Vincents and Camelins may have been, socially speaking, just a cut above this group of immigrants. Susanne Vincent married Mathieu Camelin on 21 November 1695. Camelin, from Couche in Poitou, is characterized by Pastor Gillet as "Sieur" and "marchand" and, according to a later gloss on a map dated 1678, owned significant tracts of land just east of the town square and over the western bridge across the Barrow in Kilmalogue townland. The Camelins had at least three children: Susanne (b. 1696), Mathieu (b. 1699), and Charles (b. 1702). Camelin was a prominent enough citizen by 1733 to have been included as a signatory on a petition addressed that year to the Duke of Dorset. A "Susanne Camelin" who died on 24 February 1740 might have been either the mother or the daughter and, after this date, the Camelins and Vincents drop out of the Parish records.

Claude Guiot, who was an elder at the French Church from 1694 to 1696, married Jeanne Pastré and both died in 1711, within five days of each other. A Daniel Guiot was a baker by profession. The Guiots originated in the Valley de Pragelas in Dauphiné, as did Jean Bonin ("Tronche en Pragelas"). His first wife Catherine Jordan, whose family may have hailed from the Briaçonnais, died on 3 January 1696 and was followed by their daughter, aged about two-and-one-half years, three months later. Bonin remarried in 1703 to Marie Ouly, daughter of a refugee family from Chalans, Switzerland. The couple had at least two sons and left Portarlington after the birth of the second, Isaac Pierre, in 1705. By 5 September 1706 the couple resided in Dublin, where they formed part of the French Non-Conformed congregation at "Golblac Lane" (sic), at least until February 1711.

Pierre Vuilly married Claudine Comte, and two sons were born to the couple at Portarlington before Pierre's untimely death on 8 October 1698. Claudine remarried to Joseph David, a fellow-Burgundian whose family came from the same village in Bresse where his wife's had originated. The Davids had two children while at Portarlington and, after 1703, became one of the many families to depart from the town during the years of the War of the Spanish Succession.

There were quite a few Comtes at Portarlington; in fact there were four younger married couples bearing that surname in the 1690s alone. The most prolific of these was that of Pierre Comte, "laboureur", who married Marguerite Neuache and is believed to have died in 1733. The couple had thirteen children, eleven of whom survived past infancy. One daughter married Jean Debreuil of Portarlington in 1726, while another married outside the Huguenot community: to Francis Shannon of Dublin in 1728. Pierre's son Jacques (b. 1707) also married exogamously to Grace Cowin, who bore him at least two children prior to her death in 1741. Even before then, the surname was in the process of being anglicized to "Count".

Portarlington has long basked in a rosy glow, and the glamorous image of the refined "Irish Athens" and the genteel society reputedly established by the Huguenot colonists has assumed the status of legend. But how accurate is this picture which has developed its own momentum and been perpetuated into recent times? Documentary evidence from the early years of the settlement's foundation paint an opposing picture: that of struggle, uncertainty, constant flux, anxiety, isolation, and disease – elements present in all pioneering societies. According to one source – admittedly anecdotal – the first group of families to disembark from their river-vessel to the designated settlement were stoned by some of the (Irish Catholic?) locals.

One petition dispatched by the settlers in April 1694 was addressed to the Consistory of the French Church at the Lady Chapel of St. Patrick's in Dublin. It describes the dire straits that many of the Portarlington Huguenots found themselves in: with the greater portion of their assets exhausted on traveling expenses; in the taking up of leases; and the day-to-day cost of living expenses. With charitable donations depleted and no forthcoming government assistance, they asked that the French Patrick's Consistory appeal on their behalf to the Lords Justice that each colonizing refugee might receive seed and whatever else necessary to give him, and his family, a decent start. Similar provisions, the petitioners went on to note, had been made for colonists settling on land owned by Sir Richard Cox and Lord Blayney. The petition received a favorable response from the members of the Consistory, who even went a step further by writing to Galway himself (who at that time was away directing military operations in Piedmont).

In the autumn of 1695 another petition was presented, this time in Parliament, on the Portarlington colonists' behalf – its sponsor was Lord Moore, MP for Drogheda. The main complaint centered around lack of funding. It was argued that construction on the French Church had not been completed and that the community did not as yet have the services of a schoolmaster, a surgeon, or an apothecary. There was shortly to be at least partial realization of these appeals: work on the French Church was finished the following year; the need for a surgeon was filled by the advent of the pensioned veteran, Moise Marcombe; and a persistent legend, unconfirmed by documentary evidence, credits a Monsieur Faure (Faurel?), father of a pensioned lieutenant, with becoming the first school-master. Whether there was a direct link between petition and fulfillment in this instance is, however, unclear.

Accommodations could, and in some cases did, pose a problem. Construction on dwellings could not keep pace with the influx of new residents and many colonists had to be lodged in outlying hamlets. At least two died while residing in rented domiciles awaiting the completion of the cottages in Portarlington that would never be theirs: Ensign Josias de Castelfranc demised on 15 July 1695 at the village of Lea, and Lieutenant Moise Ferment passed on at his room in the house of Lieutenant Jean Procureur des Champs in Doolagh (15 July, 1697).

St. Paul's (The French Church) at Portarlington, founded by the Earl of Galway. The church has been in existence since 1694 and was enlarged and remodelled in Victorian Gothic style in 1852. Courtesy of St. Paul's Canon, Leslie Stevenson.

La Lande House, Portarlington, built *c.* 1710: Francois Daulnis de La Lande was a Huguenot military pensioner who moved with his family to Portarlington prior to 1702. His daughter Henrietta ran a French School at this house during the 1720s. Courtesy of Mr. Ronnie Matthews, Portarlington.

HUGUENOT CHURCH

The original French Church (St Paul's) was built in 1696 for the Huguenot settlers brought to Portarlington by Henri Massue, Marquis de Ruvigny, Viscount Galway, who was granted land here to reward his services in King William III's army.
The French language was used both for Divine Service and for entering the Register of Baptisms, Marriages and Burials until about 1816.
They built fine houses with high-pitched roofs and tall chimneys, presenting blank walls to the street front with the main windows facing beautiful gardens and orchards which included oranges, lemons, black Italian walnuts and jargonelle pears.
There existed for a time in Portarlington a soap factory, a linen industry, a Glass-works and a Malthouse, but the settlement was more famous for the purity of the French spoken here and its French Schools which included Ecole St. Germain (now Searson's Hotel) and Arlington School (now Travel Goods Ltd.)
The Church was completely rebuilt in 1851.

Plaque commemorating the Cathedral of St Paul's in Portarlington.

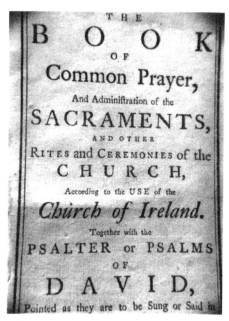

Les Pseaumes de David (Dublin 1731): Dublin was, by far, the site of the largest Huguenot concentration in Ireland and there was always demand for new editions of French and English Psalters and Prayer Books. Courtesy of the Lisburn Historical Society.

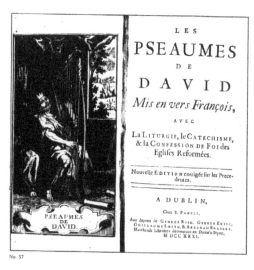

No. 57

No. 58

Sermons sur divers texts de l'Ecritude Sainte (Dublin 1728): The author, Gaspard Caillard, was French minister at Dublin and (later) Portarlington and was noted for the eloquence and erudition of his pulpit sermons. Courtesy of the Lisburn Historical Society.

(Left) Dublin: Gallery to Archbishop Marsh's Library: From 1701 to 1719 the Library building was home to the eminent scholar, public official and clergyman Elie Bouhereau, who also served as the first librarian of this, the oldest operating library in Dublin. Courtesy of the Library Keeper, Mrs. Muriel McCarthy.

(Below) Title page and inside page of Louis Crommelin's *Essay towards the improving of the hempen and flaxen manufactures in the Kingdom of Ireland* (Dublin 1705). Courtesy of the Irish Linen Centre and Lisburn Museum.

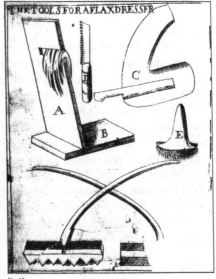

No. 15

No. 16

As it was, even the remains of the dead posed a problem. Galway had not provided for a burial ground and the deceased had to be transported for enterrement in Lea. This could prove to be a dangerous proposition during outbreaks of epidemic, and at least one such ("la grande infection") is recorded to have occurred during these years. Though the Earl of Galway donated land behind the French Church as a cemetery in 1698, it seems rather bizarre that it took him so long to respond to such a basic community need. Or perhaps events in Europe and in Ireland were impelling him to see Portarlington, and the entire Irish Refuge for that matter, in a far more direct and serious light.

The Settling of Portarlington: 1698–1702

It was at this juncture that Portarlington would begin to experience its greatest period of growth – and its brief demographic zenith. Much of this would be occasioned by the Peace of Ryswick, another one of these global events whose significance has been perhaps underplayed. It was deadlock: Louis XIV had not broken; in point of fact the threat seemed more substantial than ever – inasmuch as the united power of the Grand Alliance had not been enough to budge him an inch. The Huguenots lost all hope of immediate return and the French regiments were about to be disbanded. Of course, "Fortress Ireland" might need further buttressing; and then, in 1697, the Earl of Galway returned to Ireland as one of three Lords Justice. In point of fact, the Huguenot Earl was by far the most politically pro-active and influential of the three; and it could be stated for all practical purposes that this French noblemen functioned as Viceroy of Ireland from 1697 to 1701.

In 1698, Portarlington's first pastor, Jacques Gillet, departed and was superseded by an intimate in Galway's circle, the strong-willed Benjamin de Daillon, Sieur de la Levrie. Daillon's stormy ministry began in the wake of Portarlington's greatest surge of Huguenot arrivals – those pensioned off after the Peace of Ryswick, who constitute the third identifiable wave of colonizers. Over royal opposition, the British Parliament passed a bill on 15 September 1698 authorizing the disbandment of all Huguenot regiments. Those who were to be retired were placed on a reduced Irish establishment. The 1698 pensioners who shortly found their way to Portarlington included: one lieutenant-colonel, one major, eight captains, seventeen lieutenants, six cornets, five ensigns' two corporals, one quartermaster, five troopers, and two of undetermined rank. One striking difference between those disbanded in 1698 and the 1692 retirees is the fewer number of disabled and aged veterans within the former group. The 1698 veterans had a greater proportion of younger, more vigorous men who, settling down to start families, infused a new dynamism and vitality into their colony. Only three are recorded as having been wounded, another three as being "aged", and only one other as being "sickly". Fourteen were definitely pronounced fit for future service, according to a report of statements and declarations of the French pensioners, undertaken by the Treasury in 1702 (the same report indicates none of the 1692 group as possessing the same degree of fitness for service).

The Ryswick veterans included a greater number of younger family men than their colleagues of 1692. Thirty of the Ryswick settlers reared families: 18 of these had less than four children, while 12 had more. One has to sometimes wonder about the accuracy of some of these statements of health, however. For example: one Captain André Labat, despite having been characterized in 1702 as "old & sickly", was nonetheless successfully supporting a family at the time and survived for another thirty-four years to1736, when he died in Kilkenny.

There were others who for one reason or other arrived at Portarlington in and around 1698 but who were not pensioned in that year. The best known was Captain Isaac Dumont de Bostaquet who was born in Pays du Caux, Normandy in 1632. He married three times and had a total of nineteen children. His military career began during the Fronde Uprising of 1648–52 when he formed part of the Huguenot Loyalist forces supporting Louis XIV and Cardinal Mazarin against the rebels. A member of the provincial noblesse d'épée, Bostaquet successfully made his escape from France overland to Holland in 1687 with a rifle bullet in his arm (the result of a failed attempt by sea – fortunately the bullet dislodged itself from his flesh during the course of the journey). He was a long-time friend/retainer of the Ruvigny family and served in Galway's Horse before retiring (reluctantly) on half pay in 1692 on 6 shillings four pence per diem. Settling first at "Bray" (Bride) Street in Dublin, Bostaquet was an elder at French Patrick's from 1694 to 1697. Prior to 13 November 1698 he leased a house and farm from the Earl of Galway at Portarlington, bringing with him his third wife, neé Marie de Brossard and one daughter, Judith Julie. Bostaquet is notable as the author of *Memoires Inedits de Dumont de Bostaquet, Gentilehomme Normand*, one of the rare personal life-accounts left by the Huguenot refugees.

The three (De) Foubert brothers also arrived around 1698. The founder of the family fortunes, Abraham Fabert, or Favert, had become chief magistrate for the city of Metz in Lorraine, and director of the ducal printing press. In his first capacity he was sometimes called upon for protection/assistance by the substantial Calvinist population of Metz. Three of his grandsons pursued military careers and, after the Revocation, fled to Holland, where one of them, Henri, was commissioned as a major and named aide-decamp to William III. Henri himself was wounded at the Boyne and, along with his brothers Philippe and Jacob, retired on half pay in 1692. The three came to Portarlington around 1698. Jacob later departed for London but Henri & Philippe and their descendants went into the linen manufacture at Portarlington with some degree of success – other family members settled in Cork. Another soldierly/clerical family from Metz which was at least briefly associated with Portarlington at this juncture in time was that of Le Chenevix. In 1682 Philippe Le Chenevix and his wife Magdalena were naturalized and denizened in England, Philippe having come thence from a calling as pastor from the Church at Limay, near Mantes-la-Jolie. The pastor dwelled temporarily at Portarlington –for how long is uncertain – but seems to have made little impact. His namesake son was a major in the Second Carbineers and fell at the Battle of Folkstadt in 1704. The Major's son, a third Philippe, had moved to Dublin by July 1723 when he married Marie la Rinbilliere, and is described on the certificate as being "of the city". Rising to the rank of lieutenant-colonel in the British army, he was to likewise become a combat fatality in 1747 during the War of the Austrian Succession.

In spite of all that was to follow, it was the period 1698–1702 that defined the nature of what was at this time the second-largest Huguenot concentration. The military nobles (écuyers) were to set the tone and to provide community/political leadership into the 1740s when individuals such as: Josias de Robillard, Seigneur de Champagne, Charles de Quinsac, Jean Clausade, Jean David Boyer, Pierre Goullin, Daniel le Grand du Petit Bosc, Pierre de Franquefort, Guyon de Geis, and David D'Arrippe dominated the affairs of the Sovereign Court of Portarlington Borough.

The écuyers made a tremendous impact on the settlement, so much so that it might have legitimately been termed the nobles' enclave: an incredible 44 percent of the surnames that can be found at Portarlington between 1692 and 1771 are of noble origin. Thus there is some basis to the romanticized picture of the bucolic outpost of aristocratic gentility – but the superficial image does not account for the borderline penury, underlying anxieties, homesickness and internecine disputes which certainly plagued the colony into the 1720s.

Worship at the French Church, under the direction of the scholarly Daillon, followed a strict Non-Conformed Calvinist line, with the constant nostalgic refrain: *"Suivant la discipline et forme ancienne et ordinaire de nos églises de France."* The venerable pastor, who had suffered imprisonment for his faith in the Conciergerie in Paris and was now in his early seventies, was to be a protagonist in a religious schism which was to fissure the refugee community and to contribute towards the Portarlington settlement's demographic regression in the years after 1703.

Daillon seems to have worked in tandem with a major landowner and "grand seigneur"Robert D'Ully, Vicomte de Laval. The De Lavals claimed descent from King Henri IV and, prior to 1685, held title to extensive seigneuries in Picardy, chiefly lands adjacent to the Chateau de Gourlencour. These were declared forfeit when the family refused to abjure the Calvinist faith. De Laval and his eldest son were imprisoned at Laon in 1688 and though the Vicomte made good on his escape in September 1689, the son remained in confinement until 4 March 1705. The elder De Laval moved to Portarlington in 1695. His rank, coupled with sufficient wealth to acquire tracts of land within the town land itself, soon marked him as a community leader. Shortly thereafter a son, and last child, David Daniel, was born to the Vicomte and his wife Madeleine de Schelandre. De Laval was a church elder from 1697 to 1702; he comes across as a somewhat aloof figure, aware of his unique status among his fellow colonists and proud of his putative kinship to the House of Bourbon. He lived in a relative degree of grandeur, intent on preserving the past. Folk memories of the proud Vicomte endured for over a century. According to a well-quoted description he was fond of sporting "knee buckles . . . sword . . . shoe stock buckles . . . of silver, with diamonds . . . a cloak of scarlet trimmed with ermine", and always walked with his hat carried under one arm.

But the advent of yet another global conflict brought about by the dynastic rivalries of the great European powers, and political twists and turns, were to intrude into the world of Daillon, De Laval and other denizens of the Midlands settlement and force many to make some extremely difficult choices.

Conflict and decline, 1702–1720

Four major factors were to disrupt the French colony at Portarlington, transform its way of life, and trigger a serious demographic retreat:

(1) The Act of Resumption of 1700;
(2) The struggle over conformity vs. dissent within the French congregation;
(3) The War of the Spanish Succession; and
(4) Low agricultural productivity.

Of these it was the second – the religious controversy – that had by far the greatest effect, and it was to be brought about by the first cause, so they must be considered together in order to fully understand, what occurred during the pivotal year of 1702, and why. The Act of Resumption came about because of the conflict between crown and parliament over the King's right to grant forfeitures of confiscated estates. The practice of the monarch's dispensing land which had been the property of attainted traitors had been long-grounded in precedence (the transfer of Clanmalire's holdings to Arlington having been but one example), and it was a procedure which was firmly held in many quarters to be a natural prerogative of the throne's, and hence not subject to scrutiny of either populace or Parliament. The usual mechanics involved appointed royal commissions which were empowered to enquire into the conduct of individuals suspected of Jacobite sympathies during the Williamite reduction of Ireland. On the basis of the evidence uncovered by the commissions, juries of freeholders would render a verdict. Parliament would then act upon the attainder or outlawry of the individuals in question and, this having been passed, the high-traitor's property was transferred into the hands of the Trustees for Forfeited Estates, who in turn would issue their own reports. In the case of Jacobite land forfeitures, enquiries continued between 1691 and 1699 and a report of the Commission of Irish Forfeitures issued a figure 1,600,000 Irish acres of land.

The controversy between the Crown and the House of Commons over the right to dispose of confiscated estates was extremely drawn-out. In granting his forfeitures, William inevitably incurred criticism over his large grants to non-English retainers. including Galway. Even greater controversy swirled around his generosity to his mistress Elizabeth Villiers who was presented with some of King James II's private estates. Parliament adjourned in March 1693 and a number of three-year "in custodiam" grants were bestowed by the King. When no substantial opposition emerged, the grants – Galway's among them – were made permanent in 1696/1697.

In the years following the Peace of Ryswick, when there was no war to serve as a distraction, pressure mounted in the Commons generated by: William's perceived preferential treatment of foreigners; fear of individuals like the Earl of Galway, who were consolidating strong local power-bases; and an honest desire on the part of some to relieve the burden on the English taxpayer by auctioning off some of these forfeited estates, thus obtaining funds for the Exchequer. In 1698 the Junto of Whig ministers in Parliament fell from power and the definition of limits to royal authority to grant forfeitures became a hotly-contested issue. The Commission of Irish Forfeitures' Report in 1699 led directly to the Act of Resumption of 1700. The act was tacked onto a land tax bill which many of William's supporters were reluctant to oppose just to maintain grants that they already had some difficulty in justifying. The Act cleared and placed the estates into the hands of a seven-member commission nominated by the Commons. Each case was judged on its own merits and if declared null and void – as was the case with Galway's forfeiture – it would revert to the Trustees for Forfeited Estates to be auctioned.

The immediate effects of the Act's implementation and the annulment of many forfeitures was to throw all legal positions into disarray. The ambiguity of the situation even gave the heirs of former proprietors some hope that they might either be compensated, or that they might actually regain the estates. Earlier, Sir John Trant, son of the now-deceased Sir Patrick, requested of the Earl of Galway that he return the lands to the Trant family Galway's classic and oft-quoted reply was that Sir John might avail of his high standing with the King of France to secure, in compensation for his family's losses, some of the Ruvigny seigneuries in France which Louis XIV had confiscated. The Trants again pressed forward their claims following the passage of the Act of Resumption, but once more to no avail. Apart from creating a tangled legal situation, the critical impact of the Act of Resumption on religious dissenters (including Portarlington's Huguenots) who had a stake in confiscated property was profound. It kindled a feeling of renewed insecurity. Having endured persecution, exile, war, and economic hardships of varying degree, the Huguenot tenants were now faced with possible eviction. If Galway's grant itself was void, then it followed that the leases he granted were also rendered void. The property that the settlers had taken for granted during the administration of their protector was now, to King William's deep regret, no longer in the hands of the Huguenot Earl and, despite all the improvements they had made, might be snatched away. The vast majority of the settlers subsisted on slender means and were rearing young families. Many possessed little else besides their pensions, and what they had invested in their property. What then, was the extent of capital investment for the average Portarlington householder at this time? The number of new dwellings, townhouses, and farm cottages on which rates were being paid may have stood at something over 150; certainly at least 130. We may assume that, as their families grew and their fortunes brightened a little, the *laboureurs* and artisans of the community (over 30 families by 1703) would build house extensions, workshops, barns, stables, mews, wells, fences and mills. Carpenters were certainly there to complete these tasks. For the *laboureurs*, one might also have to count in: livestock, flocks, poultry, orchards and apiaries. And, insomuch as much of the land was low-lying and subject to flooding, one would have to account for all efforts expended in draining and preparing the ground for tillage or pasture. Some refugees built and maintained malt houses. In town we may discover evidence for the existence of butcher shops, blacksmith forges, bakeries, a wig-maker's establishment, general retailers, carpenters' workshops, and a linen manufacture.

The Portarlington Huguenots as refugees of conscience had the advantage of some degree of sympathy and being singled out for protection by articulate advocates. Some were sincere and acted out of disinterested motives, such as the anonymous authors of *Jus Regium* and *The National Remonstrance of the People of Ireland Against the Act of Resumption.* Others had an agenda: the Anglican Bishop of Killaloe, Thomas Lindsay, whose petition to Parliament of 22 May 1702, while it professed to advocate protection to the refugees nonetheless included a ploy by which the High Church Bishop of Kildare, William Moreton, could impose conformity on the French congregation. The Bishop of Killaloe's relief proposal contained a clause requiring the Trustees for Forfeited Estates to "convey, assign, and make over" to the Bishop of Kildare the two churches and the two schools and to appoint ministers and schoolmasters "from time to time".

The Relief Bill was passed, and included the clauses that the Bishop had proposed. Galway's erstwhile grant was purchased at auction by the Hollow Sword Blades Society of London, who left the settlement intact and ultimately sold their interests to Sir Ephraim Dawson, M.P. for the Queen's County.

Though the property and lease titles were now secure, the Bishop of Killaloe's clauses had opened the door to mischief. The Bishop of Kildare was then emboldened to impose Anglican conformity upon the French Church and this ignited a rancorous dispute with Pastor Daillon that would split the congregation and – it is not too strong to say – brought about an antagonism within the community that would fester for decades, even though the combative Daillon was replaced by the malleable Antoine Ligonier de Bonneval, and would, some six contentious years later, leave for Carlow.

It is fair to consider Daillon's deposition as a point of departure. From 1703 to 1720, the French population dropped, families disappeared from the *French Church Registers,* and what scanty influx of families there were could not compensate for the hemorrhage of defections. While the effects of the malaise arising out of legal ambiguity over the leases and the virtual schism within the French Church cannot be calculated with absolute precision, there is no doubt that it was profound. The Daillon/Moreton incident and its consequences are examined in a later chapter but for the moment it may be stated that the appearance of substantial numbers of erstwhile Portarlington settlers on record as members of the Non-Conformist congregations in Dublin between 1703 and 1720 (at least twenty-eight out of thirty-seven families who are known to have defected from the Midlands colony to the Irish capital) offers researchers certain insights into the dynamics of intra community tensions and migrations.

The War of the Spanish Succession left a noticeable imprint. The rival claims to the throne formerly held by the defunct Spanish branch of the Hapsburg once more enkindled the dynastic rivalries whose embers had been glowing under the thin bed sheet of the Peace of Ryswick. The last of the line, King Charles II – a mental and physical anomaly so pitiable that he was known as "Charles the Bewitched" – died in 1700 and most of Europe lined up behind the claims of either Philip of Anjou, grandson of Louis XIV, or (in the case of Britain) Archduke Charles, younger brother of Holy Roman Emperor Joseph I. Eighteen Portarlington pensioners were reactivated for service after 1702. While the actual battle-field casualties were not horrific, the decline in Portarlington's French population was probable aggravated by a drop in the birthrate, occasioned by the lengthy separation of married couples. The old Huguenot regiments were not resumed and the veterans were dispersed in amongst various units and dispatched to various theaters of operations. Fourteen went to Spain and Portugal where the Earl of Galway had assumed command; three more saw action in Flanders and Germany; and four are definitely known to have lost their lives in active service.

Lieutenant Guy Auguste de La Blachière, Sieur de Coutiers is tersely described as having died in Portugal in 1707 while serving as quarter-master in Nicholas Sankey's regiment of infantry. It is not clear whether his death occurred as a result of combat or of illness. He left behind a widow, Judith Julie Dumont de Bostaquet, and four young children. A "Captain Cudderoy" who was killed at the pivotal Battle of Almanza was almost certainly Noe Cadroy, whose father Joseph had taken a lease from the Earl of Galway for a house, garden plot and malt house in 1698, and whose brother Etienne Cadroy served in Germany and Flanders under Marlborough. Noe married exogamously to Catherine Jephson before 1705, and was survived by her, but there is no evidence that the couple had children.

According to a letter written from captivity in the city of Brest on 29 May 1709 by Louis d'Ully, Sieur de Fontaine to his sister, two other Portarlington veterans met their deaths in a sea battle between a British transport convoy sailing out from Cork to Spain, and a group of French men o' war. De Fontaine was the son of Robert d'Ully, Vicomte de Laval. His brothers, Joseph and thirteen-year-old David Daniel were traveling with him when the French squadron appeared on the third day of the voyage. In the ensuing engagement, Joseph was slain. Also perishing in the cannonade was Lieutenant Pierre de Chizadour, Sieur de Bette, who had in 1702 first been declared fit to serve, then in 1706 restored to pension as being "incapable of service", only to be reactivated and placed on that ill-starred convoy in 1709. The surviving d'Ully brothers and Captain Jean Nicholas were taken prisoner and later exchanged. While they were incarcerated at Brest, Captain Nicholas took a fatherly interest in the young d'Ullys, giving them each a half crown with the exhortation to practice economy.

Altogether sixty-seven surnames vanished from Portarlington during the period 1703–20. While a total of twenty-three individuals (12 écuyers and eleven others) joined the community at this time they were more than cancelled out by defections, among them veterans who, having fulfilled their duties, were retired after the Peace of Utrecht in 1714 and left Portarlington shortly thereafter. By 1720 the pioneering age, Portarlington's heroic era, was over. Though the Portarlington saga itself was far from over and the French community and their descendants would maintain a considerable presence during most of the eighteenth century, the fire and flavor of the garrison outpost anchoring the Irish Midlands against internal and external foes was forever spent. The Peace of Utrecht and the tacit *entente cordiale* between France and Britain which developed during the postwar years frustrated the hopes of all those Huguenot refugees who had never abandoned the idea of returning in justified triumph to a purified and repentant French motherland. Though they were to preserve their language and their identity for a longer time span than other comparable refugee communities, the Portarlington colonists inevitably found themselves surrounded by an English or Irish-speaking sea, and facing up to the challenge of living out their lives in exile, adapting to a foreign way of life.

References

Primary sources

Archbishop Narcissus Marsh's Library: Bouhereau Diary 30 Z2.
British Library: Additional Ms. 9718, n. 580; Additional Ms. 34,079, folio 52, n. 881; Egerton Ms. 917 n. 620 p. 29.
Calendar of State Papers (Domestic) 1690–1691; 1691–1692, 1693, 1696.
Historic Manuscripts Commission Publications. Buccleuch & Queensbury Ms., 1889; House of Lords Ms., Vol. V.
Huguenot Society of London-Quarto Series. Vol. VII, XIV, XVIII, XIX, XLI.
Irish Statutes. Vol. III, pp. 243–4.
National Library of Ireland Manuscripts: 90, 12, 092, Ms. Map 21 F 55 1; D. 6516–6596; Microfilm n. 2976 p. 2597.
Public Record Office of Ireland (Dublin): Caulfield Ms. 4976 IA 53–87.
Royal Irish Academy Archives (Dublin): Dumont Ms.
St. Paul's, the French Church (Portarlington, Ireland): *Original French Church Registers.*

Books/pamphlets

Anonymous. *Hibernia Notitia.* Anonymous. *Jus Regium.* London 1701.
Anonymous. *The True Way to Render Ireland Happy and Secure.*
Dumont de Bostaquet, Isaac. *Memoires Inedits de Dumont de Bostaquet, gentilhomme Normand.*
Read, Charles and Washington, Francis, ed. *Formulaire de la Consecration et Dedicace des Églises et Chapelles selon l'usage de l'Église d'Irlande.*

Secondary sources

Agnew, David Carnegie. *Henri Massue, Marquis de Ruvigny*, pp. 36, 97, 224.
Agnew, David Carnegie. *Protestant Exiles from France*. Vol. I, pp. 151, 163–8; Vol. II, pp. 105, 107, 121, 233.
Arnaud, Eugene. *Histoire des Protestants du Dauphine*, Vol. III, p. 361.
Bligny, Bernard. *Histoire du Dauphine*, p. 71.
Borrowes, Sir Erasmus. "Portarlington" in the *Ulster Journal of Archaeology*, Vol. III pp. 62, 65–6, 218, 328, 337–8.
Butler, William F. T. *Confiscation in Irish History*, pp. 219–20, 227.
Carre, Albert. *L'Influence des Huguenots Francais*, pp. 2–6.
Deyon, Solange. *Du Loyalisme au Refus*, pp. 9–10 18, 20, 26–7.
Floy, James. "The Huguenot Settlement at Portarlington" in *PHSL*, Vol. III, pp. 12, 15–16, 19, 21.
Gilbert, John. *A Jacobite Narrative of the War in Ireland*, pp. 263–5.
Lee Grace Lawless. *The Huguenot Settlements in Ireland*, pp. 15–17, 20–1, 69, 72, 99, 117–19, 132, 135–6, 141–2, 149, 152, 172–3, 236, 256–8.
Ligou, Daniel. *Le Protestantisme en France*, pp. 193–5.
Luthy, Herbert. *La Banque Protestante en France*. Vol. I. pp. 28–31.
Matthews, Ronnie. *Portarlington: The Inside Story*. Privately printed, 1998 (provides a local perspective pertinent to the town's lore and ambiance).
O'Hanlon, John Canon and O'Leary, Edward. *History of the Queen's County*, pp. 15–18, 31–4, 283–4.
Petrie, Sir Charles "A French Project for the Invasion of Ireland at the beginning of the 18th Century" in *The Irish Sword*, Vol. I (1949–53), pp. 9–13.
Poole, R. L. *Huguenots of the Dispersion*, p. 109.
Robb, Nesca A. *William of Orange*, pp. 438, 454.
Simms, J. G. "The Bishops' Banishment Act of 1697" in *Irish Historical Studies*, Vol. 17, pp. 186, 188.
Simms, J. G. *The Williamite Confiscation in Ireland, 1690–1703*, pp. 31–3, 86, 88, 96, 110–11, 113.
Smiles, Samuel. *Huguenots in England and Ireland*, pp. 230–1, 312–13, 343, 401–2, 421, 434–5, 437–8.
Stoye, John. *Europe Unfolding*, pp. 367–8.
Swift, Jonathan. *Unpublished Letters* (Hill, George Birbeck, ed.), pp. 51 56, 61.
Traill, H. D. *William the Third*, pp. 168, 180.
Tribout de Morembert, Henri. *La Reforme a Metz, II: Le Calvinisme, 1553–1685*, pp. 147, 164, 195.
Vigne, Randolph "The Good Lord Galway" in *PHSGBI*, Vol. XXIV, no. 6, pp. 534–40, 543–5.

5

"FORTRESS IRELAND": THE DUBLIN CORE, 1692–1745

" . . . that part of my family that was left behind in France remains constantly in my thoughts, and I plead to God that he might bless them, as He does those of us who are more fortunate because we can worship God in freedom; and that He may combine their wishes and ours for our eventual deliverance and reunion."

— Isaac Dumont de Bostaquet (Dublin, 1693)

Between 1692 and 1712, Huguenot immigrants into Ireland had fanned out in a most uneven axis East/West from Dublin to Tallow and North/South from Belfast to Cork, into perhaps as many as 28 separate colonies/communities. There is a good deal of debate over how many there actually were, who specifically settled there; and how long and to what extent they were "Huguenot communities" in any substantial sense of the word. Waterford, Carlow, Wicklow, Kilkenny, Portarlington, Cork, Youghal, Bandon, Killeshandra, Innishannon, Collon, Birr, Gorey, Tallow, Lisburn, Lurgan, Dundalk, Lambeg, Belfast, Castleblayney, Drogheda, Arklow, Enniscorthy, Gowran, Waringstown and Dublin have all (on the basis of a greater, or much lesser, degree of evidence) been claimed as Huguenot settlements set up during the Ruvignac era, and later.

What is established without a doubt, however, is the pre-eminent position of Dublin. The Huguenot community (or more properly speaking, "communities") in the capital city was the largest, most diverse, and most influential – close to half of the estimated 10,000 French Protestants to come into Ireland resided there, and an even greater proportion would have passed through. It was in every sense the "core" around which "Fortress Ireland" was cocooned, and its sustaining lifeblood.

Much has been – justifiably – made of the noblesse d'epeé who settled and reared families in Portarlington, but what is an interesting fact is that a greater number elected to dwell in Dublin. For example, of 121 officers who were retired to half pay in 1692, after the Treaty of Limerick, 85 are known to have settled (initially, at least) in Dublin. These écuyers, and the French Church pastors, provided an axis of leadership for the refugee communities. However, Dublin's case was far removed from that of Portarlington's. In the Midlands colony, the settlers in effect moved into space which had been abandoned, and the numbers of individuals of the military nobility were disproportionately large and domineering as measured with the rest of the population. In Dublin, of course, where the French were just one more element in a vast, fluid and diverse population, and the écuyers were a pronounced minority within a pronounced minority, the situation was far more complex; "Fortress Ireland" soon became a less pressing priority. In spite of hopes to the contrary, too, the failure of the Earl of Galway to exert unitary leadership over the refugee community assured, on the other hand, that this would remain a contributing and dynamic force in urban affairs. It would be equally wrong, however to cast aside Galway's role, his political rise and fall, and the presence of écuyer families. It may serve one best, therefore to at least examine this piece of the puzzle first, before dissecting the Huguenot element inside the city neighborhood by neighborhood.

The Huguenot Earl: a capsule biography

But just who was the Earl of Galway? He was born, Henri Massue de Ruvigny in 1648, and as the eldest son of Marquis Henri Massue, received at an early age the thorough grounding in the diplomatic and social skills necessary for survival at Louis XIV's gaudy and protocol-driven court. It is stated that he received his military training at the hands of the eminent Marshal Turenne. His father had become Depute-General for the Huguenot Community in succession to the Marquis d'Arzelliers in 1653, and in 1678 the younger Ruvigny was appointed to be co-Député-Général alongside his father. The role of the Ruvignys in the years preceding the Revocation is highly controversial. Certainly, they were of the opinion that a policy of accommodation and appeasement towards Royal pressure upon their community was the best possible strategy to follow given its vulnerable minority status. In this they were often bitterly opposed by the proponents of resistance who harked backwards to Duplessis-Mornay and forward to Pierre Jurieu and Jean Cavallier, and could be vehement in their denunciation of Ruvigny *père et fils* as having sold out to the King and/or, at best, being hopelessly naïve about the reality of the situation. The Ruvignys incurred the most heated criticism from their co-religionists over their actions (or rather inaction) regarding the execution of the militant leader Roux de Marcilly. As the Ruvignys did not lift a finger or say a word in protest, many perceived them as being all too willing to sacrifice potential rivals in their attempts to curry favor with Louis, and to offer a sop to the Dévot Party at Court. While charges of appeasement would most certainly be extremely unfair, the fact remains that the Ruvignys were persistently mistrusted by at least half of their own community; that this mistrust followed them into exile; and that this surely explains why an effective exilic leadership (or "*Huguenot Internationale*") never materialized, and how, even during the height of his power and influence, the Earl of Galway singularly proved unable to even forge a consensus amongst his Dublin co-religionists.

Unable to stem the tide of oppression, or even in the end to mitigate the effects of the Edict of Fontainebleau, the Ruvignys were nonetheless offered a special dispensation from its provisions, in consideration of their past loyalty and services to the Crown. They would be permitted to dwell in France, enjoy the same lifestyle and royal favor that they had been accustomed to, and even be allowed private services. Even when conscience compelled them to turn this down, the King's munificence did not cease: the income from Ruvigny estates would continue to go to flow their way, and the entire household could take their time making the transition to exile, taking with them whatever personal property they desired; thus the Ruvignys settled into a comfortable exile at Greenwich, England. The Ruvignys had a particularly deep and abiding connection with England, the Marquis' sister Rachel had married the Earl of Southampton, and both the father and son had undertaken extensive diplomatic missions to London during the reign of King Charles II. The elder Ruvigny died in 1689, passing the title to his son; but upon the younger Ruvigny's acceptance of a commission to serve under King William III in Ireland, Louis XIV confiscated the family estates and the income thereof was discontinued.

Ruvigny's star rose dramatically in the wake of his cavalry charge at Aughrim (see Chapter 2); subsequently he was active during the Second Siege of Limerick. In effect, he and Godert de Ginkel assumed the favor that King William had once shown to Schomberg before the Disaster at Dundalk. In February of 1692, having now assumed legendary status as a first-rate military leader, Major-General Ruvigny was appointed commander-in-chief of the army in Ireland, and granted the titles of Baron Portarlington and Viscount Galway. Though on the surface Viscount Galway's position within the now-burgeoning Huguenot refugee population of Dublin (and indeed of Ireland as a whole) might have been presumed to be unassailable, signs appeared quite early-on that tended to refute this notion. The uniqueness of his situation, as Député-Général, as the most visible Huguenot presence at King William's Court, his active advocacy of Huguenot resettlement in Ireland and elsewhere, and his tangible accomplishments in the diplomatic and martial spheres: all these things would have been in his favor. Notwithstanding, however, and perhaps because of the "baggage" he carried from his accomodationist past, coupled with an inability to relate to the intensity of religious fervor amongst the "rank & file" membership within his own community, his attempts at exerting leadership over a united Exilic colony foundered badly. The resounding rebuff of his unity proposals by the Dublin Non-Conformists in April 1693 (see Chapter 7) was a blow from which he never recovered. Though Galway's position was pre-eminent, its limitations had been set and the former Député-Général himself would in the end allow this to go unchallenged and would not repeat the attempt, or make any other such attempts for that matter. Still, as long as Galway was in a viable political position, the vision of a "Huguenot Internationale", or at least the forging of a consolidated *"Corps du Réfuge"* in Ireland, was deemed to be a possibility.

Shortly thereafter Viscount Galway departed for military action on the Flanders front of the War of the League of Augsburg and generally distinguished himself at the Battle of Landen (the same clash during which his former Irish adversary Patrick Sarsfield died, allegedly uttering the poignant words: "Would that this had been for Ireland!"). His career seemed to take a downturn, however, when he was dispatched to Piedmont in what was, after three years, to prove a losing attempt at stabilizing that theatre of operations and persuading the vacillating Piedmontese Duke, Victor Amadeus II, to persevere as a member of the Alliance against Louis XIV. But Victor Amadeus, who was playing both sides against the middle and had been lukewarm at best to the Allied cause chose in the end to throw in his lot with the Sun King. Galway was recalled and, the following year, the Peace of Ryswick signaled an inconclusive end to the conflict.

Galway did not escape political attack and censure for the collapse of the Piedmontese initiative but it became patently obvious that King William did not share in this opinion, and placed the blame largely on Victor Amadeus' artful prevarication. Shortly after the signing of the Ryswick agreement, Galway was promoted to lieutenant-general; made an Earl (of Galway); and named to be one of the three Lords Justice of Ireland.

The Earl of Galway's first term as Lord Justice of Ireland (1697–1701) marked the zenith of his political power and influence. He was without doubt the dominant force in Irish affairs during those four years. His fellow Lord Justices were far less assertive: The Earl of Jersey was a chronic absentee who spent the greater part of his time in Britain; and the young Duke of Bolton was an administrative neophyte. Undoubtedly, the presence of the Huguenot Earl at Dublin Castle contributed in large measure to the growth, expansion and prosperity of the Dublin Refuge in particular, and by extension the Huguenot diaspora across Ireland, and beyond. Galway was most instrumental in facilitating the immigration and settlement of the écuyers. As at Portarlington, he was able to manipulate the Irish establishment pension lists to secure all sorts of advantages for the Huguenot veterans retired after the Treaties of Limerick, and especially, Ryswick.

The rise and fall of Galway's political career as Lord Justice will be discussed in a subsequent chapter but by the time of his controversial resignation in 1701 he had presided over a period of spectacular Huguenot expansion. In Dublin alone, four separate French Churches, two Conformed, and two Dissenting, were thriving and the Huguenots had insinuated into every profession, neighborhood, and walks of life in the Irish capital. Though it is difficult to come to concrete figures, and one has to deal with a fluid, rapidly-turning situation, the Huguenot population for Dublin may be conservatively projected as having expanded to 2,200 by 1701; 2,900 by 1710; and 3,600 by 1720.

The Huguenot Earl's role in the War of the Spanish Succession proved singularly unrewarding: to him fell the task of organizing the Allied Expeditionary force for the ill-fated Iberian Campaign to enthrone Archduke Charles of Austria as King of Spain. He was certainly outgeneraled by the Duke of Berwick at the pivotal battle of Almanza, which was merely the culminating blow in a series of calamities. Dissension in the Earl's multi-national Allied Forces hindered his efforts; coordination amongst the various under his command was always tenuous, Portuguese units in particular exhibited a tendency to look first to their own self-preservation, and would rapidly retreat in crucial situations. Galway was severely wounded on three occasions, all Allied defeats: at Badajoz (1705), where his forearm was severed by cannon-shot; Almanza (1707), where his right eye was put out by a sword-slash; and the Caya River (1708). The Archduke's cause collapsed; and the Peace of Utrecht (1714) would ultimately award the Spanish crown to Louis XIV's grandson, Philip of Anjou (who thus became King Philip V), on condition that the French and Spanish thrones would never be united under a single monarch. Long identified with the Churchill (Marlborough)/Godolphin faction of the Whig Party, which had pressed hardest for prosecution of the war, Galway was called to task before the Tory-dominated House of Lords and reprimanded for his role in the disaster at Almanza. Unlike Marlborough, however, he was not imprisoned or, in the end, tainted with charges of corruption, and would return to some measure of favor under King George I.

From 1702 to August 1715 his involvement in Irish affairs, even as regards the ever-expanding Huguenot community, had been negligible. However, in the twilight of his years, he was recalled from retirement at Rookley Estate in England to serve a second stint as Lord Justice of Ireland.

Anatomy & Impact: What the evidence indicates

Quite apart from the more spectacular events of the Ruvignac Age, yet complementary to them, was the implementation of a quiet revolution – an insinuation of Huguenots and Huguenot capital into the life and blood-stream of Dublin City. The activities of French Calvinists in all walks of urban life and particularly in the burgeoning property market of the early eighteenth century may be traced. The findings certainly tend to explode some of the more pervasive myths and half truths as to the actual role the played, and the true nature of their communities.

From 1701 to 1745 a demographic pattern emerges which denotes a steady, at times even spectacular, growth up to 1717, after which time there was a decade of stagnation. Around 1728, from what evidence may be gathered, there seems to have been a slight decline in the number of French Protestants who overtly demonstrated their separate identity by worshipping at one of the Huguenot churches. This trend accelerated until, by the early 1740s, Dublin's French colony is quite evidently on the wane, especially in the city's north side. This decline was somewhat, though far from entirely, mitigated by an increasing number of Huguenot families attending Anglican parish churches.

From 1708 onwards, one can glimpse with a much keener insight into the exact nature of the Huguenot contribution to Dublin's expansion and the precise distribution of French Calvinists throughout the urban area. This is due for the most part to the presence of numerous entries in the Irish Registry of Deeds from that date. Hitherto, information on residence, property ownership and development and records of transactions is sketchy and often curtailed to scattered documents or the odd occasions when a post-1708 deed refers back to an earlier transaction. From such data as is available, coupled from what can be gleaned from extant parish records, it is safe to dismiss the long-cherished image of a Huguenot enclave in the Liberties.

Patterns of concentration and property ownership

In fact, when specific patterns of property ownership and residency are traced it becomes quite clear that, at the precise moment when

Huguenots were presumed to be so much in evidence in the Liberties, this particular area of Dublin was one of least concentration. Of 951 property transactions occurring between 1708 and 38, only 66 involve plots and buildings in the Liberties. If the truth be known, the most active areas of Huguenot property ownership and development during these thirty years were: St. Stephen's Green, north, south, east and west (79 transactions), Aungier Street, including Beaux or "Bow" Lane (63), Grafton Street (49), Eustace Street and Dirty (now Temple) Lane (30), Dame Street, including St. Andrew's Lane and Whitmore Alley (34), Strand Street (39), Great Britain (now Parnell) Street and Ballybough Lane (21), George's Lane (now South Great George's Street) (21), Longford Street and Lane (21), Ormond Quay (18), Cuffe Street (19), Church Street in Oxmantown (15), Abbey Street (15), King Street, North (15), Jervis Quay (13), and Liffey Street (13) – none of which are encompassed within even the outer boundaries of the Liberties. The secondary areas of concentration and activity included: Blind Quay including Smock Alley (11) Big Butter Lane (now Bishop Street) (10), Bride Street (12), Bachelor's Walk (11), Chequer Lane (11), Capel Street (11), Drumcondra Lane (10), Henry Street (10), Kennedy's Lane (11), Stafford (now Wolfe Tone) Street (10), Digges Street (10), Smithfield (9), Fishamble Street (9), Essex Street (8), Fleet Street (8), Francis Street (8), James' Street (8), Jervis Street (8), and Peter Street (8). Of these, only Francis Street, Kennedy's Lane and James' Street are located within what is strictly defined as the Liberties area.

The twenty principal Property-owning/developing families were: Digues Latouche, Maret de Larive, Espinasse, Jalabert, De Susy Boan, Chaigneau, Boivin, Picard, Vauteau, D'Apremont, Correges, Blosset de Loches, Debrisay, De Castelnau, Mazotin, Caillaud, Pomarede, Corneille, Boust Laboutrie, and Rouquier. Of these, ten were écuyer families, five were merchants, two were brewers; one a leather-tawer; another a wigmaker; and one a baker.

The Digues Latouche Story

David Digues Latouche (Senior) was by far the most intensive of the Huguenot property developers, as befits the founder of an immensely successful banking and financial enterprise. Yet the circumstances that led to the foundation of his business empire are obscure. Having been discharged from active service in La Caillemotte's (Belcastel's) Regiment in 1692 as an ensign, he was transferred to Princess Anne of Denmark's Regiment (English) of infantry, which later became Liverpool's Regiment; and was finally retired in 1697 on half pay – with no apparent financial backing other than his War Office pittance of two shillings per diem. Within the space of a few months, however, he had already launched a successful banking enterprise, as well as acquiring a controlling interest in a Dublin cambric/tabinet factory in Castle Street. How he came to obtain such a substantial amount of capital in a short time is an intriguing question and has yet to be conclusively answered. It is possible that the legendary account might be indeed correct: that Latouche had earned such a reputation for honesty and had shown such capacity for handling financial matters amongst his co-religionist colleagues during the years that he served in the officer corps that they were predisposed to entrust their assets into his hands for safe-keeping whilst they relocated their families from England, Brandenburg and the Netherlands to Ireland – and afterwards. Of course, the fact that he was "one of their own" would have given Latouche a certain edge insofar as the burgeoning Huguenot colony was concerned. In view of the House of Latouche's later reputation as bankers to the Anglo-Irish nobility; the continued influx of Huguenot veteran officers into the city; and the inclusion of several old comrades-in-arms in some of his speculatory schemes: this renders this hypothesis all the more attractive. Yet this still appears a bit simplistic and one has the uncomfortable feeling that the answer actually encompasses a vaster scope. One clue might lie in the often complex web of unofficial trusteeship arrangements between Huguenot exiles and certain of their familial or personal contacts as remained in France. This impromptu system, which can be credited with removing large amounts of capital out of Louis XIV's realm, depended on the ability and willingness of an individual to function as "trustee" or "steward" for an expatriate's property and assets. For instance, the head of a noble house or business in France who might elect to leave his country in order to practice his faith without harassment would leave his estates and/or commercial holdings in the care of a designated "trustee" who was willing to pay at least lip-service allegiance to Roman Catholicism. The designee was often a member of the exiled party's family – in the case of Isaac Dumont de Bostaquet it was his eldest son who remained on the estates in Normandy – and of course this had the most desired effect of keeping the properties and revenues derived from them entirely within the bonds of kinship. Sometimes it may have been an unwritten arrangement between friends. These "trustees" were to hold titular possession until the day that the rightful (Protestant) owner might return but, until then, they were to dispatch the revenues to their houses-in-exile. The Roi Soleille was even less adept at stemming the hemorrhage of capital from France than he was at sealing his borders to prevent the tide of Protestant humanity from breaching his net. Huguenot assets arriving via letters of credit flooded the banks of

Holland and Great Britain, and both pre-established and newly formed financial houses under Huguenot ownership operating in London or Amsterdam flourished on exilic capital during the two decades after the Revocation.

The success of the Latouche Bank may be ascribed in great measure to its being available to perform a similar function for refugees in Ireland; and being in the hands of a personage with the necessary credibility and networking skills to turn a fluid situation to maximum advantage. Latouche would then have readily had the capital to invest in such industries as poplin, silk & linen weaving, and property development. In this last-mentioned enterprise, the Huguenots were not unique – certainly the Anglo-Irish nobility had long been, and would continue to be, in the forefront in employing the vehicle of property speculation to foster the expansion of the capital city and other urban areas. But Huguenot wealth did contribute to the transformation of Dublin during the half-century after the Peace of Limerick – and this in a manner and to an extent that was disproportionately significant when measured against their actual numbers. The Longford Estate comprising: present day Aungier Street, Longford Street, Longford Lane, Beaux Lane, Goat Alley, Digges Street, Cuffe Street, Love Lane and several smaller by-ways were opened in large part through Huguenot money.

Of course a transitory, not a permanent exile, was presupposed when the arrangements were put in place. In Waterford at least, the hope for the reopening of France to its Huguenot children was so avidly kept alive that the French colony there is asserted to have irreversibly decimated itself because so many refugee descendants sailed back to their forebears' native land after Louis XVI's Edict of Toleration of 1787 officially reversed the Edict of Fontainebleau.

In the case of Dublin the picture that emerges of its Huguenot expatriate community of c.1700–40s is hardly one of depression and destitution – despite some occasional protestations from the Huguenots themselves to that effect. Rather, it appeared for the most part to function as an active and invigorated force. When all is taken into account the old Whig-historian theory that Louis XIV's excessive reliance on Catholic piety to influence his religious policy worked to the economic benefit of towns like Dublin and to the continuing detriment of his own realm, even to the point of factoring into French military reverses, might not be all that remotely far from the truth.

In 1715 Latouche entered into business partnership with three other firms, those of: Nathaniel Kane, Thomas Howe, and Richard Norton. By 1726 only Kane and Latouche remained as major partners and the banking concern became known as "Kane & Latouche". Though it has been suggested the Latouche financial empire owed much to David the

The Dublin Core

Elder's being propped and carried along by Kane as a junior partner, and having the good fortune to outlive Kane himself, this point cannot be credibly argued inasmuch as the Latouche enterprise was already a force in its own right on the property market prior to this amalgamation.

Between 1708 and 1738 the House of Latouche was involved in 151 major transactions. Latouche's first speculative enterprises occurred in the Eustace Street/Temple Lane area, where from 1713–24 the company brought out the leasehold interest on 27 plots, at least 20 of which had been developed and let, or re-let, by 1729. Latouche was instrumental in opening Grafton Street where between 1716–28, eleven parcels of ground had been bought and built upon. But Latouche's primary focus devolved on the Longford Estate from 1720–35. During the course of those fifteen years, Latouche was involved in 101 transactions (34 in 1726–8 alone – which marked the span of the most intensive activity). The streets in question, which were effectively developed in what was perhaps the most massive undertaking of its sort in Ireland during the first half of the eighteenth century – even more so than the opening of the Dawson Estate which occurred around the same time – included: Aungier Street, Longford Street, Longford Lane, Bow (Beaux) Lane, Goat Alley, Love Lane, Digges Street, and Digges Court. Longford Lane, Digges Street and Digges Court were almost entirely Latouche developments. There actually seems to be some truth to the old legend that Digges Street and Digges Court were named after Digues Latouche, for the variant spelling "Digues" does appear in the original leases of the 1720s. The actual process differed, but the pattern of development favored by Latouche usually involved the subletting of waste ground to a contractor, who in turn would sell back his interest on the property and any improvements he might have undertaken (most often gabled semi-detached or terraced structures) to Latouche at a profit, while Latouche would proceed to lease the property at a higher rate to the next tenant. One example among many should serve to illustrate the procedure: David Latouche, Senior leased a parcel of ground in Aungier Street, East ("near Goat Alley) on 16 October 1724 to Oliver Ball, carpenter, who resided in Anglesey Street, at a peppercorn rent for the first seven months and thereafter at nineteen pounds, seven shillings per annum. Ball, having built a detached house, then sold back to Latouche for the sum of two hundred pounds on 7 June 1726. On 19 October 1726 Latouche rented the plot and structure for three months' peppercorn rent and 28 pounds per annum thereafter to substantial merchant named John Hall. This pattern would be repeated: Ball was engaged in this fashion twice more; John Masterson, carpenter, eight times; Nicholas Mansfield, carpenter, four times; Nicholas Carter, bricklayer, three times; Francis Taylor, glazier, once; and even John Delahunty, victualler, once. The waste ground initially brought up by Latouche was owned mainly by: Jacob Poole, Quaker – and a clothier by profession (15 lots); Michael Cuffe, a member of the Longford family (4 lots); and James MacCartney, esquire (4). The rough outlines of a Latouche network with fellow Huguenots can also be discerned, the known participants including: the nobles Adam and Paul de Glatigny, Bartelemy de Landre and Cornelius Lescures; Abraham Viridet. *Lecteur* of the Dublin Conformed Churches and grandson of Moses Viridet; Jean Darquier, surgeon; and Antoine Rafugeau & Jacques Chaigneau, merchants.

Certain Huguenot families of Dublin

Adam Danoué de Glatigny, who at times interacted with David Latouche the Elder, was a veteran who served for twelve years in Holland, Ireland and Flanders and was pensioned off after Ryswick as an ensign in La Meloniere's infantry. Glatigny lived in Capel Street, where he had purchased three houses from the Pain family. He was one of the parishioners of the French Conformed Church that met at the Chapter House of St. Mary's Abbey (known variously as "French Mary's", "the French Church of St. Mary's" or "Little French Patrick's") where his two sons were baptized: Paul – 1712 and Philippe David – 1717. Two of his daughters married, and died, in Dublin: Elizabeth (1701–63) and Susanne (1703–78).

Jean Ycard, who became an Anglican minister and eventually rose to the dignities of Dean of Achonry and Dean of Killala, brought a house on the east side of Clarendon Market on 10 June 1710 from Francis Knox, gentleman. The house, which Ycard took as his domicile, had formerly been in the possession of two Huguenots: Jean Caillot, army quartermaster; and Madame Olimpe Laffarel, wife of Lieutenant Colonel Louis Laffarel. Dean Ycard married Susanne de Soret and the couple had at least two children who died at a tragically early age: Benjamin (1699–1701) and a daughter (1704–5). Ycard died in Dublin on 25 July 1733, and his wife Susanne on 25 April 1740.

Isaac Vauteau merits special mention as being one of the few Huguenots who actually dwelled and owned most of his property in the Liberties of Dublin. Vauteau was a leather tawer (*chamoiseur*) who arrived in Dublin during the early 1690s and who seems to have had, or have been able to have had sent over, a considerable amount of capital. As early as 1697 he had obtained leases from the Earl of Meath for five plots on Mill Street, upon which he built gabled townhouses, one of which may have become his residence. One of these structures was still standing as of July 1985, though derelict and minus the gable. Vauteau's property interests were mainly industrial in nature and included lease-hold plots at Pimlico, Great Ship Street, Crane Lane, and Stafford Street. Isaac died on 16 March 1717, aged 94. His eldest son, Jean Jacob was bequeathed the four houses in Pimlico and his younger sibling Isaac II received the buildings, sheds, and workshops on Great Ship Street, the remainder going to his widow Marie Madeleine to be divided amongst the remaining heirs upon her death. Jean Jacob married, probably in June 1706, Elizabeth Le Gaigneur. The couple had two sons both named David, who survived for only two days, and only three months, in 1708 and 1709, respectively. Isaac II, who died in 1733, apparently had only one surviving son, Pierre (1700–78), who was the last of the Vauteau family's male line. In 1758, Pierre had acquired the lease to five some-what ancient houses in the portion of the Dean and Chapter of Christchurch Cathedral, lying between Bride Street and Little Ship Street. Pierre became a freeman of the Merchant's Guild in 1727 and an elder at French Patrick's, leaving a bursary of thirty ponds per annum for the preaching of a special sermon at St. Luke's Church every Wednesday evening. His wife Madeleine, neé Bureau passed on 26 January 1787, at which time the family died out.

Pierre Picard, brewer, is variously described as being of the Blackpitts or of Meath Street. He owned at least three plots on Aungier Street, five houses in Big Butter Lane; 39 feet of ground on Grafton Street, a house and back in Marrowbone Lane, and ground in Meath Street. Pierre received the franchise in 1708 and was a member of the Non-Conformist congregation. A son George was born to Pierre and his wife Madeleine on 27 July 1702, and their daughter Madeleine married Jean Bues on 21 April 1717. Catherine Picard from Dié in Dauphiné who married Pierre Audouin and made a public repentance for having attended Mass, may have been a relative. Pierre had died by 1733.

The most ambitious of the Huguenot brewers was Paul Espinasse, who at one time seemed on his way to establishing a minor urban brewing empire. He purchased interests in the taverns trading under the names of: the *Sign of Robin Hood* (Ormond Quay); the *Blue Boar's Head* (Arran Street); the *Brewer's Arms* (James Street); and additional property on Liffey Street, Aston Quay, Peter street; Back Lane, Arundell Court, Chequer Lane, Charles Street, Garden Lane, Jervis Street, Pudding Row, and St. James' Gate. At the last of these locations Espinasse obtained a leasehold interest from Mark Ransford for a lot commonly known as "the Pipes", where he set up yet another brewery. Upon Espinasse's death in Drogheda in 1750, as the result of a fall from a horse, the lease reverted to Ransford and was obtained nine years later by Arthur Guinness I.

Pubs, taverns, alehouses and distilleries seemed to be popular (and doubtless lucrative) investments for Dublin's Huguenots. The fore-mentioned Pierre Picard owned the *Sign of the Red Cow* on Abbey Street which he purchased from a tallowchandler named Gawen Wren on 3 November 1724 for one hundred pounds. Daniel Guyon obtained the *Playhouse* tavern on a corner lot on Aungier Street on 5 September 1729 for two hundred pounds. On 22 February 1710 the merchant Jean Vabres purchased a 31-year lease on the *Turk's Head Inn* on Bridge Street only to sell his interest to the Reverend John Fontanier, rector of St. John's Church in Sligo on 16 April 1713. Vabres worshipped at the Non-Conformed Churches and for some unknown reason, had by 1713 altered his surname to Saint Sauveur. He and his wife Anne had seven surviving children born between 1710 and 1718. Jean Chaigneau, merchant, lived in 1724 at the *Three Tuns* on the north side of Blind Quay, and had purchased the building for two hundred pounds from John Porter, Lord Mayor. In 1717 Pierre Garesché took possession of a 21-year lease for the *Duke's Head* in Christchurch Lane. David Latouche, Senior obtained the leasehold of no less than four public houses in Dame Street: the *Shrewsbury's Head,* the *Crow's Nest,* the *Maidenhead,* and the *Three Dogs' Head.* David Calveirac de Terson and Charles Boileau de Castelnau, pensioned Williamite officers, acquired between themselves four taverns on Francis Street: the *Red Cross,* the *Royal Coffin,* the *White Swan,* and the *White Cross.* By 1730 the De Thierry de Pechels family possessed no fewer than six inns scattered along James Street: the *Black Bull, Kilkenny Castle, Fox & Geese, Three Goats' Head, Dog & Duck,* and the *Lamb & Phoenix.* Later, the *Blackmoor's* on Mary's Lane, off Church Street, became one of their holdings.

Other such establishments to come into French Protestant proprietorship were: the *Pyde Bull* at Smithfield (Desminieres); *Sign of Salutation* on Dame Street (Gervais & Sauvaget); *King's Head* on Fishamble Street (De la Rue & Boursiquot); *The Boote* on Francis Street (Boivin & Lunel); *The Vine* on Dame Street (Pellisier); another *Pyde Bull* on Glibb Lane (Aigoin); *Jacob's Ladder* on Cork Hill (Guyon); *Ram Inn* on Chequer Lane (Villebois); another *Three Tuns* on South King Street (Maignon); *Bunch of Grapes* on Swan Alley facing Crane Lane (Pineau); *Duke of Marlborough* on Skinner's Alley (Drolenvaux); another *King's Head* on Mutton Lane (Guimet); *Two Friends Tavern* and *Ruben's Head* off Crow Street (Perrier and Rivett, respectively); and the *Black Lion* on North King Street (Gerrard).

The Chaigneaus were perhaps the most pervasive and widely-scattered of all the Huguenot families in Ireland, and unraveling them is a challenge. Some family members had arrived even prior to the Revocation: Louis Chaigneau, merchant was sworn into the Freedom of Dublin City before

Lord Mayor Abel Ram at Christmastime 1683, and Isaac Chaigneau, currier, joined him in 1686. The family was mercantile and came from the area of Saint Savenien in Saintonge. During the 1690s–1700s there were at least six nuclear families of Chaigneaus which revolved around and interacted within the extended family structure. Indeed, as is often the case in similar situation, there is one example of consanguinity or near-consanguinity. Etienne Chaigneau, son of David Chaigneau and Susanne Tabois, married his cousin Jeanne, daughter of Josias Chaigneau and Jeanne Feuilleteau on 4 October 1704 at French Patrick's. The marriage, tragically, was not destined to endure for long, for Étienne died at age 35 on 26 February 1706. Chaigneau holdings in Dublin included lots on: Arbour Hill, North Anne Street, Blind Quay, Dirty Lane, Dame Street, Essex Street, Eustace Street, George's Lane, Kennedy's Lane, St. Stephen's Green, Stephen Street and Prince's Street.

"French Walk" & St. Stephen's Green

The southern portion of St. Stephen's Green was being opened extensively to development during the 1710s–20s. The western and northern sectors were the first to be built upon (during the seventeenth century) and the southern, still later, the eastern, were left for the succeeding generation. Huguenots were involved in 71 separate real estate transactions on all sides of the Green over the period 1708–38: 35 on the south; 19 on the west; 9 on the north; and 8 on the east.

The House of Latouche held a meager six leases around the Green and in actuality, the prime developer there (especially on the south side – "Leeson Walk") was Alexandre de Susy Boan. De Susy Boan was in several respects an extraordinary individual: he was in fact a clergyman and a convert from Roman Catholicism who had elected to embrace the French Calvinist faith after the Revocation of the Edict of Nantes had been proclaimed. On 14 September 1709 Henri de Rocheblave died while serving for a second time as the French Patrick's minister. Although De Susy Boan had been consecrated into the ministry by the Anglican Bishop of London in 1708, and had been recommended to the Dublin congregation by Pastor Joseph De La Motte of the French Church of the Savoy, his proselyte's status impelled the elders to proceed cautiously and take a bit more time investigating a pastor-elect than was customary. But he was at length approved before the following year was up and served at French Patrick's from 1710 until his death in November 1741. He was apparently able to draw upon much more capital – possibly from a French source – than the average Huguenot Church of Ireland minister, for between the years 1710–38 he held ten leases on plots at South St. Stephen's Green (upon one of which he constructed his own dwelling), and one on the west side. De Susy Boan and his wife Sophie Louise (neé Addié) were married in 1713 and had two children: Alexandre Frederique (born 1718–19) and Louise (died 17 January 1777).

The western edge of St. Stephen's Green was by the 1750s known as French Walk, presumably for the incidence of Huguenot residents/proprietors there. This is one legend whose veracity is very largely confirmed upon examination; resident property owners on the Green's west side included: Salomon Blosset de Loches, Pierre Combecrose, Jacques Girardot, Anthoine de la Sautié, Simon Chabert, Jacques Fontaine, Charles de Cresserons, Guillaume Le Fanu, Theodore Desvories, Samuel de Thierry de Pechels, Jean Arabin de Barcille, Pierre Poussin, Auguste Le Goux de Laspois, Daniel de La Fontan, Jacques Boursiquot – and possibly Henri de Rocheblave and Jacques Peltier.

Besides De Susy Boan, proprietors on the south side of the Green included: Daniel de Bouchers de Benâtre, Guillaume Darquier, Maximilien Dubois Descourt, Baron de Favière, Isaac Belloc, Jean de Brasselay, Pierre de Gualy, Michel Duchesne, Élie Gervois, and Jean Lamaria Duponcet.

The north side of St. Stephen's Green is often rendered as Beaux Walk on mid-eighteenth century maps. This had nothing to do with the Huguenots but derived from the popular notion that it was fashionable for people of "quality" to stroll up and down on Sunday afternoons. Indeed, Huguenot proprietors there were not so much in evidence: only Paul Blosset de Loches, the De Creissel sisters, and Pierre St. Leger. The eastern end (Monk Walk) was even more sparse: Israel Jalabert, Paul Landré, and members of the ubiquitous Chaigneau family.

The Blosset de Loches clan were from Val d'Isère in Dauphiné: Salomon senior was born at St. Boudille-et-Priet; Salomon junior at Clelles; and Paul at Langefords. The elder Salomon was among the more substantial of the veterans and had retired in 1698 on two commissions (Colonel, and Brigadier-General in La Melonière's). He died on 20 October 1721. Paul went on to serve in the War of the Spanish Succession from 1706 to 1709, when he was placed on half pay as a colonel. Paul passed away on 13 November 1719. Salomon junior was born in 1683 and taken into exile as an infant. In 1696 he entered the service as a cadet, rising to captain by 1706, and retiring in 1712. He died in 1749, though his wife, Jeanne Chateaigne de Cramahé, survived until 1783. From their base in St. Stephen's Green the family obtained property throughout the city.

Pierre Calvin de Combecrose, who served in Galway's Cavalry, was allotted a captain's pension in 1699. Mention of a Madame de

Combecrose is made in August 1705, but by 5 September 1709 when Pierre purchased a 120-year lease on a plot of ground on French Walk, she is not alluded to. There are no indications of Combecrose children or descendants. Pierre built a domicile on the plot and sold it on 9 June 1724 to another Huguenot noblemen, Jean Girardot. Pierre de Combercrose died in Dublin on 23 May 1732. Girardot is very likely to be identified with Jacques Girardot Duperon who was born in Paris and naturalized under act of the Westminster Parliament in 1699. Apart from the fact that he changed his residence from London to Dublin by 1723, he remains a shadowy figure who maintained slight contact with the Huguenot churches. It is known that he purchased six houses in Castle Lane in 1725, which he sold in 1729, and then mysteriously drops out of the record, apparently leaving Dublin as abruptly as he had arrived.

The De Chabert family originated at Gagnoles in the Languedoc. Simon de Chabert was pensioned as a reformed lieutenant from Lifford's regiment in 1699 and is recorded as being in Dublin on 1 June 1703 when he married Françoise D'Hours from Manguio in Languedoc. The couple seems to have had no surviving children: a daughter, Louise Françoise, died on 19 April 1705, aged seven months; and a son, Esaye (1706–22) did not survive into adolescence. In March 1721 Simon moved into a new house on the north side of Glover's Alley, renting it from the proprietor, Farmer Glover. De Chabert passed on in 1738, and his wife in 1746. Farmer Glover's land off St. Stephen's Green, West, was being developed along the laneway which still bears his name, though on certain signs it was more colorfully known as Rapparee Alley. Besides Chabert, Huguenots who resided and held plots along its rather jagged course were: Pierre Massromet and Jean de Branday.

The écuyer Antoine Peuch de la Sautié was disbanded from the cavalry after the Peace of Limerick and resided briefly in Dublin before settling at Portarlington for at least 19 years. He and his wife Isabeau de Jean reared five children and he claimed possession of 25 acres of land, a cabin and 20 head of cattle. Some time after 1714 he removed to Dublin where on 10 February 1721 he had purchased a 31 year lease on a dwelling "and backside" fron Alexandre de Susy Boan at 12 pounds 10 shillings per annum at Stephen's Green, West. Peuch de la Sautié is reputed to have died in 1743.

Pastor Jacques Fontaine is well-documented as the author of one of the few surviving refugee memoires (printed under the title *Mémoire d'une famille Huguenot, Victime de la Révocation de l'Édit de Nantes*). Fontaine arrived in Dublin late in his rather turbulent career. Since coming to Ireland he had caused quite a stir as a non-conformist preacher; vociferous antagonist of the Earl of Galway and the Bishop of Cork; sailcloth manufacturer in Cork City; and fisheries entrepreneur in Bearhaven, County Cork. After having been released by the French following his capture in a raid on Bearhaven, Fontaine came to Dublin (1709) and took up residence at French Walk in what was, by his own description, an old house reputed by locals to be haunted (though in point of fact the house itself could not, at the outside, have been much older than 50 years). There he established and ran a school where he taught French, Latin, Greek, Mathematics and Religion into the 1720s.

Fontaine is not to be confused with his close neighbor Daniel de la Fontan from Vendôme who was retired as a captain of cavalry in 1692. He and his wife Judith de Pierrefite and their daughter Jeanne were amongst the earlier Huguenot residents of the Stephen's Green area. Daniel lived on the south side of a street leading into Stephen's Green West, which was named La Fontan's Street after him (as far as can be determined, he was its first inhabitant). By 1750, however, the name of La Fontan's Street was no longer in usage and the thoroughfare was known as York Street. Among those who acquired property on La Fontan's Street was David Digues Latouche, Senior, who in turn rented two plots to Theodore Desvories and one to Pierre Poussin. Captain de La Fontan lived to the age of 53, and was buried in Dublin on 4 May 1719, his wife having predeceased him since 7 October 1710.

Theodore Desvories was a Huguenot minister who was ordained into the Church of Ireland and first appears in Dublin on 30 May 1717 when he married a daughter of the late Captain Auguste Le Goux de Laspois, who is variously styled as "Caroline" or "Charlotte Anne". On 30 June 1718, the couple took residence at a brick house adjoining Captain de La Fontan's dwelling on the south side of La Fontan's Street. The first six of their eleven offspring, at least, were born there: Auguste Antoine (14 October 1720); Jean Theodore (11 November 1721); Charlotte (22 October 1722); Theophile Jacques (18 March 1724); Pierre (26 August 1726); and Louis François (August 1727). Two other girls – Caroline and Susanne – may also have been. From 1720–8 Desvories was assistant minister at French Patrick's to De Susy Boan, Pierre Bouquet de St. Paul, Pascal Ducasse, Abraham Viridet and Amaury Philippe Fleury. While there, Desvories played a leading role in the operation of the Huguenot Charitable Society, and was responsible for founding one at Portarlington in 1732. Before 14 August 1729, Desvories accepted a call to Portarlington where the incumbent. Antoine Ligonier de Bonneval was in declining health. He would succeed Bonneval as French Church minister and three more children were born in the Midlands colony: Anne Marianne (29 May 1730); Pierre (19 August 1731); and Guillaume (7 March 1733). Of their eleven children, four at least appear to have died prior to reaching adolescence.

Charles Le Fanu de Cresserons was born in Caen, Normandy in 1655 and served with an English regiment (Peterborough) stationed at Jersey until 1699. From 1706 to 1709 he served with La Fabrèque's Regiment in Spain and Portugal, earning the rank of major and retiring to St. Stephen's Green on a very substantial English establishment pension of 63 pounds, 17 shillings and sixpence per annum.

Auguste Le Goux de Laspois received notoriety as one of the most vehement opponents of non-conformity within the Huguenot Refuge, while an elder of the French Patrick's consistory. He was born in Blois around 1666 and enrolled in La Caillemotte's Regiment, rising to the rank of Captain by 1692. He married Charlotte Petitot, and the couple had six children born between 1695–1706, four of them, tragically, died in infancy or childhood: Auguste (June/August, 1695); Jacques (December 1696/February 1699); Auguste (January 1698/June 1700); Marie (September 1706/June 1711). Two girls survived but one, Jeanne, died unmarried in 1722. Only Caroline/Charlotte Anne, who married Theodore Desvories carried on the family lineage. Captain Auguste succumbed in Dublin on 20 August 1709 at the early age of 43 and Charlotte Petitot Le Goux de Laspois accompanied her daughter and son-in-law to Portarlington, where she passed on in 1738.

Samuel de Pechels, Sieur de la Boissonade had a swashbuckling history before settling at Stephen's Green. He was born in the Huguenot stronghold of Montauban in the Languedoc in 1654 and, refusing to escape, resisted all pressure to abjure. In 1686, he was first imprisoned and tortured at Montauban, then transferred to Cahors and Marseilles, whence he was transported to the Caribbean island of Hispaniola. This was in itself often a virtual death sentence, but Samuel managed to escape, and found his way to England by 1689, in time to spend two years in Ireland with the Williamite expeditionary force. Pensioned after Limerick on a lieutenant's annuity, he was joined by his wife, the Marquise de Thierry Sabonières, and his son Jacob (b. 1679 at Montauban), who had fled from France via Geneva. The couple's other offspring, three sons and two daughters, appear to have remained in France. In 1702 Samuel claimed assets of only one hundred pounds but may well have been concealing his full fortune, or else have come into an unexpected bounty, since he was able to purchase the lease on a plot in the prestigious residential area of Stephen's Green West from Salomon de Blosset de Loches in 1705. Samuel died in Dublin in 1733, his son Jacob also pursued a military career, rising to the rank of lieutenant-colonel in 1739. His wife, Elizabeth Boyd, had been born of Huguenot parents in Craven County, South Carolina, The family owned a 202-foot frontage plot in Grafton Street until 1731, and interest in several pubs on James' Street.

One of the most prominent of the denizens of *French Walk* and the progenitor of one of the most enduring of Dublin Huguenot families was Bathelemy Arabin de Barcille from Ries in Provence (though it has been attested that the family originally hailed from Dauphine). Arabin de Barcille had entered the military and so distinguished himself that Marshal Schomberg had appointed him *aide-de-camp* at the rank of Captain. He seems to have temporarily lost favor after the aged Marshal's disgrace and death but by 1693 had been restored to his old staff position by Lord Galway. Arabin de Barcille was retired to half pay after the Peace of Ryswick, and in 1699 he married Jeanne Reneé de St. Julien de Malacare. The couple seems to have been possessed of substantial assets: Barthelemy purchased a forfeited estate at Mogvaughly in the County Westmeath from the Commissioners of the Hollow Sword Blades Society in London prior to his death in 1713. His son Jean, born in 1703, was also destined to serve as Captain of cavalry and in 1727 acquired a parcel of land in Gregory's Alley off St. Stephen's Green West.

Grafton Street, the Dawson Estate & Dame Street

Grafton Street, which was being opened for development as a fashionable residential District during the 1710s–30s was also notable for the number of Huguenot families who resided or invested there, and again most of the surnames are of noble origin. De Pechels, Duponcet, Chabert, De Creissels, Picard, Blosset de Loches, Debrisays, Gervais, Digues Latouche, De Gualy and Ducasse have already been mentioned. Additionally, there were: De Questebrune, Garesché, Desvignoles, De Puichenin, De Lamillière, Trapaud, Lecoq St. Leger, Audouin, Vincent, Moissey, De Maistre, De Durand, Pineau, Molié, and Lafausille.

Relatively few Huguenots had a part in the development of the Dawson Estate, where a great number of the original "Huguenot Houses", ironically enough, survive in altered and more-or-less well-maintained condition. The Desvignoles, De Faviere, Aubrespy and Ducasse families had interests and holdings in Dawson Street; Gerverau, De la Rousèllire, De Favière and Boucoiron in Duke Street.

Around Chequer Lane off to the west of Grafton Street (now Wicklow and Exchequer Streets) there was yet another concentration of Huguenot involvement; with the Blosset de Loches, Espinasse, Villebois, Pennettes, Paisant, Digues Latouche, Perrier, and Debrisay families among the most active. Raymond Pennettes, who became a native of Dublin as early as 1717, was a merchant from Clérac in Guyenne and married Jeanne Guron on 1 January 1719. Raymond had at least three children: Marianne (born 31 December 1723), Raymond (13 August 1728), and Marie (23

November 1730). On 10 August 1732 he secured a 9-year rental at six pounds per annum from David Digues Latouche of a plot of ground on a laneway running from the north side of Chequer Lane and situated in the end closest to George's Lane. The alley on which the land was situated would be known as Pennettes' Lane and Pennetes was to construct a warehouse on its west side and clear a 13-foot wide passage into George's Lane – which was evidently done.

Anthoine Perrier, son of Jean Perrier, vintner, had immigrated to Dublin with his parents by the 1730s, though, unlike his father, he had chosen the baker's profession.

Anthoine acquired the leasehold on a small house or cottage on Chequer Lane with a granary, shop, bake-house with oven, shed, stable and "use of house of ease in yard behind house". On 23 February 1737 he contracted a marriage with Marthe L'Éveque, who had lost both her father and step-father. The prosperous écuyer, Theophile Debrisay, acting as guardian for Marthe and her mother, Jeanne L'Éveque Jameson, was to present Anthoine Perrier with 300 pounds in cash, as dowry, and to buy out the lease on his Chequer Lane property so that the couple could enjoy freehold possession of their shop and domicile. Jeanne L'Éveque Jameson survived to the ripe old age of 95, dying on 23 October 1777, and being entered at the Peter Street burial ground. A Lucy Perrier is denoted in 1753 as the owner of the *Two Friends' Tavern* on Chequer Lane.

Jean Paisant had an exceptionally tragic history, from what the records indicate. A native of St. Jean D'Angely in Saintonge, and a window-fitter by profession, he lost one child, a 20-month old daughter named Deborah on 1 November 1701. On 12 September 1706 his wife Jolie Loe gave birth to twin sons. The mother and one of the twins died on 20 September, and the remaining son four days later. On 26 October 1709 Jean had remarried, to Marie Perochan, and in 1730 he sold his interests in two houses on Chequer Lane to Anthoine Perrier.

The Dame Street area was another sector of the city where the refugees left quite an imprint. On Dame Street itself, many Huguenot proprietors may be identified: Pomarede, Tabois, Chaigneau, Gervereau, Laveauté, Gervais, Sauvaget, Vialas, Boivin. Digues Latouche, Darquier, Lambremont, Martin, Maret de Larive, Servant, Pellisier and Pineau.

During the turn of the eighteenth century the Dame Street periphery was a favorite spot for barber surgeons. Members of the professions who were Huguenots included Michel Lacomte of Essex Gate, Louis Deblonde of College Green, and Maurice Baudouin of George's Lane.

Dame Street itself fairly abounded with shops of identifiable Huguenot proprietorship. Two of these were owned by women: the *Merry Shepherd* by Marie Gerrard, milliner (1712); and the *Dove* by Jeanne Hautenville (sometimes rendered Hattanville), silk mercer (1732–7). Jeanne's

husband Daniel, a stag-maker by profession, was running an establishment known as the *Red Ball* on Dirty Lane in 1731. Jeanne died on 12
June 1772, aged 78. The family also acquired commercial property on
Capel Street, where Samuel Hautenville was managing an enterprise
called the *Dove and Olive Tree* (1751).

The Vidouze family were jewelers; their shop, the *Ring and Cornet*, was
located on Dame Street, and their residence was on the east side of Fownes
Street. Jean Celles, apothecary, had established himself at Essex Gate by
20 June 1724 at the sign of the *Spread Eagle*. He had been, however, well
known in the refugee colony long before this time, being patronized as
early as 1704 by none other than Dr. Elie Bouhereau. Celles would seem
to have lost either two children, or a child and his wife, in 1706; but lived
to the age of 90, passing on 24 June 1759.

At Blind Quay there were two tobacconist establishments run by
Huguenots – the only Huguenots in Ireland known to engage in this
profession – the *Blackamoor's Head* by Thomas Paget (alleged to be the
son of a "Colonel Pagès"), and the *Hand and Snuff Box* operated by a
certain Ferrand or Fernand (1723). Also at Blind Quay the widow
Lappiere had a grocery shop called the *Olive Tree* in 1750. This widow
was probably a Mademoiselle Favre who had married George Lapiere,
and whose son Jean was born on 3 September 1736. The child's godfather was Jean Paget, who may have been related to Thomas Paget the
tobacconist.

Urban Entrepreneurs:
An Embarrassment of Riches

While it is sometimes a treacherous exercise to rely on surnames alone
(some French names might be those of resident French Catholics; and
French-sounding names might actually be Anglo-Norman) enough data
is available to establish the French Protestant element as a sufficiently
substantial portion of the city's business sector.

Among the small businessmen of Dublin we find, for example: Joseph
Aget, bookseller, trading under the *Golden Hand* in Capel Street; Jean
Guiot, grocer, at the sign of the *Three Sugar Loaves* at the corner of
Mary's and Capel Streets; the perriwigmakers Louis Reignier and Pierre
Mazotin at the *Sign of Hand and Peruche* on Castle Street; drawing master
Guillaume Briand at the *Raphael's Head* on Aungier Street; and jeweler
Jean Letablere at the *Gilded Cup* on Francis Street.

Family reconstructions for other Huguenot residents of Dublin through
church records, property deeds, and other documentation exists, and may
be the subject for a more specialized volume, but enough has been

revealed, certainly, to refute stereotypical assumptions concerning the true nature of Dublin's Huguenots.

Statistics may be compiled for such social professions/occupations/situations as can so far be ascertained, but these are readily subject to revision. The categories and names are undoubtedly incomplete and in some cases overlap; certainly they must admit of a potential for considerable leeway as new research will continue to clarify the situation. Even if given these shortcomings, a much more diverse and dynamic Huguenot population than has previously been acknowledged is confirmed. During the 1692–1745 period there can be detected within the Huguenot Refuge at least: 290 noble houses; 68 merchants; fourteen surgeons; six physicians; five grocers; seven shoemakers; eleven tailors; one lawyer; three bakers; four wool combers; four hat-maker; two silk weavers; four saddlers; one cooper; one church porter; one ironmonger; three printers or engravers; two clothiers; one armourer; one button maker; one glazier; six watch makers; one cabinet maker; four schoolmasters; three sailors; one blacksmith; three leather tawers; seven wigmakers; one notary; three masons; one sea captain; one serge weaver; ten goldsmiths; one jewelry merchant; two weavers; one gardener; one linen weaver; four glovers; five innkeepers; three hosiers; two skinners; one pewterer; one sugar refiner; one coachman; two founders; two stationers; one cutler; three gunsmiths; one sword cutler; one organ builder; one drawing teacher; two linen drapers; two tobacconists; one milliner; five booksellers; three woolen drapers; four mercers; two lace-makers; one perfumer; one stay maker; and one haberdasher.

The overall impression, undoubtedly a misleading one, is that of bustle and prosperity; there is little evidence of real failure or destitution. However, one can not escape the impression that life's negatives intruded upon the Huguenot community as readily as others. Two individual whose surnames might indicate Huguenot origin are noted in the Poor Lists of the Dublin City Workhouse. Jeanne (?) Dugatt and Richard Boyers are both described as being "a foole".

When the French provincial and regional breakdowns for the French Calvinists of Dublin are concerned for this same period 1692–1745 extant records indicate that the most numerous contingent came from Languedoc (77 families), followed by: Saintonge (66); Guyenne (43); Poitou (20); Normandy (18); Dauphiné (16); Switzerland (15); Flandre (10); Isle de France (9); Béarn (6); Brittany (6); Orleanais (4); Lorraine (4); Angoumois (3); Picardy (3); two each from Blesois; Comte de Foix; Anjou; Champagne; Touraine; and Provence, and one each from: Alsace; Limousin; Burgundy; and Berry.

As far as Dublin's Huguenots were concerned the 1740s witnessed in large measure the passing of a generation, the first generation of the

Ruvignac Refuge. From 1735 to 1749 at least ninety-six of the more or less noteworthy individuals among those who had arrived in droves during the decade 1692–1701 had been laid to rest. On 17 October 1745 David Digues Latouche the Elder was suddenly stricken, perhaps by apoplexy, while at prayer in the Chapel Royal at Dublin Castle, and died soon after being taken home to Castle Street. That same year, on 11 November, the Huguenot prelate Gabriel Jacques Mathurin was elected to be Dean of St. Patrick's Cathedral in succession to Jonathan Swift. Each event, in its own particular fashion, signaled the respective eclipse of the elder generation, and the incipient transformation of the Huguenot element into an integral part of the Anglo-Irish establishment. A second generation of French Protestants in Ireland, for whom France was becoming an ancestral memory, and whose perspectives on Ireland, France and Anglicization differed from those of their parents, was ready to assume direction over the life of Dublin's Huguenot communities.

References

Primary sources

British Library: Additional Ms. 9718.
Dublin Registry of Deeds: Ms. Deeds for Dublin, 1708–38.
Huguenot Society of London-Quarto Series. Vol. VII, XIV, XVIII, XIX, XLI.
National Library of Ireland Manuscripts: 76, 104, 3019, 4126, 8007, 8341, Microfilm n. 2976 p. 2597.
Royal Irish Academy Archives: Dumont

Ms.Books/pamphlets

Anonymous. *Hibernia Notitia.*

Secondary sources

Agnew, David Carnegie. *Henri de Ruvigny*, pp. 36, 46, 225.
Craig, Maurice. *Dublin, 1660–1860*, pp. 20, 101–10.
Deyon, Solange. *Du Loyalisme au Refus*, pp. 9, 27–8, 92, 96–7, 159–60.
Gerard, Frances. *Picturesque Dublin*, pp. 60.
Hylton, Raymond Pierre. "Elites and Assimilation: the question of leadership within the Dublin *Corps du Refuge*, 1662–1740" in Vigne, Randolph and Littleton, Charles, *From Strangers to Citizens*, pp. 427–34, expounds upon certain leadership issues, including Galway's role.
Fontaine, Jacques. *Memoire d'une Famille Huguenote: Victime de la Revocation de L'Edit de Nantes*, p. 290.
Le Fanu, T. P. in Lawlor, Hugh Jackson, *Fasti*, pp. 291, 294.
Le Fanu, T. P. "The Huguenot Churches in Dublin" in *PHSL*, Vol. VIII, pt. 1, pp. 33–4, 112.
Le Fanu, T. P. & W. H. J. *Memoire of the Le Fanu Family.* Privately printed 1924, pp. 27, 32, 38.

Lee, Grace Lawless. *The Huguenot Settlements in Ireland*, pp. 113.

Ligou, Daniel. *Le Protestantisme en France*, pp. 74–5.

Luthy, Herbert. *La Banque Protestante en France*, Vol. I, pp. 28–33.

Maxwell, Constantia. *Dublin Under the Georges*, p. 116.

Pezet, Maurice. *L'Épopee des Camisards*, p. 83.

Smiles, Samuel. *Huguenots in England and Ireland*, pp. 345–8, 354–5, 420.

Vigne, Randolph "The Good Lord Galway" in *PHSGBI*, Vol. XXIV, no. 6, pp. 534–45.

6

"Fortress Ireland", the Huguenot Earl, and the "Hinterlands": Lingering Questions

"By the rivers of Babylon, there we sat down, yea we wept, when we remembered Zion.

We hanged our harps upon the willows in the midst thereof. For there they that carried us away captive required of us a song, and they that wasted us required of us mirth, saying 'Sing us one of the songs of Zion.' How shall we sing the Lord's song in a strange land?"

Psalms 137: 1–4.

"Fortress Ireland" proved to be neither success nor failure. The Duke of Berwick's invasion scheme never materialized. Whether this was due more to the presence of the Earl of Galway's garrison colonies or to the fact that Louis XIV had other fish to fry may be debated but, in view of the *Roi Soleille's* prior dismissal of the Irish theatre of operations as a mere sideshow, the latter assumption is far more likely. And as the Grand Monarch breathed his last at the end of 72 years on the throne, the threat of invasion receded. As Anglo-French tensions eased, a semi-official *entente cordiale* shepherded by Cardinal Fleury and Sir Robert Walpole developed and endured into the 1740s, by which time the rationale for "Fortress Ireland" had been reduced to irrelevance, and its authors long departed.

Many of the écuyer families and their descendants stayed on in the areas they colonized in Ireland for a greater or lesser period of time, and these are usually well-documented, as is invariably the case with the upper echelons of society. But as a general rule when we get past the two major strongholds of "Fortress Ireland", the problems of verifying details as to who the Huguenots were, and precisely where and how substantially they settled and contributed, are much more challenging. The Huguenots were very conscious of Biblical paradigms, and Psalm 137 was one of those scriptural texts that struck closest to home. But whereas the exiled Jews in the Psalm were centered in Babylon, the Huguenot situation was more complex: instead of one "Babylon" there now existed multiple "Babylons" in widely-scattered locations – many in regions where road networks and communications were notoriously inadequate. To maintain a communal cohesiveness as a *Corps du Réfuge* under such circumstances proved well-nigh impossible; and this time, unlike the situation with the Jews, there would be no King Cyrus to facilitate a return to the Holy Land. It may therefore be not so much a question of an Irish *Corps du Réfuge* falling apart, but it may perhaps more accurately be stated that it never had a chance to fully realize itself in the first place.

It is *a propos* the Huguenots beyond Dublin and Portarlington that a legendary gloss has endured most tenaciously, primarily because of the current scarcity of documentation.

Pitifully few church records, either in the original, or in transcript, have survived. Correspondingly, there is a genuine dearth of studies, and some of those which exist are of more-or-less uncertain quality. In the 19th & early 20th centuries there were articles by Thomas Gimlette on Waterford; by Charles De La Cherois Purdon on Lisburn; by several authors in the *Journal of the Cork Historical and Archaeological Society*; references in Smiles, Agnew and Lee (the latter of which remains definitive for the so-called "minor colonies"); and of course those eternal "lists" of surnames which have sometimes proven to be more misleading than helpful. There is at present much anecdotal material that needs to be winnowed out. A great deal more in the way of meticulous scholarship is needed here. Cork (David Dickson and Alicia St. Leger) and Lisburn (W. H. Crawford, Angelique Day, and E. Joyce Best) have at least been well served in recent years – but this has pretty well been the sum total of work lavished on the "hinterlands" communities.

Galway as Lord Justice, 1697–1701

The Earl of Galway served two terms as Lord Justice of Ireland: 1697–1701 and 1715–17. It was during the first of these when, backed by his patron, King William, he had the power and opportunity to make the most measurable impact. It was the failure to complete the grand scheme that he and his suzerain had envisioned that stunted the advance of "Fortress Ireland" and has thus far left those Huguenots beyond Portarlington as historical "orphans". That which was left unsaid, what was not realized, what has remained unfinished – these are often as significant as what may actually have occurred.

Like all historical triumphs and failures, the entire onus cannot be placed on a single individual; but any avenue to understanding what went awry must travel through certain key personages. There was some interesting work on the ambitious Huguenot colonization strategy of the 1690s, but this was carried out over a century ago by the Baronne de Chambrier in volume III of the *Proceedings of the Huguenot Society of London*, and there has been no sustained study on the Irish dimension of the subject since then. The project itself was to be highly ambitious in its scope, was to include Vaudois (Waldensian) as well as strictly Huguenot settlers, and in terms of sheer numbers, envisioned at some 3,000 individuals. For a variety of reasons, the results fell far short of expectations. Perhaps its aims were set unrealistically high from the outset. When the colonization project failed to achieve much of what had been originally envisioned, there was certainly a more than ample amount of blame to be passed around. However, this setback did not deter Galway's standing in Royal favour, or his advancement.

On 12 May 1697 he was promoted to the rank of Lieutenant-General of the army, the title "Earl of Galway" was officially conferred, heraldic arms were drawn up, and the newly-minted Earl took position as one of what would be a trio of Lords Justice of Ireland on 31 May 1697. He was definitely the most proactive of the three Lords Justice of presided over Irish affairs at any one time: Lord Edward Villiers (brother of William III's mistress), who was soon made Earl of Jersey, was more often than not away from Ireland on diplomatic assignments; his replacement (18 May 1699) Charles Paulet, Marquis of Winchester – soon to become Duke of Bolton – seemed content to follow Lord Galway's initiative in most matters. Nor did Archbishop/Lord Justice Narcissus Marsh have any major disagreement with Galway, though his successor (23 August 1699) Charles, Earl of Berkeley did, on at least one significant occasion.

As with all political figures who held such an extensively responsible role, the Earl of Galway's career is tinged with controversy that has survived, or even intensified, through the passage of centuries. Hagiographers and detractors existed then, and their words have impacted into the present day. The Huguenot Earl has been variously described in terms of being a spectacularly successful administrator, an unscrupulous operative, a bigoted persecutor, a naïve neophyte, a farsighted and unsung statesman, a benevolent and patriarchal figure whose good intentions were undone by circumstances beyond his control, a would-be Strafford to William III's Charles I, a dangerous, over-mighty subject or potential turncoat, "an extraordinary man in every respect". There have, unfortunately, only been two scholarly, impartial studies of the Earl of Galway in his governing capacity, but those are of sterling quality: Patrick Kelly's "Lord Galway and the Penal Laws" (in *Huguenots*

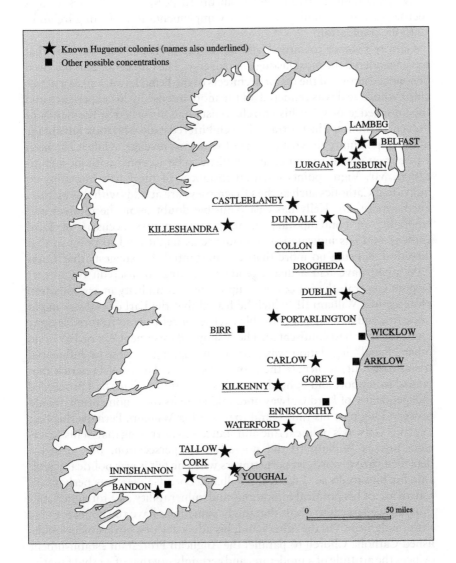

The Ruvignac Huguenot colonies

and Ireland: Anatomy of an Emigration), and Randolph Vigne's "The Good Lord Galway" (in *Proceedings of the Huguenot Society of Great Britain and Ireland,* xxiv, 6). Only the latter, however, attempts to assess Galway's administrative career from broad perspective; Patrick Kelly's focuses strictly upon his role in policy implementation effecting Ireland's Catholic population.

Galway's stance towards Catholicism has perhaps been the issue that has engendered the most lasting controversy. The Huguenot Earl has been denounced as one of the major architects of the Penal Laws, and as a persecutor whose zeal was rendered all the more intense by his experience and the knowledge of what his co-religionists had absorbed at the hands of French Catholics. The portrait of an embittered exile who took advantage of the opportunity to wreak a sort of vicarious revenge, while it has been a persistent one, is too patently simplistic to be accepted without qualification. Mr. Vigne points out that instances of the Earl's humanity to individual Catholics such as the O'Dempseys are at odds with this picture. Furthermore, Dr. Kelly has cast plausible doubt upon the motives and credibility of contemporary or near-contemporary accusers of Lord Galway and has indicated such evidence as might tend to point in that direction as being no more than circumstantial. He suggests that Louis XIV might have had a dual agenda in seeking to discredit his former Depute-General: that of covering-up his own complicity in assassination plots against William III (which he feared that the Earl of Galway might unearth), and of having a plausible excuse for refusing to restore Ruvigny estates that he had confiscated. The Bishops' Banishment Act of 1697 and other "Penal" legislation was part of an ongoing process by influential Irish Protestants to negate the provisions of the Treaty of Limerick that tended to support and uphold the rights of Catholics. This had proceeded independently of Lord Galway and, taking on its own momentum, would proceed long past his time – and that of King William. Perhaps this best explains Galway's political role and stance – as mirroring that of his sovereign: just as William III did not advocate persecution, but turned a detached gaze towards its perpetrators when he felt it was politically realistic for him to do so. Like King William, Lord Galway was perhaps all too aware of his political limitations and vulnerability as a foreigner, and thus allowed much to occur that might sometimes have run counter to his better judgment. On the other hand, his advocacy of a government-established Catholic Church to parallel the Anglican Protestant establishment evinces the attitude of a moderate, and certainly not that of a rabid fanatic. What Professor Kelly accomplished was Galway's exoneration as far as being an active persecutor of Irish Catholics. However, the possible culpability involved in being a passive agent for persecution (a point raised, but not totally resolved by Dr. Kelly) remains at issue.

Allegations that the Earl of Galway's efforts on behalf of his co-religionists went beyond merely planting them into sheltered refuges in Ireland and had as its ultimate goal the establishment of a Huguenot-controlled "statelet" capable of playing a major strategic/political role are still just that – unsubstantiated allegations. However, contemporaries did view the rising power of William III's foreign-born favorites with some degree of anxiety; this would certainly hold true for such a well-positioned satrap as the Earl of Galway. Regardless of what true intentions might have been, very often it is the perceptions, accurate or otherwise, that have the most bearing on the outcome of events. If certain elements had been predisposed to suspect the grand design of a Williamite coup with Lord Galway as a key player, nothing would have swayed them from this belief, and "Fortress Ireland" would have further confirmed them in their own suspicions.

Of more substantial import are the accusations that he used his office to suggest changes to the pension rolls on the Irish establishment to favor his former officers. He did do this; Dr. J. G. Simms believed that this had been the main reason for his appointment as Lord Justice. It is, however, extremely difficult to see how this could be construed as wrongdoing. It was undoubtedly part of the duties of the Lords Justice to be concerned with the pension rolls, and one cannot impeach his right to provide whatever input he deemed necessary. Nor was he the sole arbiter, the process for implementation and approval went beyond him. There is in fact ample grounds for belief that in this, as in other matters, he was complying with the King's wishes or directives. William III had often expressed his desire to provide for his retired veterans to the greatest possible degree.

Pressure from Parliament had forced the King to completely dissolve the Huguenot regiments; he had hoped to keep at least some of the veterans in Ireland as a permanent, active-duty garrison. What was to be done with these veterans, and those who had already been retired to half-pay since 1692? In Britain the political backlash against the admission of further refugees (particularly those with military expertise) was becoming intense, and the government was under pressure to devise another solution. By the time the Irish establishment list had been revised, augmented and otherwise hammered into final form on 17 September 1700, it is clear that a great deal of political influence and leverage had been exerted by the Earl of Galway in order to obtain the maximum favour for his co-religionists. Certain formulae recur in cases where Lord Justice Galway makes a petition on a refugee veteran's behalf. More often, petitions were addressed to William Blathwayt, Secretary of the War's Office, but on occasion to Richard Cardinnal, also at the War Office. Such appeals for exceptional treatment were often placed in the context of emphasizing an individual's past valor under fire. There were at least 83 such petitions lodged during the time that the list was formulated (from July 1698 to September 1700). There were, however, other instances where the plea was addressed to the War Office through reasons of poverty, wounds and incapacity, past sufferings at the hands of French Catholics, family considerations, social position, exchanges of pensions between comrades-in-arms, or a straightforward sacrifice of a pension in order to assist a friend or relation.

What sort of alterations were effected through Lord Galway's entreaties on the pension lists, and do they actually demonstrate overriding or unreasonable favouritism, as the Earl's detractors would have it? On occasion it was recommended that two veterans be allowed to exchange pensions. Claude Dubochet, who had a Dutch pension and desired to settle in Ireland wanted to trade it off against the spot on the Irish establishment held by Elie Dusaux, who wanted to reside in Holland. Lieutenant Guy de St. Auban also wished to retire to the Netherlands to join his aged mother by exchanging his pension with the Dutch bounty of Charles de Rocheblave, whose brother Henri held Church of Ireland benefices, having been named Vicar of Narraghmore in the Diocese of Glendalough in 1696, and Vicar of Usk in 1698. Colonel Frederick Hackbreist, who preferred to remain in Switzerland, was willing to surrender the pension he would have received had he chosen to settle in Ireland to Cornet Gedeon de Castelfranc "out of friendship, without any consideration". The same personal reasons apparently motivated Peter Ormond's quitting his half pay for the benefit of Captain Pierre Raboteau, and Count Maurice's relinquishing his to Lieutenant Jean Montledier.

Ensign François Delormes left his place on the establishment rolls in favour of a woman, Esther Falgueroles. Certain veterans were nominated for slots inclusion in the list, or for augmentation of their *per diem* allowances for reasons of past sufferings and disabilities. Lieutenant Paul Pineau had been forced to quit active service in 1693 because of age and infirmity but his squadron (Galway's Horse) had nevertheless allowed him surreptitiously to continue on full pay. Lieutenant Japhet de Puichenin is described as being a very poor man with a large family and Galway suggested that he receive an additional sixpence from the portion originally allocated to the recently-deceased Ensign Jean de Valada. Ensign Pierre Dorignac is introduced as a nephew of Lieutenant-Colonel Samuel de Boisrond "who is unable to maintain him. It would be an act of charity to allow him one shilling (*per diem*)". Jacques Mouvray "a very indigent man, old and sickly" is recommended for a further sixpence, as is Jacob Monjaux. Jeremie Vialas; Michel Le Comte ("disabled, twenty-two wounds in one fight, and cannot be without a servant . . . "); Isaac de La Garde; and Gabriel Foronce (for whom it was simply thought appropriate to add sixpence in keeping with his possession of a reformed captain's commission) were all designated as special cases. There are particularly touching examples of fatherly concern on the Lord Justice's part, for individuals, or their families, who had fallen under distressing circumstances.

Some were put forward for special consideration for having been held prisoner in France and thus having endured considerable anguish because of their faith: Jean La Roque, Durand de Therond, Etienne Saurin, Jean La Salle, and Pierre Bordemarque. The last was a native of Dunkirk and was singled out for being a released galley slave, which within the context of the Huguenot dispersion was viewed as a mark of honor. Others were set apart for favoured status because they fell within an "inner circle" of officers who were on intimate terms with their commander, and/or with important courtiers, and/or King William himself. Isaac Dumont de Bostaquet is the best-known of these "insiders". Others included: Louis La Malquiere "Monsieur de La Malquiere est bien connue du roi, avancement merite"); André de St. Philibert ("de fort bonne maison"); Daniel Maucos who was sponsored by Lord Albemarle; Joseph Blancard by Pierre Jurieu; and François Gaillon by General John Churchill.

Contrary to any charges of political manipulation, Galway's pleas and suggestions bear the stamp of pragmatic justice, flexibility towards individual circumstances, loyalty to those to whom he felt a semi-paternal connection, and – again – a genuine sense of humanity.

Lord Galway's colonizing zeal seems to have reached beyond Ireland. In 1700 he was involved – to what extent is uncertain – in at least two expeditions of Huguenots to the New World. One of these was a project for dispatching a group of officers along with "500 men sent by the King" under the supervision of a certain Mr. Arshfield, described as an "honest gentleman", to colonize New York. This expedition was first mooted on 16 May 1700, but by 13 July of that same year had still not embarked. There is no further mention of the New York scheme and what might have come of it. However, there is a concrete connection between Lord Galway and a successful 1700 colonizing voyage to Virginia led by Charles de Sailly, who had acted in concert with the Baron De Virazel as the Huguenot Earl's agent during the 1690s, had perhaps dwelled for a while at Dublin and Portarlington, and had served on the Dublin committee to coordinate and implement the planting of refugees who had fled from France via the Swiss cantons. De Sailly and the Marquis de La Muce definitely brought Huguenot families to Manakintown, Virginia; just to the west of present-day Richmond. One reference also implies a possible involvement in the settling of Huguenot families in Boston, Massachusetts.

During the final two years of his first posting as Lord Justice, Galway's initial zest appeared to have gradually paled into disillusionment. His fledgling political knowledge of the Irish and English systems of patronage, pressure groups and special interests certainly hampered his effectiveness at implementing lasting policy reforms. The Prior Controversy, which largely boiled down to another attempt at advancing one of his Huguenot retainers might have been the decisive factor. In a letter dated 13–23 June 1699, Galway wrote to Matthew Prior, then Chief Secretary for Ireland, first expressing his delight that Mr. Prior was coming from France to England to go directly into the King's service and, secondly, dismissing him from his position as Chief Secretary, berating Prior for having failed to fulfill his official tasks in Ireland. There was apparently more that lay behind Galway's actions than his official explanation indicated: it was mooted that he intended to move the Assistant Secretary, Humphrey May, into Prior's position, and elevate his own personal secretary, the Huguenot physician Élie Bouhéreau, into May's place as Assistant Secretary. Dumfounded, and initially taken aback, Prior fought back fiercely to preserve his tenure of office, appealing both to former Lord Justice Jersey, and to the Earl of Portland, pleading that it had been through the King's orders, and not by his own choice, that he had been stationed for such a length of time in Paris and that the Earl of Galway, who was only one among three Lords Justice, had acted arbitrarily in not consulting with his two colleagues and had subjected him to "hard usage". Prior then went on to very deftly cite precedent for Irish office-holders residing outside of Ireland itself; thus demonstrating that the practice was not unusual, nor was his case unique. Having effectively weakened the legal foundations for the Lord Justice's actions, Prior then repeated the accusation that Galway was seizing upon a chance to accommodate his co-religionist, Bouhéreau. Prior's argument convinced Lord Jersey, who took up the Secretary's cause and promised to intervene with Lord Albemarle. Notwithstanding, the Huguenot Earl remained adamant in his position that Prior, as an absentee holder of two offices, could not feasibly exercise the function of First Secretary of Ireland. The squabble was then blown into a political controversy which drew others into its vortex – Lord Justice Bolton sided with Galway while Lord Justice Berkeley and Secretary William Blathwayt supported Prior's claims. A King's order reinstating Prior was not immediately acted upon by Galway, who insisted on verifying its authenticity. The dispute became increasingly rancorous as Galway continued to insist upon his position even after the transmission of a second Royal order dated 19–29 September 1699. The delaying tactics ultimately paid off for the Earl of Galway, who was able to persuade King William to reverse his stance. It was finally on 24 November 1699 that the matter was seemingly resolved with the Monarch's dismissal of Prior, and the appointment of May as his replacement. Though no documentary confirmation has yet been unearthed to support this, the likelihood is that Bouhereau was indeed advanced into May's former office of Assistant Secretary. It has been suggested – initially by Mrs. Muriel McCarthy, Keeper of Archbishop Marsh's Library – that Dean Jonathan Swift's ties of friendship with Matthew Prior might have immediately occasioned his famous and trenchant observations on Lord Galway's character: *"A deceitful hypocritical factious knave – a damnable hypocrite of no religion."*

July of 1700 marked a downturn in the Earl's overall health and vigor when he had to endure an extremely painful onset of the gout, and he would never be the same from that time on. His physical condition sapped his energies, would sideline him for lengthy periods of time, and might arguably have impacted upon his judgment (a case can certainly be made in this regard over his ultimately disastrous strategy and military reverses in the Iberian Theatre of the War of the Spanish Succession). His condition of debility would worsen, much aggravated undoubtedly by his horrific battle wounds that cost him an eye, and an arm. Already stretched by the Prior Affair, Galway's energy and morale were further strained by the fall of the Whig Junto with which he was affiliated, and the subsequent lessening of influence at Westminster, as evinced in the Act of Resumption's withdrawal of his Land Forfeiture (and, some would argue, the gutting of his power base in Ireland). To what extent his departure from office in April of 1701 was a resignation, and to what extent it was an ouster, is a debatable point. Insomuch as King William himself had had his authority curtailed and policies repudiated by electoral and parliamentary maneuvering, and as much of the Earl's own power depended on Royal favor, a change of regime at Dublin Castle would have, in any case, proven to be an inevitability. On the other hand, there is some evidence of weariness and despondency on Lord Galway's part. He seemed genuinely relieved at the prospect of Lord Shrewsbury coming to Ireland to take up the post of Lord-Lieutenant. It was not to be, for Shrewsbury pleaded ill health and never made the journey; and Lord Galway's tenure of office was necessarily prolonged for several months.

Galway's Subsequent Career

The circumstances would never again be so favorable; by the time that Galway was called back to the post of Lord Justice, the moment had passed. Time had in effect run out on the idea of a controlling Huguenot presence in Ireland. As stated in Chapter 5, the Huguenot Earl was involved very little with Irish affairs from 1702 to 1715, at a time when the French Protestant population burgeoned and expanded. He would still occasionally intercede on his co-religionists' behalf, at one stage beseeching the Second Duke of Ormond for continued consideration for Bouhéreau on Queen Anne's new Irish establishment (King William's list had allocated Dr. Bouhéreau two hundred pounds *per annum*).

Then came the catastrophic Iberian campaign of the War of the Spanish Succession. The Earl had by then become identified with the Marlborough/Godolphin war faction within the Whig Party and when military reverses and a general public malaise led to the faction's downfall and the triumph of the Tories under Robert Harley, he was caught up in the web of political recrimination. Though his disgrace was light, when compared to others, and he did not suffer a term of imprisonment, he had to endure the humiliation of appearing before the House of Lords to answer questions relating to his handling of the debacle at Almanza, and was twice censured by the Tory majority. This done, however, the harassment eased and upon the succession of the Hanoverian King George I in 1714, Galway was restored to favour (q.v.: Chapter 5).

In March of 1715, rumors circulated that the Stuart Pretender (James Edward, son of James II and Maria of Modena) planned to make an attempt to reclaim the throne. Ireland was seen as a potential landfall and on 27 August 1715 the Earl of Galway was persuaded to come out of retirement to serve another term as Lord Justice, partnering this time with the young Charles Fitzroy, Duke of Grafton. The desirability of someone of Lord Galway's military stature and first-hand knowledge of Ireland being at the helm (in fact the person most qualified to, if need be, activate "Fortress Ireland") was obvious for all to see. On 6 September 1715 the anticipated Jacobite Rising, initiated by the Earl of Mar, broke out in Scotland. The rebellion was brought to a head in this manner not by premeditated strategem but by Mar's personal political misfortunes, and thus caught the Jacobite émigré community unawares. Would a variation of Berwick's plan for landings in Ireland have been attempted if it had not been for Mar's precipitous actions? A descent from Scotland to Ireland was feared and it is certain that news of Louis XIV's death (31 August) and the impeachment of the Second Duke of Ormond contributed to the general sense of alarm. In the event, nothing drastic occurred in Ireland. Galway and Grafton dispatched troops to Ulster and to the Duke of Argyll in Scotland; Jacobite propaganda was widely disseminated in Dublin; and the Lords Justice were apprehensive over the general dearth of arms and ammunition around the Irish capital. Galway, as he had before, still continued to work at securing special benefits for his retired officers, but the verve and energy were largely spent, and he would retire – this time permanently – after less than two years.

It is incumbent upon all historians to make at least a cursory evaluation on the legacy of such pivotal individuals as the Earl of Galway. What we don't often admit is how difficult it sometimes is to tread the narrow path between placing such a person on a pedestal, while avoiding the equally pernicious fallacy of iconoclasm. The Huguenot Earl was a statesman who possessed the essence of greatness – that much cannot be doubted. Not being native to Ireland, and even being less-than-familiar with the intricacies of British politics, he could not have been expected to, in four short years, have attained the level of effectiveness of, say, the Dukes of Ormond. If at times he seemed uncertain or indecisive it may well have been the result of this unfamiliarity, and a desire to avoid disastrous blundering through hasty decisions – he cannot be tagged as being naive. But the evidence indicates that he was conscientious in serving his adopted people, that he exhibited a remarkable work ethic even during his months of infirmity, and that he put forth the utmost effort within the limits imposed on him by often trying situations. Even a critical contemporary observer like John Dunton, who never hesitated to speak his mind, attests to his sincere piety and diligence and informs us that, every morning, the Lord Justice would go to pray at the north side chapel that lay within the Dublin Castle complex and would then receive petitioners "listening with all the sweetness and readiness that the petitioners can wish for in so great a man".

But Where Were They?

When we get into what might so-to-speak be the "hinterlands" of Huguenot settlement there is a disparity of opinion as to precisely which locations can legitimately be so classified – a situation further aggravated by tantalizingly sparse clues and stray references. At this juncture in time, it may be possible to get as many opinions on this as there are scholars or enthusiasts. There are, as has been noted, some who hold that there were Pre-Ormondite Huguenot settlements in Ireland, but no records support this. One can thus discount totally the Rochelle Street merchant's "ghetto" in Dublin; Sir Henry Sidney's shadowy Flemish plantation at Swords; and the Earl of Strafford's phantasmagoric Ulster weavers. Only the supposition of the presence of a community in Cork has some slight foundation, given some long-standing maritime contacts with Aunis-Saintonge, Brittany and Normandy, and James Fitzmaurice of Desmond's intriguing statement of 12 July 1569 (see epigraph at the beginning of Chapter 1). However, even this is heavily qualified in view of the ambiguous nature and context of the quote, and the fact that no other documentation supports the existence of a substantial number of Huguenots in Cork for over a century thereafter.

During the Early & Late Ormondite periods there is some greater-to-lesser evidence for 6–7 concentrations of Huguenot settler/refugees:

Dublin, Chapelizod, Carrick-on-Suir, Clonmel, Waterford, Wexford and, much more doubtfully, Enniscorthy. Outside of the capital, however, the numbers seem to have barely been consequential and, with the possible exception of Waterford, the colonies were short-lived. Chapelizod had faded by 1677, and the two other industrially-based centers at Carrick and Clonmel appear to have experienced an even briefer existence (or perhaps not really to have gotten off the ground at all). It is known that Dr. Jacques Du Brois de Fontaine had a hand in attempts to procure settlers for the Carrick colony, as might have had Jacques Hierome, who would become a resident and vicar, and ultimately died there in 1682. Wexford in 1684 with 10 Huguenot families composed of 42 individuals seemed to have the potential of developing into a thriving maritime outpost, but there is no subsequent mention of the settlement and all indications are that it had broken up within as little as a decade.

It was the Ruvignac wave that brought by far the greatest numbers, but here there is even more that is open to debate. Some twenty-eight locales have been identified as Ruvignac "Huguenot settlements", evidence of the veracity of their claims differ substantially. If we were to accept the legitimacy of all of them, the total number of Huguenot colonies, when the Early Ormondite, Late Ormondite, and Ruvignac are combined, and duplication is taken into account, would stand at thirty-three.

The "canonical" list of Ruvignac communities put forward by Grace Lawless Lee includes: Dublin, Portarlington, Cork, Lisburn, Waterford, Carlow, Kilkenny, Lurgan, Lambeg, Belfast, Youghal, Tallow, Bandon, Innishannon, Killeshandra, Collon, Castleblayney, Wicklow and Dundalk. Other individuals, local lore and legend, or documentary footprints might justify the inclusion of: Arklow, Birr, Drogheda, Kinsale, Gorey, Gowran, Counties Limerick/Kerry/Tipperary, Waringstown and Donnybrook.

Dublin and Portarlington were the most substantial, and best-documented; Cork, Lisburn and Waterford would fall into the second tier, though since we are without parish records and there are substantial gaps in the municipal records, the researcher is at a marked disadvantage. The others range from most probable (Carlow, Youghal, Castleblayney, Dundalk), to probable/unproven (Kilkenny, Lurgan, Lambeg, Waringstown), to legendary-speculative (Killeshandra, Donnybrook, Belfast, Birr, Gorey, Wicklow, Enniscorthy, Gowran, Kinsale), to the very-likely mythical (Arklow, Drogheda, County Limerick), to very late examples which do not strictly qualify for the designation of "Ruvignac" (Collon, Inishannon). Distinct Huguenot churches existed at: Dublin (4), Cork (2), Portarlington, Lisburn, Carlow, and Waterford. Certain other centers are known or believed to have been served by French ministers who perhaps held services either at Anglican Churches of Dissenter

Meeting Houses: Dundalk, Wexford, Kilkenny, Innishannon, Arklow (?), Castleblayney (?). Wexford, a Late Ormondite cluster of families, is considered here because it may well have prolonged its existence into the Ruvignac years. Much depends, too, on how one defines a refugee "community". Is population the only measure? What of the existence of an independent church or congregation? And for how long a time-period was it necessary for such a community to exist in order to be thus designated? It seems certain that many of these purported "communities" could only "pass muster" as such if the minimum definition of fifty individuals in a proximate area were reduced. Wexford and Kilkenny definitely seem to have been in this category. This was the criteria used at the time for determining whether or not a group of French Protestants might require a place of worship, or at least the services of an independent French pastor. Documentation is a recurring problem. When we examine some purported instances of Huguenot settlement we are sometimes left with cheesecloth pieces of evidence so thin that we must for the moment only take note of them and strongly recommend that further investigative work needs to be undertaken to determine if there is any substance to these claims and, if so, what truth can be separated from hearsay. The various listings of Huguenot names, compiled painstakingly by early amateur antiquarians, and utilized by genealogists, have often times proven to be misleading. The problem here is that, while these lists do include many surnames which can be verified to be of genuine Huguenot origin, there are many others that are quite doubtful. The value of these lists is limited by the fact that these antiquarians tended to include any surname which seemed to be ever-so remotely French, rarely resorting to independent documentation to corroborate these claims. Thus we have to qualify possible errors arising from 17th–18th century vagaries in spelling, surnames of Anglo-Norman origin, or persistent but often misleading local folklore and tradition. Separating the tares from the wheat after so many generations and so much in the way of destruction of primary source material is a daunting prospect for any researcher. Because of the prestige attached to anything that can be classified as "Huguenot" the tendency has been for claimants to be inclusive rather than the other way around. Until further concrete research has been done, the more cautious approach would seem to be best.

A separate and nagging factor is the fact that many Huguenot settlements were short-lived; the French Calvinist colonizers having moved on to (presumably) greener pastures and thus offering little opportunity for bequeathing much in the way of tangible evidence for their presence. Generally, the centers whose port facilities had enjoyed a long-standing prior connection to overseas trade networks (Cork, Waterford, Dublin) fared much better than industrial/utopian based concentrations and

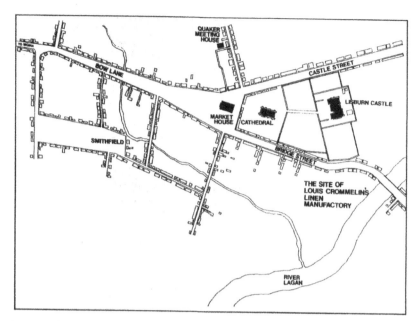

Conjectural Map of Lisburn, *c.* 1700. Courtesy of the Irish Linen Center and Lisburn Museum.

"Printers at Work". From a Lisburn Museum publication. Copyright Lisburn Borough Council.

Louis Crommelin as found on gravestone.

Waterford: The Bishop's Palace on the Mall. It was completed under the auspices of the Huguenot prelate, Archbishop Richard Chenevix, a descendent of Williamite military veterans. Photograph courtesy of Mrs. Petra Coffey, Newtownmountkennedy, County Wicklow, Ireland.

Waterford: Tray of traditional "Blaas", a specialty of the region. It is believed that the Huguenots introduced the soft bread rolls that are unique to the Waterford area. Though the origin of the name is subject to debate, many attest that it derived from the French "blanc". Photograph courtesy of Mrs. Petra Coffey, Newtownmountkennedy, County Wicklow, Ireland.

Cork: Site of the French Cemetery: Located at Carey's Lane the lot enclosed behind this wall and as yet not publicly accessible is what remains of the French Church burial ground in use from 1733 to 1901. It is only one of two (the other being Merrion Row in Dublin) nonconformist Huguenot cemeteries in Europe and is the focus of energetic preservation efforts by the Friends of the Huguenot Cemetery, Cork. Photograph courtesy of Mrs. Petra Coffey, Newtownmountkennedy.

Holy Ghost Friary, Waterford: The Medieval Franciscan Friary (also known as "Greyfriars") housed the Huguenot community's French Church from 1693 to 1819. Photograph courtesy of Mrs. Petra Coffey, Newtownmountkennedy, County Wicklow, Ireland.

inland garrison colonies (with the major exception of Portarlington). A natural rather than artificially-planned economic basis seemed, in the end, to offer a more solid avenue for success.

Apart from the settlements in Ulster (primarily those situated along the Lagan River Valley at Lisburn, Lurgan & Lambeg), Huguenot settlement fanned out in an almost exclusively southeastern radius from Dublin; and some of this was surely the product of deliberate encouragement on the part of those who fostered the "Fortress Ireland" strategy. Most of these centers were urban-based, in harmony with the background of the majority of Huguenot immigrants; the purely agricultural settlements were those that fared among the most poorly (Castleblayney, Innishannon).

In the case of Arklow, we are limited to no more than a local tradition alluded to by Dr. John De Courcy Ireland (this tradition may possibly derive from the period 1685–8, when Moses Viridet left French Patrick's to become Church of Ireland rector at Arklow); and barely much more from Grace Lawless Lee in reference to the alleged settlement at Wicklow town. The name Lefebure (Lefebvre?) is mentioned and the statement made that, like the Huguenots in Chapelizod, they lived too close to the French Community in Dublin to sustain a distinct identity, and merged into the much larger element in the capital city. This makes scant sense from a logical viewpoint; the comparison is not valid: Chapelizod was a very proximate suburb, while Wicklow town lies a considerable distance away – some twenty miles. It is stretching credibility to assert that the Wicklow Huguenots needed to merge with those in Dublin, simply because they existed at such "close" quarters. Other explanations must be sought. A small number of écuyer families are strongly believed to have resided at or around Birr, County Offaly; two are known to have done so: Captain Jacques Tolemoullet and Lieutenant François Souberain.

In 1948 Sir D. L. Savory hypothesized the existence of a Huguenot-Palatine community in rural County Limerick, County Kerry, and County Tipperary. This must on examination be – at least for the moment – totally discounted. Such evidence as exists for establishing such a connection is extremely tenuous. Dr. Savory attempted to link two distinct immigrations generated by different events. The first of these was the initial influx of Huguenots into the Palatinate and other areas in western Germany after 1685, some of these refugees eventually being settled in Ireland as part of Galway's colonization scheme as administered by Henri de Mirmand. However, many more of these particular Huguenots settled in the Electorate of Brandenburg, which was far closer at hand and required no sea passage. The second and quite separate incident occurred during the War of the Spanish Succession when Louis XIV's forces ravaged the Rhineland Palatinate to such an extent that much of the indigenous

Protestant population fled. This Palatine immigrant group represented a humanitarian problem that in some ways was more acute than that of the Huguenots, who generally had the advantage of better education and an articulate international network of spokesmen; and were able to generate a deeper vein of sympathy from the general population of potential host countries. And as distinct from the Francophone Huguenots, the Palatines were German, and therefore German-speaking. Savory seems to have rather been stretching a point in order to bring the two largely incompatible Protestant immigrant groups together and postulating an amalgamated and cohesive series of colonies in Counties Limerick, Tipperary and Kerry (the latter of which is admitted to have been formed at a very late date, 1776 – far too late to be considered a "Huguenot" settlement).

All that is offered is a few presumably French-derived names: Corneil, Fizelle, Gillaud, Glazier, Gruer and Guyer and the statement that their "ancestors were no doubt Huguenots who had taken refuge in the Palatinate just before or after the Revocation of the Edict of Nantes". This is scarcely sufficient cause for employing the term "Huguenot-Palatine settlements" in this context.

Perhaps, however, it can be eventually proven that individually, and not in concert with Palatines, a few Huguenot families did come to Limerick. Dr. Elisabeth Labrousse identified several families from Mauvezin in the Armagnac region of Gascony who came to dwell in Cork and Limerick: Aiguebere, Barjau, Dubarry, Faget, Farie, Foissin, Garipuy, Momin, and Saint-Jean.

It seems established beyond reasonable doubt that there existed a small colony of Huguenots at Dundalk in County Louth, and that it was, despite the town's reputation as a military stronghold, industrially oriented. As early as 1736, James Hamilton II, Viscount Limerick (later Earl of Clanbrassil), planned with the De Joncourt brothers, Isaac Etienne and Ciprien, to establish a cambric and lawns manufacture in town, and elicited the assistance of the Irish Linen Board for this enterprise, to the tune of 30 pounds annually for seven years. There is mention of skilled weavers arriving from France and "other refugees", but no specific surnames, apart from an oddly-named gentleman: "Petit Pierre". Nor is there evidence of a separate Huguenot Church, though a chaplain (French?) was provided. The factory complex was located on Parliament Square (which one source asserts was given the name by the major De Joncourt shareholders to express their gratitude for the support that the legislative body had provided). The initial investment capital was generous: 30,000 pounds were subscribed to launch the venture; Viscount Limerick had built three-story weavers' domicile-workshops which probably resembled those built at Weavers' Square in

Dublin around the same time. The land containing the Square itself was said to have served as a flax-growing area and/or bleach yard. Cambric production was high in the 1750s, and the product was described as being quite competitive. However, all trace of De Joncourt's community had vanished by 1770, perhaps partially through marriage assimilation, and partially through failure of the cambric business there – for reasons which remain obscure.

Castleblayney in County Monaghan was the scene of a Utopian experiment, and soon went the way of all such endeavors. It was founded in 1692 and its settlers were subject to a strict regimentation. Members of the Labat family from Montpellier in Languedoc appear to have been affiliated with the colony. By 1696, the Huguenot community had disintegrated, partially, it was stated through "bad conduct" by certain individuals.

At Belfast, Lee asserts, some of the rank-and-file from the disbanded Williamite army were supposed to have taken residence. Here again, however, no names are given and the statement that the fact that they had no separate place of worship and, hence, no true identity as a refugee colony, may well be refuted by further research.

The only concrete Huguenot connection that can be established at this time with Gorey in County Wexford is the presence of a Huguenot family named Maynou in 1706. By early 1710, however, Antoine Maynou and his wife had moved to Dublin, where their four year-old daughter Susanne died and lies buried, probably in what became known as the "Cabbage Garden" near St. Patrick's Cathedral.

Tradition has also linked the Huguenots with County Cavan, and most specifically with Killeshandra. One reference, however, is extremely negative. Pierre Peze Degaliniere, later pastor at "French Mary's" in Dublin had come to Ireland at the behest of Dive Downes, Bishop of Cork. However, the good bishop seems to have disappointed the French pastor, who complained in January of 1701 at the prospect of spending winter in a "miserable burgh named Cavan". By August, Monsieur Degaliniere had moved to Dublin, where the situation was doubtless more to his liking (for more on Degaliniere's subsequent career, see Chapter 6). On the other hand, Captain Jean Antoine La Nauze appeared content to settle at Killeshandra. He had spent nine years in the service, seeing action in Ireland, Flanders and Piedmont before being reduced to half pay and becoming a physician. While on furlough in January 1690, he married Anna Hierome, daughter of the later pastor Jacques Hierome and his exogamous wife, Elizabeth Spottiswoode. It has yet to be established, however, whether or not additional Huguenot families resided at Killeshandra in numbers sufficient to justify its designation as a Huguenot settlement.

Oral tradition in legend has also linked Donnybrook just south of Dublin with a Huguenot presence, which in this instance can be confirmed. What can be ruled out is the long-standing supposition of the Anglican parish cemetery at Donnybrook being a Huguenot or even a quasi-Huguenot burial ground. It may more accurately be stated that it was an Anglophone Church of Ireland field at which a number of French Protestants happened to be interred. As many as twenty-one surnames gleaned from the parish records may qualify as being of Huguenot origin: Malherd, Le Port, Moules, Granges, Devorix, Poitevin, Paniard, Cauzier, Mahard, Clemance, Brangin, Franck, Anallis, Trevers, Lescures, Mendes, Martine, Drisman, Musson, Dellamain, and Vavasseur.

François Malherd, who was buried on 12 August 1717 is described as being "a French man" and thus perhaps a more recent arrival rather than a regular parishioner. Peter Poitevin, who married Sarah Clark on 21 May 1727, was a member of a family which worshipped mainly at Peter Street Non-Conformist Church during the 1720s–30s, though Elizabeth Poitevin married François Michel at French Patrick's (9 October 1718), and the family was one of those lingering from the Late Ormondite colony (1682). The Moules family had also taken part in Non-conformed services, as early as 1704. Marguerite Bries, neé Moules, was apparently the namesake aunt of a daughter of Jean and Anne Moules. The little girl died at Donnybrook in 1723. There may possibly have been a connection with Patrick Moule, baker, one of the earliest Early Ormondite immigrants to come to Dublin (1662). The Granges family, or at least a branch of it, later colonized Portarlington; given vagaries of eighteenth century spellings of surnames – and especially foreign ones – "Patrice Desvorix" of Ringsend may well have been related to the "Desvories" of Dublin. William and Mary Anne Paniard had at least three children: Richard (christened 28 April 1714; buried 20 January 1717); Robert (buried 24 January 1720) and another child (buried 20 August 1731). A certain Thomas Paniard had died by 23 April 1726, and William himself succumbed by 11 June 1734. Two nuclear families of Cauziers, perhaps brothers, existed at Donnybrook. Robert and Grace Cauzier had two daughters (born 1714 & 1715), one of whom survived (the eldest lived only for one day). Grace died in June of 1727 and Robert remarried in 1729. He and his second wife, Elizabeth Colson, had a daughter in 1733 – whom they christened Grace. Richard and Frances Cauzier had three children, only one of whom survived, before Richard died on 24 June 1729. James Mahard's first wife died young, and he remarried, on 4 September 1729, to Anne Denny (Denis?). Charles and Margaret Rachel Clemance were also shadowed by tragedy, losing two children (in 1728 and 1736).

The only remote, dubious Huguenot link to Enniscorthy, County Wexford is a reference made by Gimlette to a Didier Fouchant, who was among a group of foreign labourers engaged in ironwork and smelting in that vicinity around 1664–5. Lee, who quotes Gimlette, seems similarly skeptical of this – the designation "Huguenot" is never applied – and both the enterprise and putative settlement were short-lived.

The Lagan Valley

Though Lisburn has enjoyed the greatest portion of fame and publicity, the Huguenot settlements of the Lagan River Valley in Counties Antrim, Down and Armagh (Lisburn, Lurgan, Lambeg, and Waringstown) may be studied as an inter-related phenomenon. Mythology credits the "500"-odd Huguenot families for reviving a "ruined village" of Lisnagarvey, and making the whole valley hum with prosperity by introducing cutting-edge techniques in linen manufacturing and trade. The imposing Huguenot linen entrepreneur Louis Crommelin is touted as having pulled off a one-man revolution, and having laid the basis for an industry that would dominate the Ulster economy into the early twentieth century.

Stripping away the gloss, as one must do with all mythical images, it can be discovered that far from being a "ruined village" the town of Lisburn (it had long been called that) was an established enterprise area long before the Huguenots arrived in the 1690s. The population was and seems to have remained predominately English in origin and there does not appear to have existed anywhere near 500 Huguenot families – even if the northern counties are considered as a whole. Dr. Raymond Gillespie's research indicates that the Huguenot presence did not dominate the region. "Lisnagarvey", or "the gambler's (gamester's) valley" – the name seems to have been derived from the existence of cock-fighting tournaments and a Las Vegas type of ambiance prior to the 1630s – was transformed into the bustling commercial hub of County Antrim through the efforts of Viscount Conway and George Rawdon long before a Huguenot family even appeared. The Huguenots were coincidental and supplementary to a pre-existing linen-producing center, and at that were actually quite a small element within the regional population.

What is interesting is the documented presence of a few Huguenots immigrants in the Lagan Valley prior to the arrival of the Williamite armies. Bulmer/Boomer (Pre-Ormondite); Guérin, Gaston, and Vint (Ormondite) are identifiable as French Protestants but it is not until *c.* 1698 that there was a substantial enough Huguenot presence to merit the name of community, and to be granted a French Church (located on Castle Street in Lisburn) with a separate Church of Ireland minister, Charles De La Valade. Dr. W. H. Crawford's population estimate of some 120 Huguenot residents in Lisburn town in 1711, up from the traditional 70 original settlers who arrived with Louis Crommelin and his family in 1698, seems accurate (though if one were to estimate for the entire Lagan region at its height, a total of 250–300 is not unreasonable). Some twenty-nine family surnames can be identified as bona fide Ruvignac colonists, though at least four later moved to Dublin.

Though the famous Louis Crommelin might have long enjoyed an inflated reputation, he remains a formidable historical figure. Like Julius Caesar, Crommelin had a genius for self-promotion, a flair for keeping his name in the public eye – so much that even posterity was impressed, took his writings at face value, and embraced him as the founding father of the Irish linen industry. What is certain about Louis Crommelin is that he was born in 1652 at St.-Quentin in Picardy. There are indications that King William III, acting through the Earl of Galway, sent Crommelin as an expert consultant on the linen industry to Ireland to do what we may now call a "feasibility study". Though the identity of the "expert" was not disclosed in the records, it was certainly Crommelin who was appointed Overseer of the Royal Linen Board in 1698 and very likely, in and around the period 1697–9, had established a sort of residence/head-quarters in Lisburn (probably 37 Castle Street) and a production center on Bridge Street, bordering the River Lagan and a tributary stream. The success of his enterprise, and smaller ones he established at Kilkenny and Waterford, can best be described as "on-again, off-again". During the thirty-odd years that Crommelin was at Lisburn he evinced an uncanny survival instinct.

Despite indifferent success he was able to use the favor he held with Galway and the King to obtain sufficient funding to stay afloat. Then when Galway's resignation as Lord Justice and King William's death closed off this avenue, he was able to obtain the good graces (and mone-tary support) of the Second Duke of Ormond, who – like his grandfather before him – had become Lord-Lieutenant. It was for the Duke's benefit that Crommelin wrote the work upon which his future reputation would lie (in much the same way as Caesar was served by his *Commentaries on the Gallic Wars*): *Essay Towards Improving the Hempen and Flaxen Manufactures in the Kingdom of Ireland* (1705). After Ormond's down-fall, Crommelin had the good fortune to see his old patron, the Earl of Galway, return as Lord Justice, and in 1715 secured from him a pension of four hundred pounds. Up to the time of his death in 1727, Crommelin engaged mainly in the sailcloth industry at various locations throughout Ireland (notably, Cork, Waterford, Rathkeale and Rathbride). Louis Crommelin's role and importance remains a highly-charged question among scholars. He most certainly did not originate the Irish linen industry; even at Lisburn itself, this was a pre-existing phenomenon, and his *Essay* has long been criticized as propaganda which espoused ideas that were sometimes naïve in their conception. What is beyond dispute is the positive publicity that he brought to the linen industry and the fact that he played an indispensable role in initiating and sustaining not just the Lisburn colony, but the Huguenot presence throughout the Lagan Valley. That alone would secure him a noteworthy place in Irish history.

On 20 April 1707 a rampaging fire of unknown cause destroyed most of the town's buildings in, reputedly, a matter of "three hours" time. Some erstwhile colonists are said to have moved to Lurgan; others stayed to rebuild. Records were undoubtedly incinerated but this hardly explains why Pastor Charles De La Valade, who officiated over the French Church from 1704–56, did not maintain – and his successors did not preserve – more complete parish records. Thus, it is at present difficult to analyze and to chronicle the Huguenots of the Lagan Valley.

Some eighty-seven surnames and names of individuals have survived (still based upon the antiquarian lists compiled by Dr. Purdon), but many need to be taken with reservation. Those which are currently reasonably verifiable include: merchants (Henri Bringuier, Salomon Le Blanc, Louis Rochet), écuyers (De la Cherois, Mangin, De Bernière, Geneste, Jellet, De Leuze, Hautenville, De Blaquière), reed-makers (Marc Dupré), cambric-workers (Goyer), silk-weavers (Ferrier), lawyers (Guérin), printer (Boucher), linen-workers (Cordiner). Provincial origins are varied: the Crommelins originated in Picardy, but the Huguenot families who comprised the Lagan Valley communities came from every corner of France. The Mangins were from Lorraine, Goyers from Caen in Normandy, De Bernières from Alençon in Normandy, Genestes from Guyenne, Dupres from La Rochelle, Bringuier, De La Valade and Balmier from Languedoc, Hautenvilles from Rouen in Normandy, de Blaquières from Limousin, Bouchers and Gillots from Bergerac in Gascony. The excellent work done in recent years by Crawford, Day and Best need to further pursued before a final determination can be made as to the true extent and impact of French Protestant immigrants upon the Lagan Valley Region. In Lisburn itself a separate Huguenot ministry endured until 1819, upon the death of the last incumbent. Waringstown in County Down has never before been mentioned as a separate Huguenot settlement, but there is ample evidence that such a settlement of Huguenot craftsmen and artisans was sponsored by Samuel Waring – a family of weavers named Dupré was specifically noted – and worshipped with English settlers from Cumberland, Yorkshire and Northumberland at the Anglican Church of the Holy Trinity. Tradition has it that the Huguenots engaged primarily in damask weaving and dwelled in cottages alongside which they planted trees in a manner reminiscent of what they had known in France.

The Spurs: Carlow, Kilkenny & Waterford

A Huguenot community in Carlow town may have been in existence as early as 1692, but one was at least established before March 1708, when Benjamin de Daillon finally gave up his rancorous six-year dispute at Portarlington with Antoine Ligonier de Bonneval and the Bishop of Kildare, sold his holdings to Josias de Robillard, Seigneur de Champagné, and assumed – it has been believed – the position of pastor to the Non-conformist French Church there. If this is the case, it may be fair to state that some of the Portarlington colonists who joined with Daillon in condemning the conformist changes that had been imposed by the Bishop and Pastor Bonneval may have made the move along with him, particularly some of the aristocratic veterans. Does Carlow qualify as a garrison settlement? There are no referenced, specific surnames apart from those of Daillon and Lieutenant Charles La Boulay De Champs. Local folklore designated a certain tract of land as "Captain (sic) Labully's Field".

If Daillon had indeed found a measure of serenity after a lifetime of contention and controversy, it was to be of brief duration. The combative pastor died on 3 January 1709, aged 78; his wife, Pauline Nicholas, the sister of Captain Jean Nicholas, had already passed on 31 December 1708. The inscription on his tombstone read (as per T. P. Le Fanu) *Gallus Brittanus Generosa Familia Ortus, Ecclesiae Reformatae Presbyter Eruditus, Diu Ob Religionem Incarceratus.*

Assuming we can completely credit the record, by 1717 it would appear that the Carlow congregation had embraced conformity. We know very little about the Carlow Church and community after the passing of Daillon; no baptismal, marriage, burial or vestry records seem to have survived. There is a reference by C. J. Jackson to a widow "Elizabeth Lemaistre of Carlow" whose son Michael was apprenticed in 1739 to (possible relative) Charles Lemaistre of Dublin, goldsmith; and to one of the French pastors, David Chaigneau (*c.* 1744). It was not a large community, and we are fairly certain that it no longer existed as an independent entity by 1765, by which time the new Methodist congregation was established at the former French Church. What little description we have of the building itself indicates that it was rather simple, and quite small, and was "located at the end of a narrow passage from Tullow Street, bounded at one end by Cockpit Lane". It was abandoned by the Methodists by 1787, and passed from the historical record.

The Kilkenny settlement is just as shadowy. At present, there are names, but extremely little in the way of inter-connection and demographic data. Grace Lawless Lee ferreted 19 surnames that may more-or-less connected to a Kilkenny settlement, but elaborated no further as regards sources that definitely confirm they were residents of a specific French Calvinist community. During the 1690s there were elaborate plans to endow a French "university" there with Benjamin De Daillon as the Dean/Professor, assisted by "several French Divines"; and on that basis one might conclude that it was to have a theologically-based curriculum. For unknown reasons, even though King William is asserted to have taken a personal interest, the scheme never came to fruition. There was no specific Huguenot Church, and no indication as to where the congregation might have met; only that a French pastor was authorized to minister to the needs of the Huguenot population. All indications are that this again was an extremely small community which in all likelihood did not attain a total 50 individuals. Was there then a garrison settlement? It would appear that, although there were suggestions in that direction, this did not materialize. There were perhaps not enough pensioned veterans, nor the amenities sufficient to lure them from the major centers. Was there a Huguenot weavers' colony at Kilkenny? All that we can be certain of at this time was that the Second Duke of Ormond had attempted to independently set up the linen industry at Kilkenny, and that in 1707, its affairs were not doing well. The Duke petitioned the government that Louis Crommelin be allowed to move his Huguenot colony from Lisburn to Kilkenny, and Crommelin himself expressed his desire to do so – given the fact that the Great Fire at Lisburn devastated and demoralized his settlement there. Ormond's recall as Lord-Lieutenant ended the project, and Crommelin remained at Lisburn. However, Louis' younger brother Guillaume later moved to Kilkenny. Family traditions link the surnames Le Grand, Pierry and De Landre. We know of a Peter Freboul, merchant, whose son John was in Dublin learning the goldsmith's trade as an apprentice to Jacques Vidouze. Former Portarlington pensioner Andre Labat died there (see Chapter 4). Then there is the naval officer, Jean Maret de La Rive, but he died at Castlecomer, County Kilkenny in 1763, and his actual connection to the Huguenot community at Kilkenny town is uncertain.

In 1989 Professor C. E. J. Caldicott learned from the late author Hubert Butler of documents pertaining to a planned Huguenot colony in County Kilkenny at Gowran. Perhaps in the near future more information might be obtained as to whether anything concrete was realized from this venture.

The researcher is on firmer footing with regard to the maritime colonies on the southern coast. The commercial links with France long predated the Huguenots and would long outlast their presence. There is evidence of flourishing interchange with the Bordeaux region, where Irish butter, tallow and suet were in demand. All this may partially explain the enthusiasm for the Huguenot cause displayed by the city fathers. On 19 June

1682, in a resoundingly supportive municipal resolution, the Waterford Corporation authorized church wardens and assistants in each parish to conduct a house-to-house collection for the relief of French Protestant refugee victims of the Dragonnades.

Nearly eleven years later the City Corporation again demonstrated its sympathy by voting on 27 March 1693 to provide the necessary funding for up to fifty refugee families who might be willing to engage in linen manufacturing. Provided that they could hopefully bring with them at least some money and materials, Freedom of the City was offered to them, gratis. Prior, the Bishop of Waterford, Nathaniel Foy, had evinced such favor towards the Huguenots that historians later, mistakenly, surmised that he himself was of Huguenot origin. Bishop Foy was one of the activist "reform-minded" prelates of the Williamite era, working in tandem with Episcopal colleagues William King of Dublin and Anthony Dopping of Meath (and in opposition to conservatives like William Moreton of Kildare and Thomas Lindsay of Killaloe) to ardently root out inefficiency, absenteeism and pluralism. In Bishop Foy's case, his diocese, which was still tinged by the legacy of arch-pluralist Miler McGrath, and the lascivious Marmaduke Middleton, offered a particular challenge. In fact Bishop Foy was so pointedly outspoken over what he perceived as laxity and apathy that in 1696 he was arraigned by the Irish House of Lords. In 1693 the Bishop offered the use of the chancel of the Holy Ghost Friary for Huguenot worship. The arrangement bore similarities to that between the Archdiocese of Dublin and the French congregation that assembled in the Lady Chapel of St. Patrick's Cathedral and, like St. Patrick's, the Holy Ghost Friary in Waterford had a venerable and distinguished history. It was built under the aegis of Sir Hugh Purcell upon a Viking-era site, c. 1240; the chancel was apparently the first section of the Friary (which until the Reformation was used by the Franciscans) to be completed. The price for this generosity was conformity to Anglicanism, which Bishop Foy was characteristically keen at insisting upon. In the case of Waterford this seems to have been accepted without demur and the issue of non-conformity never appears to have arisen. By 1815, when the Friary roof fell in, the Huguenot congregation had been assimilated and separate French services had probably long ceased.

David Gervais from Tournon in Guyenne served as the first French Church minister, receiving a stipend of forty pounds per annum, and in 1713 was awarded the Prebendary of Lismore cathedral. Foy, who might never have countenanced this, had died in 1707. Gervais' son William died on 15 September 1714 and was buried in the French Church, and the pastor himself was succeeded in 1716 by Jacques ("James") Denis, who was in 1729 collated to the Prebendary of Donaghmore. Pastor Denis was a confidant of the Earl of Galway, who bequeathed him fifty pounds from his estate. Denis was in turn succeeded at Waterford by Gedéon Richon.

Though Waterford was regarded as a crucial "spur" to the "Fortress Ireland" strategy only 19 (perhaps 20) écuyer families took residence there, far overshadowed by the 289 at Dublin and 160 at Portarlington. These noble houses: De Franquefort, D'Augier, Sautelle, Vaury, Besard De Lemaindre, Toupelin de Delize, Duchesne, Belafaye, Chelar, Boisrond, Chenevix, De Maison, Delaune, De Languedoc, De La Malquiere, Sapillon, Petitot, Duffan, Concarett, and Churgile, while they acquired property and undoubtedly made some impact, they never did seem to dominate the refuge at Waterford to the same extent as the écuyer element at Dublin and Portarlington. Some, in fact, would later move to Portarlington and Dublin. All in all, Waterford, Cork and other "hinterlands" settlements appear to have only received "residual" military settlers, the impetus for establishing garrison colonies having been spent as the veterans planted roots in Dublin or Portarlington, with an insufficient number of individuals remaining to go further south and west.

However, the professional/mercantile element may have been more substantial. They, and the artisans, were particularly sought-after by city leaders insomuch as the Cromwellian expulsion of a substantial enough portion of the mercantile community during the 1650s had disrupted Waterford's cohesiveness and prosperity to the extent that full recovery was not realized until the early 18th century. The bits and pieces of evidence that are extant, however, tend to tantalize rather than inform. Despite the Corporation's eagerness to attract Huguenots for a linen manufactory, there is no evidence that anything notable came of this unless we count the much-later advent of Louis Crommelin's "agent" Jean Latrobe, though he very quickly came to the realization that sailcloth and rope manufacturing would prove to be much more lucrative. The sailcloth and hempen manufactory at Waterford (which may or may not have been set up by Latrobe) was in any case flourishing by 1725 and had folded by 1746. A certain Joseph Beaumont is documented as having been involved in this enterprise, perhaps as Latrobe's assistant. Grace Lawless Lee, however, credits the Huguenot Bishop of Waterford Richard Chenevix with persuading the Earl of Chesterfield to re-establish linen production in the city. During the 1730s Simon Bonique was operating a successful sugar refinery. Huguenot families like the Vashon (at least three nuclear merchant families), Derante (surgeon), Brunel, Reynette (physician), Maynes (?) (merchant), Billard, Blanche (wigmaker), Spurrier (mariner), Vallot (mariner), Chaigneau, (merchant), Sirvan (clothier), Frank, Sandoz & Dobier (clergymen), and Gall, or Gaul ("shopkeeper" – though there is a tradition amongst the descendants of James Gall or Gaul that their ancestor was Flemish, rather than French) imply that the Waterford community was one of vitality and diversity. Other surnames include: Ayrault, Sprusson, Ducla, Vinson, Shelmaindre, Gayott, St. Legere, Delaville, Coquin, Dermozan, Grandrie, Dubay, Marcel, Bellet, Lune, Guillard, and the more debatable Lisle, Ruby, Oderoft, Hagerein, Villiers, Maunsell, and Linnegar.

In keeping with Waterford's maritime orientation, there reputedly existed a Huguenot-run fishery, which carried on trade with ports in France, and Huguenot entrepreneurship has been linked to the sugar industry. Waterford by the closest calculation had some 75 Huguenot families and perhaps a total of 300 individual residents at its height.

David Dickson noted the contrast between the Huguenots of Dublin and Cork (which is also applicable in the case of Waterford) as regards the holding of municipal office. Whereas in both Waterford and Cork the Huguenots evinced a degree of activism in city politics which was out of proportion to their numbers; in Dublin there was a slacking off from what had been high profile participation. Following the Desminieres administrations in the 1660s no Huguenot attained the dignity of Lord Mayor; but between 1692–1745 this occurred no fewer than two times at Waterford (Simon Vashon, Senior in 1726; Simon Vashon, Junior in 1738) and on four occasions in Cork (Peter Reneu in 1694; Daniel Perdrian in 1712; Joseph Lavit in 1720; and Walter Lavit in 1745). Even in the tiny settlement at Youghal, Huguenots held the highest civic post in 1683 (Richard Paradise), 1721 (Edward Gillet) and 1751–2 (Joseph Labatte). Dr. Dickson attributes this to the greater willingness of the Huguenot elite in the southern cities to meld themselves into the Anglican social milieu – a theory worth investigating.

It was noted long ago by Thomas Gimlette that there seem to be no residential concentration of Huguenot families in any single quarter of the city – instead, they were spread out almost equally amongst the several parishes. That point taken, and the willingness of Huguenot families to interact so closely with their Anglophone Protestant neighbors therefore, would seem to logically contradict Grace Lawless Lee's assertion that Waterford's Huguenot families departed *en masse* to France *c.* 1790–1803, and credits this to contributing materially to the demise of the Waterford colony by 1815.

This remains yet another mystery surrounding the Huguenots of Ireland that awaits future investigation.

Tallow, County Waterford is yet another case of an encounter with historical quicksand. Brief mentions by De Chambrier and Agnew and a half-hearted reference to the surname Arnauld are all at present that there is to go on.

The Spurs: Cork City and County

Cork City is in many ways the most intriguing of the areas settled by Huguenots – and among the most frustrating for researchers. It is a case of knowing that there were many who arrived (Cork, with between 300–400 individual settlers, was probably the site of the third largest Huguenot concentration in Ireland, behind Dublin and Portarlington) but possessing such a paucity of documentary material as to make their actual history nearly inscrutable. As Dr. Dickson suggested, we may never know the Cork Huguenots like we do those of Portarlington and Dublin, but historians, like archeologists, always live in hope that documentation that has survived both the elements and the Four Courts Fire may surface. In the case of Cork, however, this hope has been all the more dimmed by a letter, discovered by C. F. A. Marmoy (and alluded to in volume xxii of the *Proceedings of the Huguenot Society of London*) dated 30 January 1827. There is reference to a flood in 1796, which inundated the French Church and destroyed the Registers. The waters of the River Lee may therefore have taken away a precious fragment of the past. This is all the more to be pitied because from all we can glean there are indications that Cork was one of the most vibrant of the Huguenot settlements.

We may reasonably surmise that individual Pre-Ormondite Huguenots should have been drawn to such an attractive, cosmopolitan commercial area, but no evidence exists of a community as such. One Richard Covert, who served as Sheriff of Cork in 1657 and as Mayor in 1662 and 1682, was presumed to be a Huguenot immigrant.

We do have evidence of Ormondite immigrants: Samuel Ablin had arrived by 1685 and would become an Elder of the French Church and City Sheriff in 1710. Antoine Semirot was a goldsmith who seems to have encountered prejudice – the Master of the Goldsmith's Guild refused to accept him. Mayor William Howell, however, overruled the Master and in 1685 swore him in as a Freeman and Guild member. Fate created its own revenge as Semirot himself became Warden (1710), then Master (1712) of the Guild, and died at a ripe old age in 1743. Between them, Grace Lawless Lee and Dr. Alicia St. Leger have identified some Ormondite surnames: Pantin (Samuel, goldsmith), Goble (Samuel & Robert gold/silversmiths), Reneu (Peter, merchant; who was a French Church Consistory member, sheriff of Cork in 1691, and mayor in 1694), Billon (Pierre, tallow chandler), Vigie (Jean Jacques Ribet, who moved to Galway where in 1703 he became mayor), Savory, Trebuseth, Rogue and Segen.

Cork City had gone through its own anxious moments during the War of the Two Kings when it was successfully invested and captured in

September of 1691 by John Churchill, then Earl of Marlborough. Shortly thereafter the Ruvignac immigration brought to Cork a substantial Huguenot presence and a French Church by January 1695. Joining the Ormondite holdovers during the last decade of the 17th century were individuals with surnames like: Addiz, Perau, Lenant, Ricards, Perdrian, De La Croix, Baron, Dupond, Ardouin, Guillot, St. Martin, St. Leger, Carré, Chartres, Caillon, Cesteau and Hanneton.

The French Church, founded originally as a Non-Conformed congregation, was first pastored by the flamboyant Jacques Fontaine, who officiated without stipend and maintained himself through a broadcloth manufacture that he set up in the city. Fontaine proved a dynamic and energetic preacher, but a controversial personality who had a knack for needling whatever established order seemed to be around at any particular moment. Like his colleague Bishop Foy in Waterford, Cork's Bishop Edward Wetenhall took a personal interest in the Huguenot worshippers. In this case the results were not as harmonious, nor was conformity so passively embraced. In 1698 Wetenhall was a party to an acrimonious debate with Pastor Fontaine over the necessity for episcopal ordination. The Bishop profited from a bitter controversy within the French Church. According to Fontaine, whose account is still the only one we have, a member of his congregation, Isaac De La Croix, and particularly his son Jean, had been involved in questionable business dealings and had taken offence at one of Fontaine's sermons which, he imagined, had targeted him for reproach. The enraged parishioner had then tried to stir up dissension, split the congregation, and had called into question Fontaine's pastoral credentials, as he had not been ordained by a bishop. Fontaine asserted that he agreed to resign in order to prevent a schism. There may be more to the story. While Pastor Fontaine was a courageous and resourceful man, another side of his character seems to occasionally reveal itself in the pages of his *Memoires*. That is, he could be stubborn, abrasive and contentious, not the easiest individual to get along with. His support within the congregation may have been less, and dissatisfaction may have been greater, than what he might have let on. While he accused Lord Galway of sacrificing him to satisfy Bishop Wetenhall's whim, his resignation seems rather premature, and perhaps petulant. For someone who later displayed such tenacity battling the French at Bearhaven and protecting his homestead, it seems out of character for him to have given up so quickly. Fontaine depicts his departure in June of 1698 as dignified, and that his threats to return if an acceptable successor were not named as having intimidated Lord Galway and Bishop Wetenhall into appointing a "Monsieur Marcombe", about whom nothing further is known. Perhaps it was always the intent of the Bishop to pry Fontaine out of position in order to facilitate the acceptance of Conformity, and the De La

Croix incident provided the convenient leverage (it may be of significance
that included among those specifically recommended by the Bishop for
Freeman's status, gratis, on 12 July 1699 was Jean De La Croix, who
barely a year before had been in such trouble with the law that he had fled
the City for a while – one may be forgiven for viewing the whole affair
with some suspicion). (See Chapter 7 for further insights on the Fontaine-
De La Croix Controversy).

The congregation had been peripatetic: first assembling at Christ
Church, then at the Cork County Courthouse, and then in a room at
Fontaine's house; it would continue to move about until 1712, when
funds were raised to construct a building designed by Huguenot architect
Etienne Dessoul de la Rochelle at Ballard's Lane and Lumley Street (now
respectively known as Carey's Lane and French Church Street). In 1733
some adjoining land was purchased for a cemetery and in 1745 a new
refugee influx brought about the establishing of a second French Church.
This church is the most baffling of enigmas: it is not known where it was
located, who its ministers and members were, or how long it lasted. It is
not mentioned again and by 1750 may have closed down. The first French
Church was to suffer the usual attrition of membership through death,
emigration and assimilation. Its last pastor, Thomas Goetval from
Switzerland, died in 1813, and the building itself was dismantled in 1897.
A portion of the cemetery has survived and has recently been the focus of
determined and thus far successful attempts to assure its preservation by
the Friends of the Huguenot Cemetery, Cork. Led by Mrs. Petra Coffey
and Dr. Alicia St. Leger, the organization hopes that, like the Merrion
Row Cemetery in Dublin, the site might in time be cleaned and refur-
bished.

In no other settlement (apart from the exceptional instance of
Portarlington) did the Huguenots show a more pervasive and active civic
involvement than in Cork. No fewer than five had, prior to 1750, become
mayor: Covert (1662, 1682), Reneu (1694), Daniel Perdrian (1712),
Joseph Lavit (1713), and Walter Lavit (1745). Seven held the post of
sheriff: Covert (1657), Reneu (1704), Samuel Ablin (1710), Augustus
Carré (1721), Joseph Lavit (1713), Walter Lavit (1733) and Wetenhall
Hignet (1730). Joseph Lavit's name is preserved to the present day on
Lavitt's Quay; he had become Cork's leading sugar refiner. Early eigh-
teenth century surnames also include: Mayne, Jervois, Bonbonous,
Verdille, D'Alterie (clothier), Allenet (sergeweaver), Augee, Laroque
(merchant), Gaggin, Loraine (porter), Parmy, Raymond, Delafaye,
Engain, Foucault (jeweller), Freneau, Bellaire, Maunsell (clockmaker),
Cadier, Dollard, De La Court, Besnard, Blanchet, Mayzyck , Marret
(joiner), Prosier, Cossart (via Dublin), Laullie, Lassarre, Pique (minister),
Mainardue, Jagaultz, and Massiot.

It is truly a shame that documentation on the Cork settlement is so thin on the ground. In the few glimpses we have there emerges a self-confidence and independence of thought that can be rather refreshing. The voting of honors and gifts conferred upon prominent individuals by the municipal corporation generally involved a formalistic, monotonous routine. On 20 January 1737, when it was proposed to extend civic honours to certain personages and to present the formidable Dean Jonathan Swift with a silver box, two Huguenots, Auguste Carré and Daniel Engain, had the audacity to have it clearly and emphatically stated for posterity that "We dissent on Dean Swift"!

It appears that Huguenots were planted near Bandon, County Cork on the lands of Sir Richard Cox (1650–1733), Lord Chancellor of Ireland, 1703–7, occasional Lord Justice, and author/historian who wrote *Hibernia Anglicana*, and that the Baron De Virazel was instrumental in facilitating their passage from Switzerland. Again, only a few names have come down: Barter, Beaumont, Chartres, Du Barry and Willis, and the colony's subsequent history remains obscure.

Though Kinsale has been omitted from most lists of possible Huguenot colonies, there seems to be at least as much evidence there to make a case for one as there is for, say, Killeshandra, Tallow, or Birr. In Kinsale, Lee has noted the surnames of Choisin, Lacroix and Lecost.

What is most remarkable for Youghal, as in the case of Cork City, is how rapidly the Huguenots, in proportion to their miniscule percentage of the population, became involved in civic leadership. Did the presence of Ormondite Huguenots in prominent positions attract the military pensioners who were positioned to guard the southwestern fringes of "Fortress Ireland"? Richard and Samuel Paradise from Limousin had arrived in Youghal during the early Restoration years: by 1679, Richard held the office of bailiff, and in 1683, mayor. Samuel was bailiff in 1693. The Casaubon family were actually fourth-generation Huguenot immigrants, having first come to England after the St. Bartholomew's Day Massacre; Thomas Casaubon was bailiff in 1672.

It was not until 1697 that, according to Smiles, some 50 veteran officers and their families arrived at Youghal. Lee believes that this is too high a number and that the total number of Huguenot colonists stood at less than 50. If there were over 50 it is indeed surprising that no French Church was built, nor was a stipend allotted to pay a French minister, as was usually the case. The Huguenots worshipped at the Collegiate Church of St. Mary where, after 1730, Monsieur Arthur D'Anvers held services from time to time. This implies that the refugees, for the most part, attended English services. Some écuyer families have been identified: Boirsrond St. Leger, De Hays, Coluon, Mazieres, Dezieres, Rouvieres. Other probable Huguenot surnames include: Delappe, Duclos, Chaigneau, Ricard/

Rickett, Guin, Falquiere, Marvault, Legardere, Lampriere, Perdue, Armour, Valletin, Carre and Labatte. Most prominent of all, however, was Edward Gillet, who became mayor in 1721, and who bequeathed his name to a steeply-sloping street called Gillett's Hill. By 1750, like all other Huguenot communities, soon or late, the Youghal colony had faded from all but memory.

Lingering Questions?

Though vague folklore is often a poor indicator of historical fact, it always pays to follow up on whatever leads it may provide. Such was the case with Donnybrook, where there had always been rumors and intimations of a Huguenot presence.

In the final analysis, did "Fortress Ireland" extend only to Dublin and Portarlington? Was it a case of the Huguenot impetus waxing, waning, and then spreading itself too thinly? The "hinterlands" of Huguenot settlement in Ireland remains a potentially fertile field for the researcher – and it will in all likelihood prove to be an ever-changing landscape. New truths will undoubtedly emerge, and presently-accepted truth may be reduced to theory, then to legend, and finally, to nothing more than exploded myth.

References

Primary works

Archbishop Marsh's Library (Dublin): Ms. 30.2.2; Bouhereau–Ellis Correspondence on microfilm.

Bath Manuscripts. *Historic Manuscripts Commission Publication*, vol. iii (1908), pp. 358, 367, 371, 375, 377–8.

British Library: Additional Mss. 9717, pp. 57, 59, 75; 9718; 34335, pp. 119–20; 38712, p. 51; Stowe Ms. 228, pp. 28–9, 86, 121–2, 130–3, 140–1, 143, 257.

Buccleuch and Queensbury Mss. *Historic Manuscripts Commission*, vol. ii, pt. 2, p. 649.

Council Book of the Corporation of Cork (transcribed & edited by Richard Caulfield), 1876, pp. xxix–668.

Genealogical Office of Ireland (Dublin): Ms. 10Y p. 13.

Dublin Registry of Deeds. Ms. Deeds for Dublin, 1708–38; Deeds for Waterford City, 1708–38.

National Library of Ireland Manuscripts: 100, 1619; 4167; Microfilm n. 5425, p. 5558.

Public Record Office of Ireland (Dublin): Mss. 2453–7; Waterford M. 4974 I.A. 58–87.

Royal Irish Academy Archives (Dublin): Dumont Ms.

Books/Pamphlets

Anonymous. *Jus Regium, or the King's Right to grant forfeitures*, London; 1701.

Dunton, John. *Teague Land, or a Merry Ramble with the Wild Irish: Letters from Ireland, 1698*. Edited by Edward MacLysaght, Blackrock, County Dublin, Ireland; 1982; pp. 16, 74.

Secondary works

Best, E. Joyce. *The Huguenots of Lisburn: The Story of a Lost Colony*, edited and compiled by Kathleen Rankin. Lisburn, Northern Ireland, 1997 (online version: http://www.lisburn.com/books/huguenots/huguenots_2.htm).

Butler, William F. J. *Confiscation in Irish History*, Dublin, 1917, p. 227.

Caldicott, C. E. J. "The Legacy of the Huguenots" in *PHSGBI*, vol. xxvi, no. 3, pp. 350–8.

Carré, Albert. *L'Influence des Huguenots Francais en Irlande*, pp. 110.

Chambrier, Baronne Alex de " Projet de Colonisation en Irlande pour les refugies français, 1692–99" in *PHSL*, Vol. vi, pp. 380, 387, 390–1, 405, 412.

Coffey, Mrs. Petra (Newtownmountkennedy, County Wicklow, Ireland); Friends of the Huguenot Cemetery, Cork. Material and insights on the Huguenot Cemetery in Cork, and efforts to preserve it (August 2004).

Crawford, W. H. "Lisburn at the Coming of the Huguenots" and "The Huguenots and the Linen Industry" in Brian Mackey, ed., *The Huguenots and Ulster, 1685–1985*. Unpaginated.

Day, Angelique. "The Crommelins" in Mackey *The Huguenots and Ulster*; and "Marie Angelique de la Cherois: life of a Huguenot heiress, 1700–1771" in Caldicott, Gough & Pittion, *The Huguenots and Ireland*, pp. 377–96.

Dickson, David. "Huguenots in the urban economy of eighteenth century Dublin and Cork" in Caldicott, Gough & Pittion *Huguenots and Ireland*, pp. 322–3, 328–31.

Evans, Joan. "The Huguenot Goldsmiths of England and Ireland" in *PHSL*, Vol. xiv, no. 4, pp. 496–554.

Gimlette, Thomas "Waterford" in *Ulster Journal of Archaeology*, Vol. 4 (1856), pp. 198–216, 221.

Ireland, John De Courcy "Maritime Aspects of the Huguenot Immigration into Ireland" in Caldicott, Gough & Pittion, *Huguenots and Ireland*, pp. 335, 340, 344, 354–7.

Kamen, Henry. *The War of the Spanish Succession in Spain, 1700–15*, London, 1969, pp. 13–17.

Kelly, Patrick. "Lord Galway and the Penal Laws" in Caldicott, Gough & Pittion, *The Huguenots and Ireland*, pp. 239–50.

Labrousse, Elisabeth (Paris). Written notes/observations shared with the author, April 1985.

Le Fanu, T. P. in Lawlor *Fasti*, pp. 285–6.

Le Fanu, T. P. "The Life and Sufferings of Benjamin De Daillon" in *PHSL*, Vol. xiv, pp. 458–78.

Le Fanu, W. R. "Families of Hierome, La Nauze and Ligonier" in *PHSL*, Vol. xix, no. 6, p. 353.

Lee, Grace Lawless. *The Huguenot Settlements in Ireland*, pp. 20–1, 28–42,

47–53, 55–6, 64, 69–91, 93–121, 124–8, 130–2, 138–9, 171, 181, 184–5, 188–190, 195, 201, 256–8.

Lenman, Bruce. *The Jacobite Risings in Britain, 1689–1746*, London, 1980, pp. 126–7.

Lumley, Ian W. J. "The Holy Ghost Friary, Waterford: an Architectural Account" in *Decies: Journal of the Old Waterford Society*, no. xx, May 1982, pp. 4–21.

McGuire, James I. (University College, Dublin): Insights shared with the author regarding Bishop Nathaniel Foy and the state of the Church of Ireland in the late Stuart period, June 2004.

Manchee, William. "Samuel Pepys and his links with the Huguenots" in *PHSL*, Vol. xv, no. 3; pp. 317–37.

Marmoy, C.F.A. "The Registers of the Huguenot Churches of Edinburgh and Cork" in *PHSL*, Vol. xxii, no. 2, pp. 281–2. (See) Petrie, Sir Charles "The Battle of Almanza" in *The Irish Sword*, Vol. 2 (1954–56).

Pittion, Jean-Paul (Trinity College, Dublin): Observations shared with the author (Fall/Spring 1981).

Reaman, Elmore. *The Trail of the Huguenots*, pp. 127–8.

Reid, James Seaton. *History of the Presbyterian Church in Ireland*, Vol. ii, p. 458.

Robb, Nesca A. *William of Orange, a personal portrait*, Vol. ii, London, 1966, p. 438.

St. Leger, Alicia. *Silver, Sails and Silk: Huguenots in Cork, 1685–1850*, pp. 3, 9–11, 3–18, 24–6, 29, 34, 37–8, 44, 48–53.

St. Leger, Alicia. "Cork's Huguenot Graveyard" in *Huguenot Heritage*, Issue 9 (2002), p. 6.

Sainty, J. C. "The Secretariat of the Chief Governors of Ireland, 1690–1800" in *Proceedings of the Royal Irish Academy*, Vol. 77, C, no. 1, p. 27.

Savory, D.L. "Huguenot-Palatine settlements in the counties of Limerick, Kerry and Tipperary" in *PHSL*, Vol. xviii, no. 2, pp. 111–33; no. 3, pp. 215–31.

Simms, J. G. "The Bishops' Banishment Act of 1697" in *Irish Historical Studies*, Vol. 17 (1970–71), pp. 185–96.

Simms, J. G. *The Williamite Confiscation in Ireland, 1690–1703*, London, 1956, p. 86.

Strang, John. "Across the Sea in Ireland" in *Huguenot Heritage*, Issue 9 (2002), p. 6.Swift, Jonathan. *Miscellaneous and autobiographical pieces and marginalia*. Oxford; 1962, p. 261. Cited by Vigne, "The Good Lord Galway", p. 533.

Vigne, Randolph. "The Good Lord Galway, the Irish and English careers of a Huguenot leader: biographical notes" in *PHSGBI*, Vol. xxiv, no. 6, pp. 532–48.

◈ PART III ◈
Unfulfilled Refuge

What went wrong? Perhaps that is not the most delicate way to put it. The schemes and visions of Ormond, of Hierome, of Ruvigny, King William, Virazel, Laval, Dumont de Bostaquet, Daillon, Fontaine and Bouhéreau, among many others, went unrealized. Maybe they were unattainable to begin with. The interaction of human beings with their environment, the fickle nature of events, and the strengths and weaknesses of ancestral memory are difficult forces to harness. The Huguenot Refuge was irretrievably split between those who agreed to conform to the Church of Ireland's forms and strictures – and those who would not. Though Conformist and Non-Conforming Huguenots could on occasion transcend their differences in order to advance the common good, they could not avoid viewing each other through a permanent divide.

The glorious return to France never occurred, and before the turn of the nineteenth century every single Huguenot community in Ireland was well on the road to absorption; and in many instances had already arrived there and become the stuff of regional folklore.

In this, neither the Huguenots themselves nor their hosts deserve to be saddled with the blame. Nor is it totally fair to take to task the religious and political leadership of the day as being unrealistic in their expectations. More accurately, it can be stated that the Huguenot dispersion – even when limited to the Irish context – proved too massive and traumatic a phenomenon to have been directed by anyone. Matters of personal, individual religious faith (as the historical record constantly admonishes contemporaries), have a disconcertingly perverse habit for defying the grand schemes of prelates and statesmen alike.

7

MATTERS OF FAITH AND POLITICS

"Quand au Dieux des deux fronts L'ours coupera la tête, Du Saturnin pays lamentera le Roy, Abrogé on verra sa Sacrilege Loy, Et la triple couronne arracher a la Bête."

— Élie Bouhéreau quoting from a contemporary (1700) "prophecy" popular amongst Huguenot exiles, written as a Nostradamic quatrain, which foretold the conversion of King Louis XIV; the abrogation of the Edict of Fontainebleau; and the imminent fall of the Papacy (characterized here as the "Beast" of the Apocalypse)

Even as Élie Bouhéreau was decrying the fact that many of his co-religionists living in exile were deluding themselves with militant radical, apocalyptic hopes, such as those expressed in the quatrains that imitated the style of Michel Nostradamus (stating that many other such millenarian prophecies were enjoying extensive circulation within the *Corps du Réfuge*), he may not have been entirely aware of the intensity of division within the Huguenot movement. He would have been even less aware of his own extremely paradoxical position between the two opposite poles of zealotry and accommodation. Bouhéreau's credentials were impressive. Born in La Rochelle on 5 May 1643, son of Elie Bouhéreau, pastor of Fontenay, young Élie completed his undergraduate studies in theology at the University of Saumur, received a doctorate in medicine at the University of Orange (1667), and then established himself as a private medical practitioner in his home town.

By all accounts, a cultured, cosmopolitan individual, he had suffered greatly in the persecution of the 1680s. Barred from practicing medicine in 1683, Bouhéreau was expelled from his birthplace, separated from his family, and for a while was a fugitive.

In January of 1686, he had engineered a death-defying escape to England for himself, his wife and five of their children, his widowed mother, his extensive personal library, and the Consistory Books of the

Huguenot Temple at La Rochelle. Fearless to a fault, Bouhéreau would later (1688) revert to his Scarlet Pimpernel type role when he secretly returned to France to spirit away his youngest son Jean.

He took a very active role in the struggle against Louis XIV, acting as Secretary/Envoy in the service of Sir Thomas Cox for the Williamite government between 1689 and 1693.

In November 1693 he became personal secretary to the then-Viscount Galway, assisting him in the mission to Piedmont from 1693 to 1696. From 1697 to 1701, during Galway's first term as Lord Justice of Ireland, Bouhereau continued in his secretarial capacity and, from November 1699 to March 1701 was probably Assistant Chief Secretary for Ireland as well.

As much as any individual, and even more than most, Bouhéreau laboured to strengthen the Huguenot Refuge, implement "Fortress Ireland", and contribute to the frustration of Louis XIV's grand designs. He had suffered loss, taken risks, and had experienced utter disillusionment over the failure of the War of the League of Augsburg and the Peace of Ryswick to effect a return to France for his fellow-exiles.

However, he found himself at odds with the majority of his fellow exiles within the Dublin community, and even probably within the entire refuge in Ireland, over how best to react to the situation in which they all found themselves. Was one to accept, accommodate to, or even become an integral part of the established order of the host country, at the risk of losing one's identity? And if this were so, how far might one be prepared to go? Did this include compromising on religious practice? Did this constitute an irrevocable abandonment of principle? In what manner? To how great an extent? Did such actions imply an acquiescence to the finality of exile, and abandonment of the vision of repatriation in a more righteous/enlightened France? Was there a fine line here between betrayal and pragmatism and, if so, precisely where was it etched in stone?

These were questions that all Huguenot exiles had to confront, sooner or later, and if one takes a superficial glance at Bouhéreau's subsequent career, the answer seems fairly clear: that he became the epitome of accomodationism. He had most readily accepted conformity to the Anglican Communion, as had the Earl of Galway himself, and regularly attended French Patrick's, burying his 90 year-old mother, Blandine Richard Bouhereau, in the Lady Chapel in 1700. On 9 July 1701, he was ordained deacon in the Church of Ireland; and priest on 21 September of that same year. On 7 March 1706 Trinity College granted him the degree of Doctor of Divinity. He became precentor to St. Patrick's Cathedral, and Librarian of the Institution founded in 1701 by Archbishop Narcissus Marsh – positions he maintained till the time of his death (he was interred at St. Patrick's on 7 May 1719). Thus, he became a quintessential, respectable, member of the Ascendancy, seemingly far along the road of acclimatization to his surroundings.

But there are hints that the contradictions of the Huguenot Refuge lingered in his mind to the end. At least a portion of the refugee, and perhaps a fragment of radical, irrational hope remained – assimilation certainly was not complete. Of telling import is his concern for the education of his grandsons, Elie and Richard ("Dicky"). That it rather peeved him that the young spoke what, in his opinion, was atrocious French reveals something, first of all, about the degeneration of the ancestral tongue within the Dublin Refuge at a comparatively early stage (1710s); and secondly that such matters were still held to be of importance and – just perhaps – a fluency in as pure a version of French as could be obtained might yet prove of use, perhaps even in the event of the long-awaited return to the homeland? That the elder Bouhereau set a high priority on this is evinced in his sending the considerable sum of at least seven pounds sterling for Élie's upkeep and education and one would assume at least a like sum for "Dicky". The location of the school(s) where the most unadulterated French could be taught was, in Bouhereau's estimation, Portarlington, where young Élie was in residence (at the home of pensioned veteran Armenault de Machinville) from at least 29 May to 24 October 1712; and "Dicky" from 28 May 1716 to 7 January 1717.

But on reflection maybe this paradox is not so surprising, given the basic dualism that had always existed for Huguenot movement as it touched upon religion, politics ethnicity and culture.

A problem from the beginning

Religious faith was, after all, at the very heart of it. And one cannot delude oneself into minimizing the intertwined nature of political governance with religion. The year 1789, comparatively speaking, occurred only yesterday, and parvenu ideals such as those expressed by the American Founding Fathers extolling freedom of religion and the separation of church and state had little relevance in the overall context of Early Modern Europe. It was belief, principle and conviction that sent the Huguenots on their perilous and uncertain travels. The ideal of integrity which these refugees clung to, decades into their exile, was something so precious that both as individuals and as a community, they felt compelled to continually and openly reaffirm their commitment to it. The need was especially strong for those who had abjured under pressure. There was of course a residual sense of guilt over having succumbed to sin; and the ceremony of *Réconaissance,* during which remorse was expressed, and the abjurees formally re-accepted into the Reformed faith, was an indispensable part of both conformist and non-conformed church services, and a way of healing both the community and the individual. Just as it would be inconceivable when discussing the Huguenots that the religious motivation should be downplayed; it is equally mistaken to neglect or fob off the very intense differences of opinion that existed within the French Protestant exilic communities over Conformity to the Established church against the desire to resist conformity to maintain the purity of the Calvinist faith. Many Huguenots – in fact the majority of those in Dublin, Portarlington and Cork – (the three largest Huguenot settlements in Ireland) in effect joined the tide of Dissent. Yet this is precisely what has been denied for the better part of two centuries. It was all rooted in the circumstances which gave rise to French Calvinism in the sixteenth century and of the very early merger between spiritual and political Calvinism.

The hijacking of the Huguenot faith by the princes, magnates and écuyers was perhaps an inevitable occurrence, given the temper of Reformation Europe. What probably need not have happened was the eruption of a vicious series of civil wars, and the identification of the term "Huguenot" with radical, even insurrectionary, postures towards established political authority. The door was open to the tragedy of the French Wars of Religion (so-named, though often they had very little to do with principles of personal piety). In 1559, a splintered lance penetrated through the eye and into the cranial cavity of King Henri II and eliminated a reasonably strong monarch, leaving four young sons who turned out to be the dregs of the Valois line and whose weaknesses brought about the venomous power struggles that scarred France for decades (see also information in the Introduction).

The tenacity of Huguenot military forces; the proto-republican nature of their church governance; and the regicidal/revolutionary ideas of individuals like Duplessis-Mornay were counterbalanced by the more moderate or "politique" elements within the Huguenot movement, who established a tenuous leadership position by the 1630s. However, the "politiques", moderates, or accomodationists (call them what you will) were under constant attack from those who may be classified as more "fundamentalist" or "zealot" in their views that loyalism to the monarch could be taken too far and that it was dangerous to appease a catholic-dominated government. When the Dragonnades and Revocation seemed to bear out their dire predictions, the Huguenot zealots carried their attacks on accomodationism (seen as embodied by the Ruvignys) into exile. In their fundamentalist reckoning, the disasters of the 1680s had befallen them because the Huguenot Community had strayed too far from the ancient tried-and-true traditions of the sixteenth century, and any deviation from these old forms of worship (such as conformity to Anglicanism) was an invitation to further Divine chastisement.

The Wishful Deception

From the start, however, the very palpable difference of opinions within the various French Calvinist communities-in-exile were watered down. In the first place, the historiography of the Huguenots of Ireland is not very ample, and those few pioneers in the 19th & early 20th centuries who ventured to research and to write about the subject were steeped in an Anglican tradition that was then under vigorous attack. Irish Republican Nationalism, a Neo-Tridentine resurgence within the Catholic Church in the wake of the First Vatican Council (1869–70), and a strong disestablishmentarian campaign being waged by the Gladstonian Liberals undoubtedly tended to tint the perspective of individuals like J. J. Digges Latouche, Thomas Philip LeFanu, David Carnegie Agnew, Erasmus D. Borrowes, Samuel J. Knox, James Floy, and even Grace Lawless Lee. The occasion of friction within the Huguenot community between Conformist ("Anglican") and Non-Conformed ("Calvinist") elements was either studiously ignored or else minimized into insignificance. Perhaps in view of the contemporary circumstances around them these writers did not, whether consciously or not, wish to admit of even an historical break in Protestant solidarity, or of discordant voices within the ranks of a portion of that community which had been so specially set on a pedestal. Whatever factors were in play, their perspective would not be seriously challenged until the 1980s by Jean-Paul Pittión and the author, and in the 1990s, by G. A. Forrest.

Anglicans & Calvinists during the Ormondite Years

In view of the misrepresentations of the past it is necessary to state firmly that the place occupied by the Huguenots, as regards religion, in the life of Ireland would revolve around this question of Conformity vs. Dissent. The conflict between these points of view was a natural outgrowth of the inherent contradiction which had always existed within the recesses of Calvinism itself over the stance that a Christian should take when confronted with an antagonistic political authority. Long before Duplessis-Mornay put these sentiments on paper, there were those Huguenots who advocated open resistance; while those who would have moderated this by admitting of some degree of compromise(*"Politiques"*) had co-existed with their more militant co-religionists from the beginning. The unresolved dualism endured the transition into exile, the Conformist and Non-Conformist worshippers adhering, in rough fashion, to the respective philosophy of passivity and that of resistance. Exile simply transposed the pre-existing problem and brought it into another Environment. Now the refugees themselves and their host country had to confront the Huguenot dualism, and arrive at their own resolution. In the case of Ireland the highly complex interaction of Anglican–Catholic–Dissenter interests represented a scenario which was already extremely volatile. The interjection of large numbers of French Calvinists could only serve to aggravate the situation – unless of course a formula for achieving common ground could be devised.

It was to be the Duke of Ormond, and Pastors Jacques Hierome and Jean Durel among others, who would adapt the compromise formula of the Church of the Savoy in London for the Dublin Huguenot colony just as it was beginning to coalesce. The resultant Anglican Ormond–Hierome system that was to anchor itself around the "French Patrick's" congregation was to endure uneasily for nearly three decades in the face of a Calvinist tendency which, though suppressed, simply refused to die.

The formula for effecting conformity to the Anglican communion of the Church of Ireland for Huguenot refugees has been described in Chapter 1 and represented a delicate balance of interests. In Ormond's estimation, it imposed the minimum possible control on the French worshippers: affording them their own minister, a separate meeting area, services in their own language, most of their traditional forms of worship, and even their distinctive Calvinist governance, with the pastor and church elders forming a consistory that oversaw the religious and social cohesion of their congregation. Ormond was an individual attempting to mediate between extremes (in fact he seemed to have made a career of it): balancing the demands of influential Neo-Laudian Anglican bishops like Jeremy Taylor of Down and Conor with the bristly traditionalist and national sensibilities of the Huguenots. It was undoubtedly an uneasy role to play, but one which the Duke had not been unaccustomed to assuming. The Restoration episcopacy had been battered during the 1640s–50s by Dissent in Britain and Catholicism in Ireland. The bishops wielded considerable influence at Court and, with a notoriously fickle and opportunistic monarch like Charles II on the throne, their antagonism could potentially to topple the "White Duke" from his viceregal seat. On the other hand, the Duke was aware that too many restrictions on their forms of worship would put the immigrants off, and they might seek to settle elsewhere, depriving Ireland of their skills and assets.

Ormond, Hierome & Viridet

Jacques Hierome was, by any reckoning, a learned and talented man. His scholarly achievements and his political skills at court have been described in Chapter 1. On the basis of this there could have been few who were more qualified for the post of French Church minister. However, it would appear that his sense of pastoral responsibility to his congregation did not measure up to the promise of his abilities. Hierome was an unabashed pluralist and a chronic absentee whose political career and business ventures seem to have occupied most of his time. Officially, Hierome served as French Church pastor from 1665 to 1677; but also held title to the following ecclesiastical appointments: the Precentorship of Waterford Cathedral (1666–82); the Treasury of Lismore (1666–82); the Prebendary of Donaghmore (1671–79); the Rectories of Churchtown (1675–9), Piercetown (1675–9), Clonegan (1679–82), and Newtown-Lennan (1679–82); and the Vicarages of Chapelizod (1667–82), Mullingar (1675–9), Rathdonnell (1675–9), and Carrick-on-Suir (1679–82). Hierome was involved in the attempted Huguenot colonization at Carrick. The extent of his involvement is uncertain, though the fact that he died there in 1682 may indicate that he might possibly have been ministering to his flock to a greater degree there, at least, than elsewhere. In 1675 we see him undertaking, with the aid of a Norwich weaver named Clubb, an industrial settlement at Callan – though without notable success. It is unknown whether other Huguenots were involved in the Callan venture, either as colonists or investors. In Hierome's defense, pluralism had been rampant within the Church of Ireland, nor was this much-maligned practice entirely without its advantages. It was rendered necessary in many instances where Irish Protestant parishes were often as much as three times larger than those in England, contained much smaller congregations, and offered insufficient salary. Thus, pluralism of benefices offered an avenue through which the communicants might at least be partially ministered to, though the situation did tend to encourage abuse, and unprincipled pluralists like the notorious Miler McGrath inspired a good deal of contemptuous cynicism amongst the Irish populace.

What is certain is that by 1670 Hierome had ceased keeping parish records, may not even have been residing in Dublin, and half the Huguenot families attested by George Blackall to have remained in the capital are defined as "Calvinist" – though it is not stated where they worshipped. Curiously, in spite of having been identified as "Anglican" by Blackall, Dublin alderman Louis Desminières was accused of forming part of a "Presbyterian party", was turned out of the corporation council in 1672, only to be restored to membership later that same year. One is tempted to raise the tantalizing question of whether there was a stronger crypto-Calvinist element than Blackall might have discerned?

In 1677 Ormond returned to power, perhaps with the intention of revitalizing the Dublin Huguenot community, and replaced Hierome with Moses Viridet.

1683

Whatever colonization schemes, if any, the Duke may have still harbored were pre-empted by Popish Plot and Rye House Crises, the Dragonnades and the onset of immigration that forged the Late Ormondite Refuge. This refuge, as hitherto mentioned, was dominated by Huguenots from southern and western regions and tended to be more assertive and less manageable.

There was indubitably a residual hangover effect from the more lenient viceregal administrations of Sir John Robartes, Lord Berkeley of Stratton, and the Earl of Essex.

All had granted wider latitude to Catholics and Dissenters; and individuals like Jean Comtesse took advantage of the opportunity this afforded to re-embrace Calvinism. In Comtesse's case this amounted to a personal rather than a practical exercise since, while he objected to continuing to worship at French Patrick's, he nevertheless – in the absence of an organized Huguenot Non-Conformist temple – chose to attend the Anglican Church of St. Peter's rather than associate himself with Presbyterianism or Independency. There were excellent reasons why a Huguenot should have been wary of associating with Presbyterianism, and these would become manifest during the Crisis of 1683.

J. C. Beckett, in his seminal work on Protestant dissent pointed out that as a general rule there existed different official attitudes and varying degrees of toleration by the Anglican establishment towards distinct groups of Protestant dissenters – they were not all to be lumped into one basket. The Huguenot Non-Conformists were actually the group that was most favorably treated (with the only exceptions occurring during the 1683 Rye House Crisis and the Jacobite Era of 1687–90). The Huguenot diaspora's dissenters were quite small in numbers when measured against other non-conforming groups. A good deal of sympathy was generated because of their amply-reported sufferings in France and their status as refugees of conscience who were often in need of assistance – at least during their initial period of resettlement. The Huguenots had generally shaken off their 16th century image, amassing a certain respect as energetic and law-abiding residents.

A rung below them stood the Quakers who, though they elicited no comparable degree of sympathy, were nevertheless considered to be too few in numbers to cause much of a disturbance, and invariably followed a non-confrontational posture with regard to state/established church authority. In 1683 and again from 1687–90, it was they who received favor over the dissenting Huguenots. The least tolerated group were the Presbyterians. Their doctrine and consistorial church organization was not only assumed to have subversive overtones, but as a religious and political force they were considered an imminent threat to the established order – owing to their strength in numbers and concentration (particularly in Ulster, which could be swiftly augmented by co-religionists in neighboring Scotland).

The Duke of Ormond had a particular aversion to Presbyterianism. In many ways, he held Dissenters responsible for the traumatic chain of events of the 1640s which had sent the Stuarts and the Butlers into exile. As one who had witnessed, and received the brunt, of the force of militant Presbyterianism he was consistently more suspicious of treasonous potential from that quarter than he was of Catholics. Problems with Covenanters in southwest Scotland who reacted against the Earl of Lauderdale's severe regime inspired Ormond to reorganize the Irish Army and dispatch troops to Ulster, where Scottish refugees were swelling the Presbyterian population and causing alarm, in 1677 and again in 1679. Ormond was of the opinion, also, that in the event of an invasion from France, the Anglophone Non-Conformists and "Irish Scots" posed a greater threat of collaboration than did the Irish Catholics. This mindset was further aggravated by the assistance rendered by Presbyterians to the elusive and nefarious Colonel Thomas Blood, who masterminded plots to kidnap (Dublin 1663) and/or assassinate (London 1670) the Duke (almost succeeding on the latter occasion). Though by the end of 1680 Colonel Blood was safely in his grave, the Presbyterian population remained under watchful scrutiny.

No sooner had Ormond re-established himself at Dublin Castle when the Popish Plot erupted in England in 1678. The Duke was at first suspicious of a parallel "Irish Plot" fomented by Catholics, but became convinced that such allegations were without foundation. However, Titus Oates' wild accusations spurred such an atmosphere of hysteria that the Shaftesbury Whigs were able to capitalize on it and there was little that the Viceroy could do to stem the tide of panic without himself falling under suspicion.

Attacks on Ormond as being too sympathetic to Papists (though he vigorously protested that he adhered to neither extreme) forced the Viceroy to acquiesce to more repressive measures than he would have wished. There was a wider political drama being played out in Britain, where the Exclusion Crisis was in full swing and the King was hard-pressed to stave off attempts to pass over his Catholic brother James, Duke of York from the line of succession to the throne in favor of a Protestant successor. In such an atmosphere, one wrong move (as the Duke was well aware) could cost someone their head.

Pastor Viridet's nerves were probably already frayed from having to contend with the challenges offered by the large Huguenot refugee influx which the 1681 Dragonnades had produced, when he was suddenly thrust into a crisis which was related to the Rye House Affair in England.

The Rye House Plot, wherein a group of conspirators allegedly planned to ambush King Charles and his brother James on the road from the horse races at Newmarket to London, was at once used by the King and the Tories to discredit the Whigs and signaled a popular reaction against Dissenters, who were implicated (by Whig association) in the murder plot. Gunmen were to be hidden at Richard Rumbold's Rye House at the village of Hoddeston in Hertfordshire on April 1, 1683 and would open fire on the Royal entourage as it passed. However the plot was foiled when a fire at Newmarket caused the King to return earlier than anticipated, and news of the conspiracy leaked out. Disclosure was followed by arrests and executions, among the latter those of Sir Algernon Sidney and Lord William Russell. As by-products, Whigs throughout England were purged of local office and Protestant Dissenters found themselves running the same gauntlet of suspicion and persecution that the Catholics had experienced during the Popish Plot frenzy.

In Ireland Ormond became convinced that the Rye House Conspiracy contained many tentacles, among them a large, undetected, Irish-based one. In Dublin, at some time in June 1683, a non-conforming minister named "Jacques" or "Jaikes" began to appeal to the newly-arrived Huguenot refugees' Calvinist proclivities to lure them away from worship at French Patrick's and join with Anglophone Presbyterians at their conventicles.

"Jacques" enlisted the active aid of a "Monsieur Leroux", a fan maker, whom he designated as his "vicar". This individual may possibly have been a certain "Pierre Leroux", and is not apparently connected to Louis Leroux, the silk manufacturer. It is probable that a majority of the French Patrick congregation defected; it was in any case serious enough to alarm Viridet, who called upon the assistance of Ormond's Lord Deputy, his son the Earl of Arran. The Duke was then in London but Arran, acting upon his father's advice as expressed via correspondence, forcefully broke up the Dissenting assemblies and shortly after 7 July had incarcerated "Jacques". Arran issued orders to the Lord Mayor to prohibit all conventicles but noted on 28 July that the "fanatics" were meeting in larger numbers than before and that Leroux had joined forces with a Dutch painter who was an elder for an English dissenting conventicle. Arran arrested Leroux and the Dutch painter and held them at Newgate Prison. By 1 August "Jacques" had been released but resumed his preaching to large crowds. At Arran's insistence the Lord Mayor seized "Jacques" at a meeting, where he expressed his belief that he had not transgressed the law. Thereupon, Arran freed him after extracting a promise that he would hold no more assemblies, which promise Arran was convinced he would break, thus providing the Lord Deputy with the justification to imprison him at Dublin Castle without the benefit of *habeus corpus* – as it indeed proved. By 4 August Arran had apparently broken the back of defiance, and on 11 August Ormond reported receiving letters from "Jacques", Leroux, and the Dutch painter from prison pleading ignorance as an excuse but containing no vow to desist. On 18 August Arran reported to his father that "Jacques" and Leroux had come to terms and had seemingly left Dublin. Not long afterwards, however another (anonymous) dissenting French minister was active for Viridet had to bring him to Arran's attention. The miscreant was jailed, released but by 2 October Viridet reported that he was still in Dublin and would now make it a habit to appear at French Patrick's after the *Book of Common Prayer* had been read and entice worshippers back to non-conformity through private conversation. It was decided to arrest him once more, but the offending pastor secretly left Dublin. Ormond, however, had by 27 October located him in London and had ordered that he be brought to his quarters. A conformist French minister from the Savoy vouched for him and though the dissident minister professed repentance, Ormond's final assessment of the man before ordering his release was that he remained a "peevish, incorrigible Presbyterian".

The 1683 episode seems to have taught the Huguenots the perils of association with Anglophone Presyterianism, and this was a lesson that was apparently taken to heart. French Protestant dissent there would be, but it would take an independent, individualistic course, so as to secure the most favorable treatment possible from officialdom. Connection with Anglophone dissent, particularly of the Presbyterian variety, would only serve – at best – as a hindrance.

From 1684–91 there is nothing to support the notion of Huguenots assembling in any other place of worship than French Patrick's; any assertion of (dissenting) groups of Huguenots holding conventicles is unsubstantiated. It is more probable that the gradual easing-out of the ailing Viridet by a series of "assistants", culminating in his replacement by the more radically-minded Josué Roussel, had the effect of temporarily assuaging dissident tendencies. Then of course there were more pressing issues to consider, chief among them the survival of the Huguenot community in the face of challenges wrought by James II's accession to the throne, the hostility of the Tyrconnel regime and the incarceration of Roussel. By 1690, the French congregation may well have been reduced almost to pre-1682 levels.

Re-Establishment & Turmoil

The French Church which emerged from the Jacobite era faced a totally altered situation: a wave of Huguenot refugees, vastly different and much larger numerically than the preceding Ormondite waves put together, was streaming into Ireland by 1692 and had rendered the old French Patrick's formula, as it stood, untenable. After Pastor Josue Roussel's death in February 1692 the French congregation was almost immediately confronted with dissension. Roussel's son Charles petitioned for the position of French pastor, in succession to his father, and he enjoyed the support of the surviving remnants of the Old Ormondite congregation. The newer (Ruvignac) arrivals, however, were beginning to immigrate to Ireland in substantial enough numbers to have an impact, and favoured the appointment of Jean Séverin. Séverin had pastored at Prouville, Isle de France and Grosménil, Normandy; and had subsequently participated in the exilic ministry in London. He had proven particularly active and effective in securing the naturalization of as many individual refugees as possible. Rejecting a chance to return to France in 1677, Séverin was appointed to oversee the Huguenot worshippers at Thorpe-le-Soken until 1687, when he left for Greenwich and there became a favourite of the Ruvigny family, baptizing a godchild of Viscount Galway's in 1691.Of those within the Ruvignac faction who supported Séverin, the most influential voices were those of the military nobles who were close to Viscount Galway – Isaac Dumont de Bostaquet appears to have been among their leaders. Roussel continued to officiate throughout the time the dispute was raging, and both sides finally obtained a hearing before the Lords Justice and Privy Council. The Lords Justice and Council belatedly (13 May 1692) consented to confirm Roussel's appointment. If, by this course of action, the Irish government sought to resolve the controversy, its hopes in that direction were soon frustrated. A little more than two weeks later, on 29 May 1692, Roussel lost a test of strength within the consistory. The Ruvignacs were able to muster a sufficient majority to nominate Gabriel Barbier as assistant minister at French Patrick's. Barbier, who had acquired a reputation for eloquent sermonizing, had been personal chaplain to both the first Marquis de Ruvigny, and his son, Viscount Galway. Given the contentious circumstances surrounding his appointment, Barbier's elevation by the ecclesiastical equivalent of a *coup d'état* which more resembled the workings of a pure Calvinist body rather than those of a conformist organization, was unanimously confirmed by the heads of family (though this was probably a façade designed to proclaim official solidarity and thus act to mask dissension and exhibit a harmonious image for the benefit of outsiders). This uncomfortable state of affairs endured for a further three months before Roussel, perhaps coming to realization that the influx of newcomers would not soon abate and that the congregation would tend to be less and less favourable to him and increasingly supportive of clergymen who would do Lord Galway's bidding, resigned his charge in August of 1692, after having held it for a stormy six months. Charles Roussel continued to serve in the Church of Ireland ministry, holding the vicarages of Carrigallen (1692–98); Drumlane; Tomregan (1685–1740); and Killeshendiney (1740–1754). He died on 14 February 1754, at the age of 102, having maintained little contact with the Dublin Huguenot colony, though his grandson Charles was then established as a Dublin merchant. A family of Roussels from Languedoc, who worshipped as members of the French Non-conformist Churches during the period 1702–21, do not seem to have been related to the Dauphinois clergyman's family.

Following Roussel's departure, there seems to have arisen a genuine need for a second pastor. Given the spectacular expansion in membership, it was no longer just a question of political maneuvering. The French Patrick's Consistory, with Galway's supporters in firm control, left the choice to the Viscount, and he rather predictably picked Sévérin.

Non-Conformity Revived

Shortly thereafter, however, it became clear that the situation had gone beyond personality and factionalism. The threat to the unity of French Protestant worship came from a new quarter, that of a suddenly reinvigorated Huguenot Non-Conformity. With the surge in immigration after 1691 and more favorable conditions for Dissent than had existed since the days of Cromwell, the larger proportion of Huguenot settlers (perhaps as many as two-thirds) were ready to embrace some form of non-conformist worship. The presence of a king who adhered to the Dutch Reformed variety of Calvinism, and the exceptionally liberal provisions of the parliamentary Act of 1692 *"For encouraging Protestant Strangers to settle and plant in Ireland"* encouraged Huguenots who preferred to adhere as closely as possible to the traditional practices of their homeland to form an independent congregation. The crucial clause read: "All Protestant strangers and foreigners who shall at any time take the oaths, and subscribe the declaration herein above-mentioned shall enjoy free exercise of their religion and have liberty of meeting together publicly for the worship of God, and of hearing Divine service and performing other religious duties in their own several rites used in their own countries; any law or statute to the contrary notwithstanding."

This paved the way for the establishment of the first permanent Huguenot Non-Conformed congregation in Ireland; no longer was the consent of an Anglican or Roman Catholic sovereign necessary, the formula was reduced to simple oaths of allegiance. It was to be admitted that conformity to the Established Church ritual, though no longer a prerequisite, was still of advantage, especially in such matters as guaranteeing the minister's source of income, securing a permanent place of worship and providing some sense of recognition and protection under the wings of Episcopal representatives. But this was not sufficient to counter nostalgia for France and for the old cherished forms of temple and consistory.

At some time in 1692 several Huguenot families rented a meeting place on Bride Street in Dublin from Councillor Thomas Whitshed for Non-Conformed worship, and shortly thereafter purchased a tenant's interest in plot # 10 on St. Stephen's Green, North for their burial ground. This cemetery, on what is now called Merrion Row, is accurately signposted "Huguenot Cemetery 1693" and protected under the Burial Grounds (Ireland) Act of 1856 and the Public Health (Ireland) Act of 1878, interments taking place there up to 1901. The impact was immediate and profound: most of the newly-arrived refugees (possibly as great a percentage as two-thirds) shunned French Patrick's to join the dissenting congregation, and soon the services of a second pastor, Bartelemy Balaguier, were needed to supplement those of the first Bride Street minister, Joseph Lagacherie.

The Dublin Negotiations & Their Impact

These alarming developments spurred the Conformed pastors and consistory into action, and Viscount Galway himself intervened. An accommodation with the French dissenters was felt to be in order and in April 1693 Galway and Sévérin opened negotiations with Lagacherie and Balaguier with the aim of welding Conformists and Dissenters into one communion. Articles of union were drawn up by Sévérin, under Galway's direction and sent to be voted on by the respective congregations (T. P. Le Fanu, however, credits Benjamin De Daillon with the authorship of the articles of union). French Patrick's approved but the Non-Conformed church membership overwhelmingly rejected the articles. It was a stinging defeat for Galway, who had expended a lot of his prestige and powers of persuasion into attempting to work out this formula. In fact, this was the incident that defined the limitations of his leadership and certainly weakened the ideal of a united *Corps du réfuge* in Ireland. Faced with this, the Viscount acquiesced with grace, but could only – prior to his departure for Flanders – call the leaders of both congregations and vaguely exhort that though unification had not been achieved, they should nonetheless strive to live together in peace "as brethren".

This admission – and in effect, capitulation – set the tone for the curious relationship and permanent split which existed from that time on within the Irish *Corps du refuge*, between the adherents of the Calvinist and Anglican tendencies. Huguenots of either persuasion were alternatively (even sometimes simultaneously) in unity and at odds with each other. There could on the one hand be the warmest of cooperation, as in the case of the continual work for the charitable relief of newly arrived, destitute refugees – wherein all French congregations might pool their human and material resources. But on the other hand, there could be incredible bitterness, made all the more vitriolic because of the internecine nature of their disagreements. Even "brethren" can sometimes indulge in heated sibling rivalry.

Growth and "Schisms", 1693–1716

French Patrick's attempts at retrenchment and redefinition in the face of the Non-Conformist challenge was given expression in the *Forme et discipline de l'eglise françoise qu'il se reunnist a St. Patrice*, which was slowly and methodically set forward and hammered out at weekly meetings of the heads of families. The deliberations covered nine months before securing approval on 7 October 1694 and passing to Archbishop Narcissus Marsh. The most important article, perhaps, was that which guaranteed a permanent stipend for the Conformed ministers, replacing the pluralistic arrangement which had proved so unsatisfactory. Other provisions standardized hours of services, required of newly-arrived refugees oaths of abjuration and *réconnaissance,* and proof of their adherence to Protantism (on the same basis as was already practiced by the Non-Conformist Church on Bride Street), and reconfirmation of the consistorial form for church governance. Furthermore, the requirement of Episcopal ordination for French clergymen was relaxed into a sort of "gentleman's agreement" between the congregation and the bishop which implied a degree of flexibility in certain situations (i.e., a shortage of pastors).

The strength of the Huguenot immigration into Ireland engendered a corresponding burgeoning in the size of both Conformed and Non-Comformed churches between 1694–1701. As French Patrick's became overcrowded, a large gallery was erected (December 1697), at the cost of fifty-seven pounds. Scarcely had this been completed when the need was felt for a second gallery (May 1698 – costing thirty-two pounds). The congregation had to assemble temporarily at St. Kevin's Church while alterations were put into place. In April of 1699 two further galleries were added and old ones enlarged, testifying to the Refuge's continuing vitality. One year later the congregation had grown too large even for the ministering efforts of two pastors, and the consistory petitioned the Earl of Galway to release yet another one of his chaplains, Jean De la Sara, to act as their third minister. De la Sara took up his charge on 28 April 1700, but resigned on 14 July 1701, to be succeeded by Charles De la Roche. De la Sara apparently went to London where he maintained contact with his Dublin colleagues for at least another year, presenting Archbishop Marsh with a copy of his sermon: *Oraison funebre de Guillaume III*.

Non-Confomist growth was even more spectacular. In 1697, Counsellor Whitshed died and, though this may not have been coincidental, another dissenting temple was established on the north side of the River Liffey. Sir Charles Meredith had obtained a grant of a parcel of land with a former Jesuit chapel, on the west side of Lucy Lane (which is believed to correspond to present-day Chancery Place). Meredith left the grant to the French congregation, and regular worship services were begun there. However, some families found it more convenient to attend church on the South side of the Liffey and thus assembled in rented accommodations at Wood Street.

Balaguier and Lagacherie shuttled between the two chapels until June of 1701 when further growth led the Wood Street worshippers to petition for a third pastor. There arose a dispute between the Wood Street and Lucy Lane consistories (the latter not admitting to the necessity of paying a third pastor). The Wood Street church seceded and brought in Jacques Gillet, the former dissenting minister at Portarlington. Gillet was shortly succeeded by a certain Monsieur Pons, former minister at Glasshouse Street and Leicester Fields in London. After the split, the Lucy Lane group became variously known as "the French Church of St. Lucy's" or "French Lucy's". In 1707, differences between the non-conformist churches were reconciled and the consistories were reunited. In 1709 the Wood Street lease expired and the owners were demanding what was considered an excessive rent increase. A subscription drive for the building of a new church with a second burial ground was organized and bore fruit when, on 19 December 1711, a non-conformist church was consecrated at Peter Street not far from St. Patrick's Cathedral. It would come to be known as "French Peter's".

A curious note appears in the Non-Conformist church registers which refers to a French church of "Golblac Lane". No such thoroughfare or alley way is to be found either in contemporary Dublin or in any manuscript source other than the one already-quoted. Nor has years of research provided a conclusive answer to this mystery. Perhaps this is a garbled reference to Golden Lane, which is located just parallel ant to the north of Wood Street, and where the Wood Street congregation may speculatively have assembled in a temporary location during the period 1709–11, while awaiting the purchase of the Peter Street site, and the construction of the new temple there.

In the meantime, increased membership sparked by immigration was also posing problems for the Conformed church. French Patrick's was having trouble coping with ever swelling numbers of Huguenot, who moreover were scattered around the city and might have found it inconvenient to regularly attend Sunday services. To accommodate its worshippers who resided north of the Liffey and preclude their defection to French Lucy's the Archdiocese of Dublin decided to reserve for their use the venerable Chapter House of St. Mary's Abbey, which was located on Meetinghouse Lane off Mary's Abbey Street. Obtaining a lease from Sir Humphrey Jervis, with the Lords Justice contributing two hundred pounds towards maintenance costs, the new Conformed congregation first assembled on 16 March 1701. Two French Anglican clergymen, Henri de Rocheblave and Pierre Pézé Degalinière, agreed to divide the pastoral duties at this new chapel – which became known as "the French Church of St. Mary's" or simply "French Mary's" – accepting the very modest stipend of fifteen pounds *per annum*.

Jean Sévérin died in February of 1704 and his demise initiated disagreements over procedure and succession which created yet another fissure in the Huguenot refuge; this time within the ranks of Anglican worshippers. This bizarre incident has been excellently documented and analyzed by Mr. G. A. Forrest; the gist of the matter centered around Pierre Degalinière's claim to Sévérin's ministry, with its sixty pounds annual compensation, on the basis of seniority. Dublin Archbishop William King, however, sided with a majority of the congregation, which favored Claude Grostete de la Mothe, who had officiated at the Church of the Savoy. The situation rapidly degenerated into dispute, the severity of which caught Archbishop King unawares. Whereas most of the French Patrick's congregation had favored Grostete de la Mothe, the majority at French Mary's had supported Pierre Degalinière – and furthermore might have harbored some resentment at being considered "stepchildren" whose needs did not weigh as heavily with the Church of Ireland as those of their more numerous co-religionists at French Patrick's. Too late, the Archbishop attempted to bridge the growing rift, but the dispute accelerated to a point beyond the prelate's moral power to mediate. Even Élie Bouhéreau, who was called upon in a desperate move to effect a reconciliation, could not avert the schism that occurred on 1 January 1705.

Thus, for the next eleven years the French Mary's church led a curious existence: separatist and individualistic, yet steadfastly remaining within the conformist ranks and while ignoring the Archbishop's directives and entreaties, paying a sort of lip-service respect to the office and to the Anglican communion. The paradoxical nature of this French Church, which simultaneously both was and was not a dissenting assembly, owed much to the character and motives of Pastor Degalinière himself. The Degaliniere who emerges out of this controversy is a shrewd well-connected politician who was adept at playing both sides against the middle. Expelled from France after officiating at Le Mans, Degalinière cultivated a close association with Samuel Pepys, and with the influential Dean of York, Thomas Gale.

A bare two months after the French Mary's secession, Degalinière and his congregation stunned the Archbishop again by entering into discussion with the Non-Conformed French Lucy consistory with the avowed purpose of unification. What is mystifying is that Degalinière's group insisted upon Archbishop King's approval as a precondition – somewhat akin to asking for approval from the chickens to allow the fox into the henhouse! This apparent self-sabotage of the project strongly suggests a ploy on Degalinière's part to wheedle a government grant that would subsidize an assistant pastor and to have his (Degalinière's) name entered in the Auditor General's Register, with the salary increase that this would secure. If so, it had the desired effect and members of the French Patrick's consistory were livid. Pascal Ducasse was soon named as the second French Mary's minister and Degalinière confounded the authorities through his dangling of the bait of dissent. Degalinière would play the game for another decade, and there were on-an-off attempts at re-forging the link between the two French Anglican assemblages. The moderating efforts of the illustrious scholar Jacques Abbadie, Dean of Killaloe, who had been Ducasse's mentor, paved the way for the end of the quasi-schism. It is probably fitting that it would be the Earl of Galway, returned to his post as Lord Justice in 1715, who succeeded where he had failed in 1693 and drew up the acceptable Articles of Union, which were agreed to on 1 May 1716. The consistories of French Mary's and French Patrick's were brought back together and designated as the Assembly of the United (Conformed) French Churches. The United Churches were to have four full-time ministers (Degalinière, Ducasse, Pierre Bouquet de St. Paul and Alexandre de Susy Boan), and a *lecteur*, Abraham Viridet.

Confrontations

Non-Conformist French Churches appeared elsewhere. Besides Dublin, we are certain that dissenting congregations emerged in Portarlington, Cork, and Carlow (perhaps, for a time, in Lisburn). Moreover, certain dissenting ministers who later accepted appointments to head Conformed congregations, such as Gaspard Caillard and Antoine Vinchon Des Voeux at Portarlington, undoubtedly carried at least the Calvinist sentiment into their day-to-day pastorate.

Nowhere else in Ireland did the Dissenter–Anglican clash within the Huguenot community have more bitter and enduring repercussions than at Portarlington. The 1702 Daillon–Moreton incident there has been mentioned in Chapter 4, but the issues involved are worth further discussion. Episcopal ordination was a primary stumbling block in both major disputes of which we have a record: the Portarlington controversy, and the flare-up in Cork between Jacques Fontaine and Isaac De la Croix.

In the case of Portarlington, the refugee community had in effect been "set up" by the legislative machinations of Thomas Lindsay, Bishop of Killaloe, who had functioned as a "stalking horse" for his colleague William Moreton, Bishop of Kildare by attaching crucial provisions onto a relief bill which had been originally intended to preserve the property and leasehold interests of the Huguenot settlers, which had been jeopardized by the Act of Resumption. The clause required the Trustees for Forfeited Estates to "convey, assign and make over" to Bishop Moreton the two churches and the schools and to appoint the schoolmasters and ministers from "time to time". In polite terms, Parliament thus handed the Bishop of Kildare the leverage to impose conformity. The petition for the Relief Bill itself reveals this to have been Bishop Lindsay's intention from the beginning and, in espousing measures to take advantage of the Dissenters' anxiety to bring them into the Anglican fold and break their "insolence", he was not alone.

Bishop Moreton was considered to harbor strong Jacobite sentiments, having served as chaplain to the Duke of Ormond before his appointment, by letters patent, to the See of Kildare. He was selected to the Irish Privy Council on 5 April 1681, but in spite of his record of moderation towards Roman Catholics, he was replaced under James II. After the Williamite conquest Moreton's Jacobitism played against him as far as being considered for an arch-bishopric. However, his conciliatory stance on Catholicism was considered a potential asset on the Privy Council, and he was reinstated. Moreton proved very aggressive against dissent, and the manner in which he enforced conformity on the Portarlington congregation reveals an imperious prelate who could be unhesitating in applying coercion, with only the thinnest veneer of diplomacy.

Even prior to the signing of the final deed of conveyance (20 September 1702), Bishop Moreton visited Portarlington and had a stormy interview with Non-Conformist Pastor Benjamin De Daillon. Stripped of such genteel language as the Bishop deigned to add, there was in essence an ultimatum: the French Calvinist Temple was to be consecrated as an Anglican church dedicated to St. Paul, and Daillon was to receive episcopal ordination. Perhaps to the Bishop's surprise, Daillon flatly refused and, effective 4 October 1702, was replaced by a Conformist ex-army chaplain, Antoine Ligonier de Bonneval. For his part, Moreton published his justification in an open letter, at first instance chiding the congregation for having "hitherto thought fit to heap for yourselves teachers utterly against the Apostolical Injunction and particularly condemned . . . in 2 Timothy 4:3".

Then, shifting his ground, adopting a paternalistic tone, and interspacing some velvet wording to slightly mask the bluntness of the situation, assured the worshippers that he would "make it my business to bring you by degrees to compliance as you shall have no reason to complain of", characterizing his scholarly opponent Daillon as a stubborn embittered man who had spurned a reasonable offer and seemed intent on maintaining a petty, consistorial tyranny. Daillon's true reservations – as recently detailed in an excellent study by Dr. Ruth Whelan – were far more conscientiously-grounded. What Moreton proposed regarding consecration and ordination would have negated the validity of the very faith for which Daillon himself, and most of the Portarlington colonists, had endured persecution and exile. In the High Churchman Moreton, Daillon discerned a more subtle echo of the Roman Catholic despotism he had spurned. Though Daillon's history had been one of cordial interaction with both Anglicans and French Conformists, what Bishop Moreton insisted upon must have seemed to have been little-removed from an *abjuration*. The Bishop of Kildare did come to Portarlington to consecrate the churches, backed by two prominent Huguenot Deans of the Church of Ireland: Jacques Abbadie of Killaloe and Jean Ycard of Achonry.

It was a *fait accomplit*. Moreton held every advantage and for most of the Portarlington Huguenots there could be no option but acceptance – the loss of home, property and living could not be risked. All they had strived for in exile was now being held to ransom. It is therefore quite remarkable, in view of the settlement's vulnerability, that some 100 adult individuals still had the fortitude to sign a petition taking sides with Daillon. Portarlington was never the same. Ligonier De Bonneval did not come into a peaceful, united flock, but one which was permanently and rancorously riven. For six years the new pastor had to confront the old across the meeting table – Daillon stayed on, supplemented by income from the Earl of Galway, as the Consistory Moderator. What must have been a most uncomfortable situation ended in 1708, when Daillon seems to have taken up his final post as minister to Carlow's Non-Conformist Temple, and hopefully enjoyed some measure of peace in the final months of his life. As for Bonneval, he remained to preside over a much diminished and divided community whose heroic age was never to be recaptured.

We have far less in the way of details about the Fontaine Incident in Cork, which has been dealt with to a certain extent in Chapter 6. However, brief explanatory summary here would not go amiss. Jacques Fontaine's *Mémoires* offer the only real clues – yet even at that certain similarities to the Daillon–Moreton escapade come to notice. Contention and controversy had followed Jacques Fontaine throughout his life like iron to a magnet. A native of Charente, he had been jailed by the authorities for illegally holding open air services, but had launched a successful appeal to the Guyenne Parlement. In 1685, after a daredevil escape from France to Barnstaple, England, he found himself in dire financial straits. Disdaining to conform to the Anglican Church, Fontaine was ordained to the ministry by the Barnstaple Presbyterians. In November 1688 he was accepted as Huguenot pastor at the Pesthouse Church in London, but soon responded to a call from the French Church at Taunton in Somersetshire. Moving to Cork in 1694, Fontaine became the pastor of the Non-Conformed Temple in January of 1695. Jean De La Croix, a Huguenot merchant, had fled the city when he had been discovered trying to smuggle butter out of Ireland without paying duty. His father, Isaac De La Croix (who had dealt with the fallout of his son's escapade), suffered acute embarrassment and became incensed when Fontaine preached a sermon which appeared to allude to this incident (Fontaine denied that this had been the intent). The elder De La Croix brought about a dispute within the French congregation which, as previously indicated, Bishop Edward Wetenhall exploited as an excuse for intervening and "suggesting" that Fontaine accept Anglican orders. Like Daillon, Fontaine refused and appealed to Lord Justice Galway. The Huguenot Earl's pro-Conformist response proved disappointing to Fontaine, who saw him as weak and vacillating, too willing to kowtow to the bishops. The pastor resigned in disgust (30 May 1698).

The Unraveling

The years *c.* 1716–40 may mark a sort of zenith for the Huguenot population of Ireland – or so at least the vitality of French worship in Dublin would indicate. There were four Anglican ministers and five Non-Conformed pastors and Huguenots from different levels of society and varying trades and professions had leavened into Irish society. Thereafter, attrition would grind both Anglican and Dissenter Huguenot worship to extinction. Decline in membership engendered by gradual assimilation into the anglophone milieu, the general eighteenth-century tendency away from proliferation of sects and breakaway religious congregations, the dying off of the first generation of refugees, and the slowing of French immigration into Ireland was manifest as early as the late 1730s.

Church attendance at French Mary's had dwindled by August 1740 to the point that the congregation abandoned the Chapter House of St. Mary's Abbey (which was relegated to the status of a chapel-of-ease), and merged into French Patrick's. Four ministers were too many, and when their numbers were whittled away by natural attrition, their positions were steadily phased out. In 1773 the north side Non-Conformists sold their building at Lucy Lane to the breakaway Free Presbyterians, and merged into French Peter's. Though the original disputes might have been forgotten, the force of tradition now made the chasm between Huguenot Dissenter and Huguenot Anglican a permanent one. On 19 February 1814, following the death of the last French Non-Conformist clergyman, Isaac Subremont, who had shepherded his flock since 1760 (and had been the sole minister during the last three decades of his lengthy tenure), French Peter's Church closed. French Patrick's did not survive much longer: in 1816, after over 154 years of existence, regular service ceased. After officiating at a memorial service on Christmas Day, 1817 the last minister, Jean Letablere, retired. He would pass on in 1822 at his residence at 22 Ely Place, and the congregation of St. Nicholas-Without-the-Walls would meet at the Lady Chapel in place of the Huguenots worshippers.

Ultimately, the exiles did not succeed in reconciling their religious principles either among themselves, or with their Anglican hosts. They could not meet the demands of the Bourbon monarchy that they had once so revered, neither did they ultimately achieve a separate unencumbered existence within their Irish refuge. But they did bequeath to their progeny the right to practice their faith, to contribute richly to their adopted land, and to alter the course of its history.

References

Primary sources

Archbishop Marsh's Library Manuscripts: 30.2.2; Z4.3.0; Z5.3.88; Bouhereau-Ellis Correspondence (Microfilm).
Calendar of State Papers (Domestic), 1660–1685, pp. 363–4.
Calendar of State Papers (Ireland), 1669–70 addenda 1625–70, p. 67.

Genealogical Office of Ireland: Ms. 4, pp. 147–54.

Historic Manuscripts Commission Publications. Rep. 2, App. 1874, p. 243; Calendar of the manuscripts of the Marquess of Ormonde, vii, pp. 65, 81, 89, 93–5, 102, 104, 106, 108–9, 139, 150, 155, 181; Buccleuch & Queensbury Ms., Vol. ii, pt. 2, pp. 502–3.

Huguenot Society of London-Quarto Series, Vol. VII, XIV.

Irish Statutes: 4 William & Mary, c. 2, Vol. iii, pp. 243–4.

National Library of Ireland Ms.: 104, 802, 2075, 2675 (pp. 32–3), 2670 (p. 12), 8007, 11970, 11971.

Royal Irish Academy: Dumont Manuscript.

Books/pamphlets

Formulaire de la Consécration et Dédicace des Églises et Chapelles selon l'usage de L'Église d'"Irlande (Dublin 1702).

Secondary sources

Aydelotte, James Ernest. *The Duke of Ormond and the English Government of Ireland, 1677–85*, pp. 17, 22, 24–6.

Bagwell, Richard. *Ireland Under the Stuarts*, pp. 8–9, 94, 100, 319–20.

Beckett, J. C. *Protestant Dissent in Ireland, 1687–1784*, pp. 124–8, 132–3, 135, 137–45.

Combe, J. C. *The Huguenots in the Ministry of the Church of Ireland.* Unpublished Doctoral Dissertation (Belfast, Queen's University, 1970), pp. 266–7, 401, 407.

Craig, Maurice. *Dublin, 1660-1860*, pp. 3–4, 38.

Deyon, Solange. *Du Loyalisne au Refus*, pp. 9, 27–8, 91–2, 96–7, 159–60.

Forrest, G. A. "Schism and Reconciliation: the 'Nouvelle Eglise de Ste. Marie' Dublin, 1705–16" in *PHSGBI*, Vol. xxvi, no. 2, pp. 199–212.

Forrest, G. A. "Religious Controversy within the French Protestant Community in Dublin, 1692–1716: An Historiographical Critique" in Herlihy, Kevin, *The Irish Dissenting Tradition, 1650–1750*, pp. 96–110.

Gimlette, Thomas. *The History of the Huguenot Settlers in Ireland*, pp. 199, 273.

Greaves, Richard. " 'That's no Good Religion that Disturbs Government': The Church of Ireland and the Non-Conformist Challenge" in Ford, Alan, McGuire, James, and Milne, Kenneth, *As by Law Established: The Church of Ireland since the Reformation*, pp. 120–35.

Gwynn, Robin. "Government Policy towards Huguenot Immigration and settlement in England and Ireland" in Caldicott, Gough & Pittion, *The Huguenots and Ireland*, pp. 211, 217–21.

Hill, Jacqueline R. "Dublin Corporation, Protestant Dissent & Politics, 1660–1800" in Herlihy, Kevin. *The Politics of Irish Dissent, 1650–1800*, p. 30.

Hylton, Raymond Pierre. "The Less-favored Refuge: Ireland's Non-Conformist Huguenots at the turn of the Eighteenth Century" in Herlihy, Kevin, *The Religion of Irish Dissent: 1650–1800*, pp. 83–99.

Johnston, Elsie "The Diary of Elie Bouhereau" in *PHSL*, Vol. xv, n. 1, p. 46.

Kenyon, J. P. *The Stuarts*, pp. 136–7.

Le Fanu, T. P. in Lawlor, *Fasti*, pp. 277, 281, 285, 287–9, 291.

Le Fanu, T. P. in *PHSL*: "The Huguenot Churches in Dublin and their Ministers", Vol. viii, no. 1, pp. 5–6, 11, 17–18, 20, 24–8, 32, 34–5, 38–41; "Archbishop Marsh and the Discipline of the French Church at St. Patrick's in 1694", Vol. xii,, no. 4, pp. 245–62; "Dumont de Bostaquet at Portarlington", Vol. xiv, no. 2, pp. 211–27; "The Life and Sufferings of Benjamin de Daillon", Vol. XIV, no. 4, pp. 458–78.

Lee, Grace Lawless. *The Huguenot Settlements in Ireland*, pp. 149, 152–3, 227.

Ligou, Daniel. *Le Protestantisme en France*, pp. 171, 174–5.

McGuire, James I. " Government Attitudes to Religious Non-Conformity in Ireland, 1660-1719" in Caldicott, Gough & Pittion, *The Huguenots and Ireland*, pp. 255–80.

Pittion, Jean-Paul "The French Protestants and the Edict of Nantes (1549-1685): A chronology based on materials in Marsh's Library, Dublin" and "The Question of Religious Conformity or Non-Conformity in the Irish Refuge", both in Caldicott, Gough & Pittion *Huguenots and Ireland*, pp. 37–65, 285–94.

Reid, S. J. *History of the Presbyterian Church in Ireland*, ii, pp. 458, 64–5.

Schickler, Baron F. de *Les Eglises du Refuge en Angleterre*, ii. p. 268.

Simms, J. G. "The Restoration, 1660-85" in Moody, Martin & Byrne, *A New History of Ireland*, Vol. iii, p. 437.

Whelan, Ruth "Points of view: Benjamin de Daillon, William Moreton, and the Portarlington Affair" in *PHSGBI*, Vol. xxvi, no. 4, pp. 463–81.

◈ EPILOGUE ◈

Legends and Facts

"The Huguenots were tolerant? We all like to think of ourselves as being tolerant."
— Irish motorist to the author, April 1985

When all is said and done, perhaps it can most aptly be stated that, for the Huguenots in exile, Louis XIV lived too long and the Enlightenment arrived too late. The Grand Monarch reigned for 72 of his 76 years and to the end, even as he was dying from the gangrene that had developed in his leg, remained adamantly opposed to restoring the Edict of Nantes and of admitting recognition of Huguenotism in any way, shape or form.

Though the various chief governors and administrators of France under the shallow and vacillating King Louis XV, from the Duke of Orleans on, were far less inflexible in their confessional attitude, the presence of a powerful Catholic *dévot* party at Court impeded any moves towards reconciliation. The Sun King's long shadow extended well into the reign of his great-great-great grandson, Louis XVI, and to the eve of the French Revolution.

By the very definition of the term, a refuge is temporary. Short of a perpetual, sustaining surge of new immigrants, and a focused, all-embracing exilic leadership, only two *déenouements* existed for Ireland's Huguenot communities. When viewed from the perspective of such hindsight as we possess, the Irish Huguenot Refuge was doomed from the onset: either very rapidly by a reversal of French governmental policy, followed by a return *en masse* to a cleansed and repentant homeland; or quite gradually through the erosive process of assimilation. Much would depend upon how long it would take to lift the sanctions of the Edict of Fontainebleau, which in turn depended ultimately on the whim of whoever happened to be ruler of France. Until the 1740s–50s and possibly (though in diminishing degree) the early 1760s there might have been some slight chance of a substantial return migration. Afterwards, with immigration of Huguenots into Ireland becoming too slight to elicit much attention, and the Anglicization and/or Hibernization of refugee descendants well under way, the only remaining path led to absorption.

If the fate of Ireland's Huguenot Refuge, as regards continuity, turned on anything, it turned on Louis XIV's refusal to countenance discussion of any revision or moderation of the provisions of the Edict of Fontainebleau during the negotiations of the Peace of Ryswick in 1697 – and the Allies' acquiescence in this. Though it could not have been foreseen, Louis' decision and the failure of his opponents to contest it in effect rendered the Huguenot exile permanent, and destined to dry on the vine: no monarch, regent or minister proving either strong enough or inclined to contradict it. Ryswick was the best and – as it proved – final chance for the exiles. No similar occasions under more favorable circumstances were to arise. The subsequent deepening of sectarian attitudes in France, Britain and Ireland brought about a hardening of positions. Violent international and internal events reinforced pre-existing alienation: the Camisard Uprising with the atrocities perpetrated by both sides; the emergence of the persecuted Church of the Desert in the Languedoc; the War of the Spanish Succession; and the ever-present threat of Jacobite/Catholic incursions into the British Isles, abetted by French or Spanish troops.

A vicious cycle fed upon itself as Anglo-French rivalry intensified. Their national origins impelled many Huguenots in Britain and Ireland to emphasize their loyalty to the British crown. The question of allegiance became increasingly important for succeeding generations. As later as 1848, upon learning of the February Revolution in France that had rapidly toppled King Louis Philippe, members of the Rambaut family in Dublin were conscious enough of their Huguenot origins to feel themselves obliged to publicly affirm their fealty to the British monarchy. Thereafter, and certainly by the time of the founding of the Huguenot Society of London in 1885, the "Britishness" of Huguenot descendants seems to have no longer been remotely open to question.

Tenterhooks and bread cakes

Whoever they were, wherever they journeyed, the Huguenots acquired a unique hold upon the Irish psyche and imagination, and one which has been so marinaded by legend and anecdote that their identity itself has often become subsumed. Whose Huguenots are we talking about, anyway? Their image is further distorted by the fact that they have been employed as time and circumstance may fit, as political footballs. The

Whig historians, following the trail blazed by Lord Macaulay, saw the Huguenots in heroic, Empire-building terms. Samuel Smiles perceived the French refugees as pioneers of self-help who lifted themselves from the depth of adversity their own efforts and virtue, and W. E. H. Lecky as exemplifying the advantages that might derive from diversity and respect for the rights of minorities. Though part-and-parcel of the Protestant Ascendancy, the Huguenots have avoided the historical condemnation of recent years. To the contrary, the mystique that has coalesced around Ireland's Huguenots has a certain unique and lively quality about it. No less a figure than James Joyce was fascinated by these French Calvinists and their legacy – *Finnegan's Wake* in particular is deeply festooned with Huguenot references.Whereas they were once held up as paragons of moral virtue ("Honest as a Huguenot" became an oft-employed cliché), sobriety, and self-discipline, they have of recent years even been limned as precursors of European unity and inter-action.* Not all of the legends surrounding the Huguenots were that positive, or innocuous. Word-of-mouth stories of course still perpetuate the fallacy that they established a weavers' ghetto in the Liberties of Dublin. Some of the tales insist that this clannish community would punish errant members by nailing then on the roofs of their dwellings with tenterhooks. Then, too, the Huguenots have sometimes been linked to the durable saga of being participants in gang warfare with the Catholic butchers of Ormond Quay in Dublin as members of the so-called "Liberty Boys". They are even accused of having perpetrated the atrocity of hanging these butchers and their apprentices on their own meat hooks! While certain members of the 16th century Huguenot Party in France might not have hesitated to do something like this, everything we can verify concerning the Huguenots in Ireland argues against this story. Nowhere in the tale are the Huguenots specifically mentioned – they have somehow been insinuated into it over the years. Also, if research has revealed anything, it is that a Huguenot Weavers' ghetto in the Liberties simply is not there to be found. Nevertheless the legend persists, to the point where individuals still assert that the accent of those remaining inhabitants of the Liberties is a French accent. Less gruesomely, we may refer once again to the interesting example of the *blah* or *blaa*, a small circular doughy bread cake baked in Kilkenny, Wexford and Waterford and which folklore ascribes to having been brought over by Huguenot refugees (see Chapter 7). Corner fireplaces in the buildings constructed between the 1680s and the 1750s are often referred to as "Huguenot fireplaces", though in an equal number of instances, the term

---

* Notably on the website posted by Dick Roche, TD, Minister of State for Europe, "Lesson of the Huguenots has Relevance to the Nice Debate" (6 October 2002).

"Quaker fireplace" is employed. The so-called "Huguenot houses" or "Dutch Billies" have also been discussed.

Perhaps the exotic elements in a society have, in and of themselves, a way capturing the popular imagination and of attracting often-fantastic stories

The "Good Guys" of the Ascendancy

Of all the elements that factored into the "Protestant Ascendancy" and formed the Anglo "Imperium", the Huguenots have proven to be the great exception. As a group they have retained a remarkable degree of respect, even admiration – such of course has not been so consistently applicable to English, Scot, Welsh, Dutch, and German colonials. The Palatines seem to come closest, but they still cannot capture the aura that has grown over the decades around the Huguenots. The uniquely French mystique might explain part of this. The Catholic Irish, too, after enduring the Penal Laws, may have seen something of themselves in the Huguenot experience. Certainly the Huguenots had going for them the role of victims, not of course a role of their choosing but one whereby they derived an unprecedented reservoir of sympathy. The tidal waves atrocity reports out of France that ebbed and flowed for over a quarter century, abetted by the characterization of the Huguenots themselves as "poore French refugees" played a significant part in the perpetuation of the Huguenot legend. As early martyrs to the cause of tolerance, their example would have surely struck a chord with Catholic nationalism. It was their sufferings that set them apart, and, at a further remove, their creativity and contributions, both verified and legendary. In a more positive imagery, the Huguenots emerged with a reputation as heroic defenders of liberal virtues. In an age which has become increasingly sensitive to international principles of human rights, the Huguenot experience has taken on added contemporary relevance.

And it is as regards the apparent mellowing of the attitude of many Huguenots over the issues of sectarian fanaticism – a mellowing perhaps in large part occasioned by their own painful experience – that the most profound and immediate chord is struck. Once, while hitchhiking to Dublin, I had occasion to engage the driver who was decent enough to give me a lift in a conversation about the Huguenots and their impact on Ireland. He set the greatest stock in the image of the Huguenots as apostles of religious toleration, commenting "We all like to think of ourselves as being tolerant." This is no isolated instance; there is certainly no lack of identification *a propos* the Huguenots and their perceived virtues of tolerance, with the debates over issues of Irish identity, European integration, new waves of immigration, human rights concerns, and peace in Northern Ireland. And in view of recent, unfortunate global developments, the international implications that link the seventeenth – and eighteenth-century Huguenot dispersion with contemporary examples of religious extremism are clear enough even to the most casual of observers.

What examples we do possess that afford us an indication of how exiled Huguenots might have viewed the broader Enlightenment tendencies of confessional co-existence and mutual respect for differing beliefs are, in and of themselves, positive ones. The Earl of Galway himself, far from conforming to his legendary image as an anti-Catholic ogre, espoused the continued existence of the Catholic faith as part of a dual-system whereby there would be two government-established churches: one Anglican and the other Roman Catholic. Perhaps he envisioned its eventual implementation through a special concordat between Whitehall and the Papacy. Jean Cavallier, the fiery Cévenol guerrilla chieftain, was an even less likely advocate for toleration – or so it might be initially thought.

Though Cavallier's *Memoires of the Wars of the Cévennes*, published at Dublin in 1726, are self-evidently of invaluable interest, it is the *Preface* that is the most moving and contemporary portion of his *oeuvre*. Astoundingly, and almost incongruously, this hardened veteran of one of the eighteenth century's most viciously fought conflicts launches a highly moving plea against any type of penal law and in favor of the open-handed toleration of both Protestant dissent and Catholicism. It is telling also, that Cavallier's list of subscribers includes many prominent Dublin and Portarlington Huguenot families.

Gaspard Caillard enjoyed a long and distinguished career as a French protestant clergyman, and a reputation as a charismatic preacher who elicited praise from John Wesley himself. He is lesser known as the author of a book of sermons in French entitled *Sermons sur divers texts de l'Écriture Sainte* (Dublin 1728). Of particular interest are the first two sermons: *"Sur l'intolérance"* and *"Sur les justes borne de la tolérance"* in which he carried forward and even expanded upon Cavallier's attack against persecuting tendencies within both the extreme Catholic and Protestant camps. Twenty-six of the more affluent Dublin and Portarlington settlers likewise readily subscribed to the publication of Caillard's volume. There are, admittedly, few examples of Huguenots recording their feelings on the subject, and much of our assessment must be based on indirect reference. It is to be hoped – and more than likely is the case – that the Huguenot reputation for tolerance is not as exaggerated an assumption as others that have clustered about their name over the centuries.

In so enthusiastically accepting the Huguenots as part of their heritage, the Irish, paradoxically, seem to have adroitly nullified what was undoubtedly a patronizing insult at the time, i.e.: that the sober, energetic, thrifty and honest Huguenot might impart these admirable traits to the "Native Irish". Instead, this slight has been turned on its head so that the Irish revel in the fact that such an admirable group has become a part of their nation's ethnic make up.

Dates & Numbers

Until we have painstakingly scoured every extant record, and deciphered each line in ink that Providence or circumstance might have been kind enough to preserve, the precision as to numbers will elude us. The "canonical" estimate of 10,000 total Huguenot immigrants into Ireland *might*, it has been suggested by Charles C. Ludington, somewhat inflate the total. Much depends (as Ludington himself readily concedes) on when one would consider that the Huguenot immigration began and ended, and if one includes the totality of immigrants rather than those who can be proven to have resided in Ireland for a substantial period of time. Does one begin in 1569? Or 1662? Or 1692? And where does it end? French Protestants are recorded as entering Ireland into the 1760s. And how does one classify the attempted New Geneva colonization scheme by Swiss Calvinists in Waterford during the 1780s? However, it is my opinion that the real total would have fallen closer, rather than far short of 10,000. Given Ludington's estimation of 7,000 Huguenot inhabitants of Ireland in 1720 (Alicia St. Leger, it should be noted, hypothesizes an even lower total emigration figure of 5,000), one is faced also with prior (Ormondite, Pre-Ormondite) and subsequent immigration, so that and even this figure must be upwardly adjusted. We are, indeed, referring to the totality of Huguenot immigration into Ireland, and not the isolated population figures for any one year. It should eventually prove to be neither less than 8,000, nor much more than 10,000.

Dublin would probably account, when all is said and done, for roughly half, or at least some 4,000 souls, Portarlington for some 650, with Cork, Waterford, Lisburn and the "lesser" areas of settlement, and scattered individuals, comprising the balance.

Early Cultural & Physical Impact

What is left of the Huguenot presence? Some of the buildings – shops and domiciles – known as "Huguenot houses" or "Dutch Billies", some of which can undoubtedly be identified as having been owned/inhabited by Huguenots, are found scattered throughout Dublin city. All, with one possible exception, are minus their original gable. The work of the Tabary siblings at the Royal Hospital of Kilmainham is extant, as is of course the architectural masterpieces of Richard Cassels (among them: Tyrone House, the original Dining Hall and the Printing House at Trinity College, Clanwilliam House and Leinster House in Dublin; Carton House at Maynooth, County Kildare; Powerscourt near Enniskerry County Wicklow; and Russborough House near Blessington, County Wicklow) and James Gandon (The Four Courts, Customs House, and King's Inn). These towering figures both had a hand in the design and ultimate construction of the Rotunda Maternity Hospital in Dublin.

Marsh's Library, Fumbally Lane, Digges Street, D'Olier Street, and La Fontan Street in Dublin, French Church Street and Lavit's Quay in Cork, and Gillet's Hill in Youghal, testify to past Huguenot connections, as do the cemeteries at Merrion Row (Dublin), Cork, and St. Paul's Church at Portarlington. Of course, the Lady Chapel at St. Patrick's Cathedral, Portarlington Church, the Collegiate Church of St. Mary's in Youghal and the Chapter House of St. Mary's Abbey survive to this day, as does much of the work of Huguenot gold & silversmiths like Guillaume Teulon, Antoine Semirot, François Gerrard, Edouard Gillet, Antoine Lefebure, Jacques Le Bas and Jean Pittar. Much more has vanished or endures in ruinous state, awaiting the demolition ball. The glory of the Latouche Bank on Castle Street off Dublin City Hall has, for example, long been reduced to a single exposed, derelict ground floor with not so much as a plaque to indicate the financial power that had once been wielded within its walls.

A Journey for Another Day

The initial apprehension, unease, and even jealousy that was surely excited by the mass arrival of French Protestant refugees during the Williamite era and beyond was painstakingly transformed to tolerance, co-existence, cooperation and, finally, amalgamation as both exiles and hosts came to blur the differences between them. It is difficult to ascertain when this process of evolution reached its crossroads, and at what point the Huguenot colonist became an Anglo-Irishman, and ultimately an Irishman, who happened to be of French descent. When France declared herself ready to re-open the doors to all her Huguenot outcasts through the Toleration Edict of Rennes in 1787, there was little movement back to the homeland, which now weighed rather lightly in the minds of refugee descendants. Of course it was true that some isolated individual families like the Belleseignes of Cork, and – if Grace Lawless Lee is accurate on this – many of the Waterford Huguenot households, did make the trek back. But for most, this was no longer a matter of great relevance.

Nostalgia for days that could never be recaptured, for ancestral memories of gathering chestnuts in the wooded hills and rough ravines of the Cevennes, of prosperous homesteads in the rich soil of Poitou, of the bustle, clutter, noise and ocean-borne smells of the ports of Normandy and Saintonge, or the sight of the Pont Saint-Georges straddling the River Mosselle flowing through Metz – all had been subsumed in favor of a new life in their adopted land. The saga of Ireland's Huguenots in the years after 1740, when it is written, will be that of their calm passage into that crucible known as Irish history.

References

Primary sources/books/pamphlets

Caillard, Gaspard. *Sermons sur divers texts de l'Ecritude Sainte*, Dublin 1728, pp. 1–61.

Cavallier, Jean. *Memoires of the Wars of the Cevennes*, Dublin 1726, pp. i–xxiv.

Secondary Works

Craig, Maurice. *Dublin, 1660–1860*, pp. 62, 88, 129–35, 236–59.

Joyce, James. *Finnegan's Wake*, New York, 1999 (Author's notes for prospective article). Kelly, Patrick, "Lord Galway and the Penal Laws" in Caldicott, Gough & Pittion, *Huguenots and Ireland*, pp. 241–2, 244, 248.

Lee, Grace Lawless. *The Huguenot Settlements in Ireland*, p. 113.

Ludington, Charles C. "Between Myth and Margin: The Huguenots in Irish History" in *Historical Research*, Vol. LXXIII, no. 180 (February 2000), pp. 4–13.

Maxwell, Constantia. *Dublin Under the Georges*, pp. 152, 238, 240.

Oral statements taken down by the author: Dublin, 16–17 May 1985.

Rambaut, Philip. *The Huguenots of Ireland* (Privately printed, London 1982), p. 15.

Rouston-Verrieres, Jean-Marie "A propos des Chevalier de Malte, une famille prestigieuse de l'Albigeois, les Dupuy-Melgeuil" in *Revue du Tarn* (Printemps 1982), p. 7.

St. Leger, Alicia. *Silver, Sails and Silk: Huguenots in Cork, 1685–1850*, p. 1.

Vigne, Randolph "The Good Lord Galway" in *PHSGBI*, Vol. XXIV, no. 6, p. 540.

Wesley, John. *Journals*. London 1872, Vol. ii, pp. 194–5.

◈ SELECT BIBLIOGRAPHY ◈

Manuscript Sources & Primary Sources in Print

*Dublin

(Royal Irish Academy)

D'Avaux Correspondence (MacSwiney Ms.; Boxes 3, 4, 7, 9).
Dumont de Bostaquet Ms. (12, N, 17).
Revenues of St. Anne's Guild (12, P, 1).
The White Book of St. Anne's Guild (12, O, 13).

(Royal College of Physicians)

Register of Fellows.

(Trinity College Library)

Archbishop King Correspondence (Ms. 750, N, 3, 1; N, 3, 2; N, 3, 2A).
Records of the Corporation of Barber Surgeons in Dublin (Ms 1447).
Registers of St. Bride's Parish, Dublin (Ms 1470, 1478, 1480).

(City Hall)

Manuscript Maps of Dublin City.
Pipe Water Application 1680–87, and Miscellaneous Acts of the Corporation.

(Registry of Deeds)

Transcripts and Memorials of Deeds, Dublin City (1708–38; 1739–88).
Transcripts and Memorials of Deeds, King's County (1708–38; 1739–1810).
Transcripts and Memorials of Deeds, Queen's County (1708–38; 1739–1810).
Transcripts and Memorials of Deeds, Waterford City (1708–38).

(National Library of Ireland)

Abstract from the Original Patent of the Borough of Portarlington, 1669, and
the Minutes of the Sovereign Court, 1726–77 (Ms 90).

* Denotes lieu of manuscript repository.

Select Bibliography

Account of Pensions which stood on the Civil List (Ms 8257).
Archbishop King Correspondence 1690–1728 (Mss 2055–56).
Charter of the Royal Hospital, Kilmainham, 19 February 1685 (Ms. 2030).
Christchurch Estate Maps (Ms 2789).
Corporation Book of the City of Waterford (Microfilm n. 5425, p. 5558).
Deeds of St. Patrick's Cathedral, 1660–89 (Ms 2675).
Defense of the Settlement of Protestants, 26 October 1689 (Ms 4606).
Eighty-two deeds, wills, and military commissions relating to Huguenot families
  in Ireland 1675–1840 (Mss D 6516–96).
Essex and Ormond Letters 1676–84 (Ms 803).
Extracts from Dublin Church of Ireland Registers (Reynell Ms 2694).
Extracts of Legacies to Churches 1713–43 (Reynell Ms 104).
Genealogies, memoires, and correspondence of Huguenot Families, 1682–1821
  (Ms 8341).
Guild List of Merchant Freemen, 1700–1802 (Ms 3019).
Guild of St. Luke's, Account Book (Ms 12,121).
Guild of St. Luke's, Membership Roll (Ms 12,122).
Guild of St. Luke's, Transactions (Ms 12,123).
Holdings of Christchurch Cathedral (Ms 2970).
Irish Army List, 1744 (Ms 1611).
Irish Gunsmiths and Sword Cutlers (Ms 9348).
James II's Approbation of Quakers, 2 August 1689 (Ms 4606).
List of Forfeited Lands, Report of the Trustees for Forfeited
Estates in Ireland, 1692 (Ms 12, 092).
List of French Clergy in Dublin 1668–1780 (Reynell Ms. 8007).
List of Printers and Booksellers in Dublin, 1726–76 (Ms 5457).
List of Protestants having fled Ireland to go to Chester, 1689 (Ms 3719).
Livres des Comptes de l'argent des pauvres de l'Eglise Françoise de Portarlington,
  1732–1865 (LeFanu Papers Microfilm n. 2976, p. 2597).
Marriages, Christenings and burials in the Parish ofDonnybrook, 1712–39 (Ms
  4167).
Muschamp Papers (Ms 10991-A).
John Peacock, *Observations in a voyage in the Kingdom of France 1675; and*
  Thomas Dineley, *Observations in a voyage Through the Kingdom of Ireland*
  1681 (Microfilm n. 7515, p. 7515).
Ormond Additional letters, 1485–1685 (Ms 4846).
Ormond Correspondence 1678 (Ms 11, 971).
Ormond Correspondence 1677–84 (Ms 802).
Ormond–Coventry Papers 1678 (Ms 11, 970).
Ormond Papers 1699–1719 (Ms 4166).
Palatines in Dublin, 1709 (Ms. 100).
Petition of the French Protestants of Waterford, 1684 (Ms. 1619).
Portarlington 1678 (Ms Map 21 F 55 1).
Proclamations Relating to Ireland, 1673–1716 (Ms 1793).
Roll of Freemen of the City of Dublin (Mss 76–79).
Robert Stearne's Transactions in Ireland, 1673–93 (Ms 4166).
Shop and Inn Signs in 17th–18th Century Dublin (Ms 4126).

Select Bibliography

Title Book for the Diocese of Kildare, 1678–1737 and 1694–1745 (Diocesan Archives Microfilm n. 4565, p. 4531 and n. 4548, p. 4410).
Tyrconnel Correspondence, 1690 (Ms 37).

(Archbishop Marsh's Library)

Bouheréau-Ellis Correspondence (Microfilm).
Diary of Elie Bouhéreau (Ms 30.2.2).
Forme et Discipline de l'Église Françoise qu'il se reunnit a St. Patrice, 1694 (Ms Z4.3.20).
List of Poor in City Workhouse, 20 March 1726 (Ms 23.1.1).
Roll of City Officers and Guilds of Dublin (Ms 22.1.7).
Tessereau Papers (Ms. Z.2.2.9 & 10).

(Public Records Office of Ireland)

Caulfield Mss (Waterford M. 4974 I.A 58-87).
Caulfield Mss. (Portarlington M. 4976 I.A 58-87).
Copy of Registers of St. Andrews, Dublin 1672–1819 (M. 5135).
Lords Justices' Correspondence 1692–1701 (M. 2453-7).

(Genealogical Office of Ireland)

Coat of Arms to the Earl of Galway (Ms. 1OY p. 13).
Forms of the Lords Justices giving audience in the City of Dublin, 1751 (Ms 4, pp. 147–54).
Pedigree of Des Voeux of India Villa, Queen's County (Ms 112).
Supporters to Ruvigny, Baron Portarlington (Ms 87, pp. 21–2).

*Portarlington

(St. Paul's Church)

Registre Contenant les baptesmes, les marriages et les sepultures Des protestants François de l'eglise reformeé qui s'assemble dans la ville de Portarlington.

*London

(British Library)

Accounts of the Army in Ireland 1689–92 (Harleian Ms 7194).
Correspondence of the Earl of Galway, 1692–1701 (Ms 9718).
Disbursements of the Irish Government, 1684–85 (Add. Ms 38,143).
Dispatches of the Lords Justices of Ireland, 1706–12 (Add. Ms 9717).
Extracts from the Diary of Narcissus Luttrell, 1678–1711 (Add. Ms 34,513).
Hanover State Papers, vol. Vii, January 1715–June 1716 (Stowe Ms 228).
Lists of Army in Ireland, 1686–1705 (Add. Ms 9726).
Papers relating to the Irish Rebellion, 1641 (Sloane Ms 1008).
Papers relating to Scotland and Ireland, 17th–18th centuries (Add. Ms 28,085).
Register of the Statute Staples in Dublin, 1658–87 (Add. Ms 15,635–7).
Robert Southwell Papers (Add. Ms 34,335).
War Office and Irish Office Correspondence, 1705–59 (Add. Mss 38,712–13).

Select Bibliography

(Huguenot Library: University College)

A List of Pensions to Huguenot Officers (communicated by Henry Wagner).

(In Print)

Calendar of State Papers
Domestic Series vol. 1660–85 (Addenda); 1683–84; 1684–85; 1686–87; 1687–89; 1689–90; 1691–92; 1693; 1694–95; 1695; 1697.
Ireland Series vol. 1509–73; 1633–47; 1647–60; 1666–69; 1669–70.
Calendar of the Ancient Records of the City of Dublin (vol. IV, V, VI; ed. John T. Gilbert).
Historic Manuscripts Commission Publications (Rep. 2; Rep. 4; Rep. 5; Rep. 6; Rep. 7 pt. 1; Rep. 11 appendix 2; Rep. 12 Appendices 6–7; Rep. 14 appendix 4; Buccleuch & Queensbury Ms, vol. II, pp. 1–2; Ormond Ms (New Series) vol. II–IV, VII–VIII; House of Lords Ms. (New Series) Vol. 2; Bath Ms, vol. 3; Egmont Ms., vol. 2; Stuart Ms, vol. 6; Finch Ms vol. 2; Downshire Ms, vol. 1, pt. 1; Hastings Ms, vol. 2).
Irish Statutes (vol. II–IV).
Proceedings of the Huguenot Society of London-Quarto Series (vol. VII, XIV, XVIII, XIX, XXVII; XLI).
Proceedings of the Parish Registers Society of Ireland (vol. III, V, IX, XI, XII).

Non-manuscript Sources

Agnew, David Carnegie. *Henri de Ruvigny, Earl of Galway.* Edinburgh, 1864.
Agnew, David Carnegie. *Protestant Exiles from France in the Reign of Louis XIV.* London, 1871, 3 vol.
An Apology for the French Refugees Established in Ireland. Dublin 1712.
Andre, Louis. *Michel Le Tellier et Louvois.* Geneva 1974.
Anonymous. *The Huguenots In England and Ireland.* Paper read before the College and Kelvingrove Literary Societies, Glasgow, 1906.
Arnaud, Eugene. *Histoire des Protestants du Dauphiné* (Geneva 1970, 3 vol.).
Aydelotte, James Ernest. *The Duke of Ormond and the English Government of Ireland, 1977–85.* Ph.D. Thesis, University of Iowa, 1975 (Ann Arbor, Michigan; University Microfilms Reprint).
Bagwell, Richard. *Ireland Under the Stuarts.* London 1916.
Barnard, T. C. *Cromwellian Ireland.* Oxford 1975.
Beckett, J. C. *Protestant Dissent in Ireland, 1687–1784.* London 1948.
Benedict, Philip. *Rouen During the Wars of Religion.* Cambridge 1980.
Best, E. Joyce. *The Huguenots of Lisburn: The Story of the Lost Colony* <http://www.lisburn.com/books/huguenots/huguenots_.html>.
Black, Eileen, ed. *Kings in Conflict: Ireland in the 1690's.* Belfast 1990.
Bligny, Bernard. *Histoire du Dauphiné.* Toulouse 1973.
Burghclere, Lady. *The Life of James, First Duke of Ormomd, 1610–88.* London 1912, 2 vol.
Burn, J. S. *History of the French and Other Foreign Protestant Refugees in England.* London, 1946.

Burtchaell, George Dames and Sadleir, Thomas Ulick. *Alumni Dublinensis*. Dublin 1935.

Butler, William F. T. *Confiscation in Irish History*. Dublin 1917.

Caillard, Gaspard. *Sermons sur Divers Textes de L'Écriture Sainte*. Dublin 1728.

Caldicott, C. E. J., Gough, Hugh, & Pittion, J.-P. *The Huguenots and Ireland: Anatomy of an Emigration*. Dun Laoghaire 1987.

Call to Hugonites. London & Dublin 1712.

Carré, Albert. *L'Influence des Huguenots Français en Irlande au XVIIeme etXVIIIeme Siècles*. Paris 1937.

Carte, Thomas. *Life of James, Duke of Ormond*. London 1736, 6 vol.

Cavallier, Jean. *Memoires of the Wars of the Cevennes*. Dublin 1726.

Clarke, Peter J. *Exploring Irish Accounting History*. Dublin 1995.

Cole, R. Lee. *A History of Methodism in Dublin*. London 1932.

Combe, J. C. *The Huguenots in the Ministry of the Church of Ireland*. Ph.D. Thesis, Queen's University, 1970.

Coonan, T. L. *The Irish Catholic Confederacy and the Puritan Revolution*. New York 1954.

Corish, Patrick. *The Catholic Community in the 17th and 18th Centuries*. Dublin 1981.

Cottret, Bernard. *The Huguenots in England: Immigration and Settlement, c. 1550–1700*. Cambridge 1991.

Craig, Maurice. *Dublin 1660–1860*. Dublin 1980.

Crookshank, C. H. *A History of Methodism in Ireland*. Belfast 1885, 3 vol.

D'Alton, E. A. *History of Ireland*. London 1906, 2 vol.

Daillon, Benjamin de. *Examen de l'Opression des Reformeés en France*. Amsterdam 1687.

De la Force, Duc. *Lauzun*. Paris 1919.

Des Voeux, Antoine Vinchon. *A Philosophical and Critical Essay on Ecclesiastes*. London 1760.

Des Voeux, Antoine Vinchon. *The Compendious Library, or the Literary Journal Revived*. Dublin: November 1752–April 1752.

Deyon, Solange. *Du Loyalisme au Refus: Les Protestants Francais et leurs Depute-General entre La Fronde et la Revocation*. Lille 1968.

Dodge, Guy Howard. *The Political Theory of the Huguenots of the Dispersion*. New York 1947.

Drelincourt, Pierre. *Speech to his Garce, Duke of Ormond . . . to return humble thanks of French Protestants . . .* Dublin 1682.

Droz, Jean Pierre. *The Literary Journal*. Dublin 1744–9.

Dumont de Bostaquet, Isaac. *Memoires Inedits de Dumont de Bostaquet, gentille-homme Normand*. Ed. Charles Read & Francis Waddington. Paris 1864.

Dunlop, Robert, *Ireland Under the Commonwealth*. Manchester, 1913, 2 vol.

Dunton, John. *Teague Land, or A Merry Ramble to the Wild Irish: Letters from Ireland, 1698*. Ed. Edward MacLysaght. Blackrock, Co. Dublin 1982.

Edwards, Ruth Dudley. *An Atlas of Irish History*. London 1973.

Erlanger, Philippe. *La Massacre de la Saint-Barthelemy*. Paris 1960.

Fleetwood, John F. *The History of Medicine in Ireland*. Dublin 1983.

Fontaine, Jacques. *Mémoire d'une Famille Huguenot, Victime de la Revocation de l'Édit De Nantes*. Toulouse, 1977.

Ford, Alan, McGuire, James & Milne, Kenneth, eds. *As by Law Established: The Church of Ireland Since the Reformation*. Dublin 1995.

Formulaire de la Consécration et Dédicace des Églises et Chapelles selon l'usage de l'Église d'Irlande. Dublin 1702.

Gachon, Pierre. *Histoire du Languedoc*. Paris 1926.

Garden, Maurice. *Lyon et le Lyonnais au XVIIeme Siècle*. Paris 1970.

Gast, Jean. *The Rudiments of Grecian History*. Dublin 1753.

Germaine, Mona. *Peter Street Cemetary* (Privately printed 1999).

Gerrard, Frances. *Picturesque Dublin: Old and New*. London 1848.

Gilbert, John T. *A History of the City of Dublin*. Dublin 1861, 3 vol.

Gilbert, John T. *Jacobite Narrative of the War in Ireland, 1689–1691*. Dublin 1892.

Gill, Conrad. *The Rise of the Irish Linen Industry*. Oxford 1964.

Gimlette, Thomas. *A History of the Huguenot Settlers in Ireland and other Literary Remains*. Waterford 1888.

Goubert, Pierre. *Cent Mille Provinciaux au XVIIeme Siècle*. Paris 1968.

Guillaume, Pierre et Poussou, Jean-Pierre. *Demographie Historique*. Paris 1970.

Gwynn, Robin. *Huguenot Heritage*. London 1985.

Haag, Eugene and E.M. *La France Protestante*. Geneva, reprinted 1966, 10 vol.

Hepburn, A. C. *Minorities in History*. London 1978.

Herlihy, Kevin. *The Irish Dissenting Tradition, 1650–1750*. Blackrock, Co. Dublin, Ireland 1995.

Herlihy, Kevin. *The Politics of Irish Dissent, 1650–1800*. Blackrock, County Dublin, Ireland, 1997.

Herlihy, Kevin. *The Religion of Irish Dissent, 1650–1800*. Blackrock, County Dublin, Ireland 1996.

Hiberniae Notitia. Dublin 1723.

Hyman, Louis. *The Jews of Ireland*. Shannon 1972.

Joutard, Philippe. *Les Camisards*. Paris 1976.

Jus Regium: Or the King's Right to Grant Forfeitures. London 1701.

Kamen, Henry. *The War of the Spanish Succession in Spain, 1700–15*. London1969.

Katz, Steven T. *The Holocaust in Historical Context: Vol. I: The Holocaust and Mass Death before the Modern Age*. New York 1994.

Kearney, Hugh. *Strafford in Ireland, 1633–1641*. Manchester 1959.

Kenyon, J. P. *The Stuarts*. Glasgow 1979.

King, Sir William Charles Simeon. *A Great Archbishop of Dublin, William King, D.P.* London 1908.

Kingdon, Robert M. *Geneva and the Coming of the Wars of Religion in France, 1555–1563*. Geneva 1956.

Knox, S.J. *Ireland's Debt to the Huguenots*. Dublin 1959.

Kretzer, Harmut. *Calvinismus und Franzosische Monarchie in 17 Jahrhundert*. Berlin 1975.

Lane, Padraig G. & Nolan, William. *Laois: History & Society*. Dublin 1999.

Lart, Charles E. *Huguenot Pedigrees*. London 1924.

Lawlor, Hugh Jackson. *The Fasti of St. Patrick*. Dublin 1931.

Select Bibliography

Lawrence, Colonel Richard. *The Interest of Ireland in its Trade and Wealth Stated.* Dublin 1682.

Lebrun, François. *Les Hommes et la Mort en Anjou au 17eme et 18eme Siècles.* Paris 1971.

Lee, Grace Lawless. *The Huguenot Settlements in Ireland.* London 1936.

LeFanu, T. P. and W. J. H. *Memoire of the LeFanu Family.* Privately printed 1924.

Léonard, Émile G. *Histoire Générale du Protestantisme.* Paris 1961.

Leroy Ladurie, Emmanuel. Les Paysans de Languedoc. Paris 1964.

Ligou, Daniel. *Le Protestantisme en France de 1598 à 1715.* Paris 1968.

Lublinskaya, A. D. *French Absolutism: The Crucial Phase, 1620–29.* Translated by Brian Pearce. Cambridge 1968.

Luthy, Herbert. *La Banque Protestante en France.* Paris 1959.

MacLysaght, Edward. *Irish Life in the 17th Century.* Dublin 1979.

MacLysaght, Edward. *The Surnames of Ireland.* Dublin 1972.

MacReady, L. T. *Dublin Street Names.* Dublin 1892.

Magdelaine, M. and Von Thadden, R. *Le Réfuge Huguenot.* Paris 1985.

Maguire, W. A., ed. *The Huguenots & Ulster.* Lisburn, Northern Ireland 1985.

Maguire, W. A., ed. *Kings in Conflict: The Revolutionary War in Ireland and its Aftermath, 1689–1750.* Belfast 1990.

Maxwell, Constantia. *Dublin Under the Georges.* London 1936.

Miquel, Pierre. *Les Guerres de Religion.* Paris 1980.

Mours, Samuel et Robert, Daniel. *Le Protestantisme en France du XVIIeme Siècle à nos Jours.* Paris 1972.

Mousnier, Roland. *L'Assassinat d'Henri IV.* France 1964.

O'Hanlon, John Canon and O'Leary, Edward. *History of the Queen's County.* Dublin 1907.

O'Hart, John. *Irish Pedigrees, or the Origin and Stem of the Irish Nation.* Baltimore 1976, 2 vol.

Orcibal, Jean. *Louis XIV et les Protestants.* Paris 1951.

Petrie, Sir Charles. *The Great Tyrconnel.* Cork 1972.

Pezet, Maurice. *L'Épopeé des Camisards.* Paris 1978.

Poole, Reginald Lane. *Huguenots of the Dispersion.* London 1880.

Rambaut, Philip. *The Huguenots in Ireland.* Privately printed, London 1982.

Reid, James Seaton. *The History of the Presbyterian Church in Ireland.* Belfast 1867, 3 vol.

Reaman, G. Elmore. *The Trail of the Huguenots.* London 1964.

Robb, Nesca A. *William of Orange, A Personal Portrait.* London 1966, 2 vol.

Roche, O. I. A. *The Days of the Upright.* New York 1965.

Roque, Jean. *Map of Dublin 1756.*

Rothrock, G. A. *The Huguenots, Biography of a Minority.* Chicago 1979.

Rushworth, John. *The Tryal of the Earl of Strafford.* London 1680.

St. Leger, Alicia. *Silver, Sails and Silk: Huguenots in Cork, 1685–1850.* Cork, 1991.

Schickler, Baron F. de. *Les Églises du Réfuge en Angleterre.* Paris 1892, 3 vol.

Scoville, Warren C. *The Persecution of Huguenots and French Economic Development, 1680–1720.* Berkeley, California 1960.

Select Bibliography

Seymour, John D. *Oxford Historical and Literary Studies, Vol. XII: The Puritans in Ireland, 1647–1661*. Oxford 1921.
Simms, J. G. *Jacobite Ireland, 1685–91*. London 1969.
Simms, J. G. *The Williamite Confiscation in Ireland, 1690–1703*. London 1956.
Skelton, Philip. *Complete Works*. Ed. Robert Lynam. London 1824, 6 vol.
Smiles, Samuel. *Huguenots in England and Ireland*. London 1889.
Stokes, George Thomas. *Some Worthies of the Irish Church*. London 1900.
Stoye, John. *Europe Unfolding, 1648–1688*. Glasgow 1976.
Strickland, Walter George. *A Dictionary of Irish Artists*. Shannon 1969.
Taylor, Charles. *The Camisards*. London 1893.
The Way to Render Ireland Happy and Secure. Dublin 1697.
Thomas, Roger. *Daniel Williams "Presbyterian Bishop"*. London 1964.
Thompson, James Westfall. *The Wars of Religion in France, 1559–1576*. New York 1909.
Traill, Henry Duff. *William III*. London 1880.
Vaissiere, Pierre de. *Gentilhommes Campagnards de l'Ancienne France*. Geneva 1975.
Vaux de Foletier, F. de. *Histoire d'Aunis et de Saintonge*. Paris 1929.
Vigne, Randolph & Littleton, Charles, ed. *From Strangers to Citizens: The Integration of Immigrant Communities in Britain, Ireland and Colonial America, 1550–1750*. Brighton & Portland 2001.
Wall, Maureen. *The Penal Laws, 1691–1760*. Dundalk 1961.
Walsh, John Edward. *Rakes and Ruffians*. Dublin 1979.
Ware, Sir James. *Bishops of Ireland*. Dublin 1745.
Wedgewood, C. V. *Strafford, 1593–1641*. London 1935.
Weiss, Charles. *History of the French Protestant Refugees from the Revocation of the Edict of Nantes to the Present Time*. Edinburgh 1854.
Wesley, John. *Journals*. London 1872.
Wolf, John B. *Louis XIV*. London 1968.
Zoff, Otto. *The Huguenots, Fighters for God and Human Freedom*. London 1943.

Journals

Decies: Journal of the Old Waterford Society.
Dix-Septieme Siècle.
Dublin Historical Record.
Eire-Ireland.
Historical Research.
Huguenot Heritage
The Irish Ancestor.
Irish Historical Studies.
The Irish Sword.
Journal of the Royal Society of Antiquaries of Ireland.
Proceedings of the Huguenot Society of Great Britain & Ireland.
Proceedings of the Huguenot Society of London.
Proceedings of the Royal Irish Academy.
Ulster Journal of Archaeology.

✦ INDEX ✦

Printed and bound by CPI Group (UK) Ltd, Croydon, CR0 4YY

09/06/2025

14685823-0003